Dear Margaret and John,

May you be encouraged and strengthened in your awareness of God's love. "He will never leave you nor forsake you"

Deut 31:6

Gene Rill

FACE TO FACE: *Seven Keys* to a Secure Marriage

Dr. Jesse Gill

WestBow Press books may be ordered through booksellers or by contacting:

WestBow Press
A Division of Thomas Nelson & Zondervan
1663 Liberty Drive
Bloomington, IN 47403
www.westbowpress.com
1 (866) 928-1240

ISBN: 978-1-4908-7863-8 (sc)
ISBN: 978-1-4908-7862-1 (hc)
ISBN: 978-1-4908-7861-4 (e)

Library of Congress Control Number: 2015906963

Print information available on the last page.

WestBow Press rev. date: 06/29/2015

Contents

Dedication

This book is dedicated to April, the love of my life. Thank you for all the ways that you create a secure marriage connection with me and for me. I am stronger because I know that I am not alone and that you hold me in your heart. I treasure you, and without your love this book would not be in existence.

Author's Note Regarding Privacy of Client Stories

All of the married couples referenced in this book are based on the types of stories that I participate in each week in my marriage counseling office and in my friendships. However, to protect the privacy of each couple with whom I have been honored to journey, I have blended together elements of multiple stories to create composites. As a result, there is no single story in this book that is a direct portrayal of a couple with whom I have worked or have known. Any resemblance to a real couple is merely due to the similarities that so many couples have with one another as they share in the human struggle to connect. The only exact stories in this book are the ones from my own marriage. My wife, April, and I have chosen to share these experiences to let you know that we too, like all married couples, have to work daily to protect and secure our marriage connection.

Introduction

The Lord God said, "It is not good for the man to be alone..."
(Genesis 2:18).

Since the dawn of human history, we have known that we were not created to live alone. We were designed for connection with one another, and created for relationship with God. This verse from the creation story in Genesis 2 speaks to us clearly about the need for both men and women to live a life connected to others. This connection begins in infancy with the critical bond between a child and parent. It extends into adolescence with the increasing connections among friends and family. And, as we enter adulthood, there is no more intimate form of connection than that which we find in the lifelong union of a husband and wife.

Marriage excites us, comforts us, challenges, and changes us. It provides solid bedrock to the family unit when a marriage stays together and thrives. Marriage even speaks to us about the nature of God's love for us, His union with His bride, the church. So why is it so hard to maintain closeness in your marriage?

There are few things in life that can compare to the joys of living in a secure and healthy marriage. By contrast, few things in life are more painful than the misery of unresolved conflict with and isolation from the very person with whom you committed to be one. Such pain and misery have driven many people to break this union, return to a more solitary life, or try to find happiness in the arms of another. An ancient sage quipped that it would be better to go and live alone in the desert than to live a life of quarreling with your mate, and an overcooked TV dinner alone is better than having gourmet feasts nightly with your spouse in the midst of constant arguments (Proverbs 21:19; 17:1, my paraphrase).

Whether you are contemplating marriage, looking to strengthen a solid marriage, or trying to save a marriage from loneliness and despair, we all have one thing in common. Each of us who embarks on the quest for marriage wants to live in communion with our beloved, to share all the beauty and pain that is life, to know that we are accepted, and to never be alone. What you want is good. What you want is normal and was even ordained by the One who brought you into existence.

When we first fall in love, the future stretches out before us like a glowing sunrise full of promise. But then conflict and pain can dim the glow, threatening to cloud our open hearts. We may lose the wonder of those first moments when we stood face-to-face. We may even despair when we fall into destructive cycles of conflict, left to wonder, *Does my spouse still love me?*

I have some good news for you that can turn you and your spouse from sparring partners back into the loving couple you once were, only wiser. This book can help you understand your spouse better and why you react in the ways you do.

The Seven Keys in this book will help you deeply understand your need to be securely connected to your spouse and your spouse's need to be connected to you. These keys will help you turn painful conflict into an opportunity to draw closer to your beloved, deepening your bond beyond what you have known before. The keys will help you unlock painful patterns of conflict and release God's attachment design for your marriage. You can learn to cling to one another in times of grief and loss, even if your spouse contributed to the loss.

I will teach you ways to tune in better, and repair things when misunderstandings arise. All along the way, you will be learning how to rest more fully in the constant and perfect love of God. If you commit to opening your mind and taking new steps along this journey, I believe that you will learn to make your relationship flourish and bring you both face-to-face once again.

May you be guided and encouraged. When you get weary, I pray that you sense the nearness of the One who designed you for connection. And, may your awareness of secure love grow strong as we embark together on this quest to build your face-to-face marriage.

CHAPTER 1

Attachment—Created for Connection

Treasure Map

Fifteen years ago I was first drawn into the drama and passion of marriage therapy. It was a challenge to listen to couples, provide compassion, and then direct them towards healthier forms of communication. I like a good challenge, so I rolled my sleeves up and leaned into the storm, eager to see something change. I was working really hard, but I wasn't seeing good results. All too often the storm just enveloped all three of us because I did not have a good map to navigate us through.

In 2003, a colleague handed me a new map, and it changed the way I do marriage therapy forever. Not only that, but this map also opened up my eyes to better understand the ways that God wired me and you for relationships from infancy and throughout our lives.

After learning this map, Scripture came alive for me as well with a strong message about how God designed us to be in relationship with Him and with one another. During Creation He tells us that it is "not good for us to be alone," and then He spends the rest of the Bible making sure that we don't have to worry about being separated from Him ever again.

We all have this deep need to know that we will never have to walk through life alone, especially when times are tough. This need draws us to God to be our rescue in times of distress, and this need is one of the key reasons why we get married. A marriage is in huge trouble when that sense of "togetherness in tough times" has started to fade. In fact, the new map says that losing this sense of togetherness is what drives couples to seek therapy.

I felt like I had discovered a buried treasure! Someone had shared a map that described what marriages need when they are going through distress. And this map helps us understand our deepest longings for God and human connection at the same time.

This map is called Attachment Theory. Every good treasure hunt starts with a journey back in time. We too must take a journey together to understand the deeper truths of this map in order to unlock the treasure inside your marriage again. We will go back in history to look at the leading person who developed this map called Attachment Theory. We will also look at your own history of attachment so that we can apply this knowledge to your marriage. Let's begin.

Human Attachment

When we are born into this world, we are so tiny, so frail, and so vulnerable. We are completely dependent on the ones who brought us into the world for sustaining our existence. God, in His wisdom, provided a means and a process for binding us to our caregivers so that our life would be sustained, so we would survive and even thrive.

The psychological term for this binding force is *attachment.* It is the drive that a parent has to comfort his or her crying child. It is felt in the comfort that the child receives when he is held and consoled in his parent's arms. Attachment is the bond that links parent and child in closeness, tenderness, playfulness, loyalty, and fierce protection.[1] At some level, attachment is present at the moment of birth, but solid attachment is forged over time through a series of stable, predictable, and secure interactions between a child and parent.

As we grow older, and when we choose marriage, this close bond is transferred to our spouse. When we marry, attachment is no longer tied to our immediate survival because we are grown and capable of caring for ourselves. However, it remains an essential part of our emotional, physical, and spiritual health, as will be described throughout this book.

Let's start our discussion about this connecting bond between humans with an overview of how the theory of attachment got its start. You will need to understand the foundation that is formed in infancy before you can apply Attachment Theory to your marriage. I understand that some readers don't like studying theories very much. I have chuckled at the thought, *Who, besides a psychologist, would get excited about studying a theory of human relationships?* But I know that understanding this theory is going to bless and enliven you. So I will work hard to help you connect the ways your adult brain is still wired and molded based on what you experienced as a child. I want you to see why attachment and your childhood have direct bearing on who you are as an adult and how you act in marriage.

The marriage tools in this book come straight from Attachment Theory.

Many of the labels I use in the Seven Keys come directly from the theory. So, you will understand the keys best if you can get a handle on the ideas involved in Attachment Theory. I believe you will also come to understand yourself in much deeper ways as you learn the theory. You might also be surprised at how much this theory helps you understand the actions of your loved ones and acquaintances too.

Attachment Theory Begins

Attachment Theory came from a rather unlikely source. John Bowlby, a proper and reserved British psychiatrist in the post-World War II era, got everything started for this emotionally connected theory of love.[2] When you look at his background, you can see why he took such an interest in attachment and loss.

John Bowlby was born into an upper middle class family in London. John saw little of his father and mother during his childhood. The leading opinion among wealthy British families at that time was that affection and attention from parents would spoil a child. As a result, John's relationship with his parents was more formal. During the school year, he only saw his mother for about an hour a day after teatime, though he saw her more frequently in summer months.

John became quite attached to his nanny, who really was his primary caregiver during his early years. Unfortunately, she died when he was about 4 years of age, and he experienced this as an acutely painful loss. As a grown man, he referenced it many times. At the age of 7, John was sent off to boarding school, which was another difficult separation experience. From these experiences, Bowlby developed a strong compassion for children experiencing separation and loss. This compassion for separated children seems to have guided his later work.

In what may best be described as a stroke of genius, Bowlby drew crucial inferences from studies of infants, and even infant animals, about the composition of the human brain and about the processes by which the emotional brain in humans is developed. Brain imaging studies and research from a half-century later have confirmed time and time again that he was right, and amazingly accurate in his predictions about how the human brain is wired for close connection with others.[3] His theory has spawned numerous research studies in children, adults, and marriage research for the past three decades.[4]

Bowlby was pioneering in his approach to the study of human development and behavior. He did not just rely on childhood memories. (Picture a bearded Freudian analyst seating you on a sofa and saying, "So tell me about your earliest memories.") Rather, Bowlby observed children in real life. He observed them in the middle of their current experiences and behaviors to better understand childhood development.

John Bowlby and the Forty Thieves

Early in his career, Bowlby studied 44 juvenile delinquents.[5] He compared them to juveniles who had emotional problems, but had not acted criminally. Among those who had committed criminal acts, he observed a trait he called "affectionless psychopathy," which is the inability to feel affection or care about other people. It was as though these youths did not have empathy or a conscience, and Bowlby wondered why.

The youths who engaged in criminal behavior had all experienced a *significant period of separation* from their mothers during their first five years of life! So, Bowlby began to focus heavily on the effects of parental separation from children in early years of child development. His emphasis on these effects gave him notoriety and positioned him to study an epidemic during the late 1940s, the separation of children from parents.

Effects of Separation on Children Due to World War II

World War II took a heavy toll on Britain, sometimes separating children from their parents for a period of time in the war effort and sometimes separating them forever, as in the case of orphans. Just after the war, Bowlby was commissioned by the World Health Organization (WHO) to look into the tragic state of the many homeless and orphaned children in Britain and throughout Europe. The WHO wanted to know whether damage was being done to children due to the loss of their parents, and whether anything could be done to improve their condition.

In 1951, Bowlby wrote a report, "Maternal Care and Mental Health," in which he outlined the alarming effects on the emotional and mental health of children who were separated from their parents. He met with professionals who were caring for homeless or disturbed children in Europe and the U.S. He reviewed evidence that showed a link between disrupted relationships in childhood and mental health problems. He concluded:

> the infant and young child should experience a warm, intimate, and continuous relationship with his mother (or permanent mother substitute) in which both find satisfaction and enjoyment.[6]

Bowlby also gave recommendations about how to reduce the effects of children being separated from parents:

1. He suggested parents be allowed to have unrestricted visits with their child when the child was hospitalized.
2. He argued for measures to support biological parents in their efforts to care for their own children in their homes.
3. He began to make the case for the foster care or adoption of children when biological parents were doing harm to children and were not able to change.

Brain Damage in Children without a Caregiver

Bowlby was among the first to bring to public awareness how devastating it can be when infants and toddlers don't get quality interaction with their caregivers. He reviewed a study of children that took place during World War II.[7] Two groups of children were observed and compared across time:

1. Children raised in an institution until the age of 3 years.
2. Children immediately placed in foster care after leaving their birth mothers.

At 3 years of age, there were significant differences between the groups. The institutionalized children did not do well, even though all their basic physical needs were met for food, clothing, and warmth. A tragic phenomenon took place! The staff were overwhelmed, the children too many, and so often the children could not be held and interacted with as consistently and constantly as the children in foster care. The institutionalized children had numerous caregivers, instead of one constant caregiver. When both groups of children were assessed at 3 years of age, the institutionalized children had language delays, an inability to form relationships, lack of guilt feelings, and a craving for affection.

Researchers followed both groups of children for the next ten years. By that point, both groups of children were placed in foster care. But the serious concerns remained for the children who had been institutionalized in the first 3 years of life, for they were still emotionally and intellectually retarded, displaying a significantly lower IQ, restless behavior, trouble concentrating, and trouble relating to other children.

The original foster care children continued to do better ten years later. Bowlby inferred that the foster care children had developed a *secure bond* with a caregiver, instead of having superficial experiences with many nurses in an institution. This secure bond buffered the foster children from the effects of the initial separation and promoted their emotional and intellectual growth.

You are truly created for connection!

Bowlby began to see that as humans we need emotional connection, touch, and bonding during the first few months of childhood, or we will not develop intellectually or emotionally. Crucial parts of our brain and physiology do not develop if we are not connected to significant others in the early years of our lives.

Let's summarize what Bowlby had learned by this point:

1. Separation from parents is a form of significant stress on the brain development of young children.
2. When a child can bond securely with one caregiver, even after separation stress, the child fares much better in later life.

Baby Monkeys in Times of Stress

Bowlby also looked at several significant findings from a primate researcher, a scientist who studied monkeys. Harry Harlow studied infant rhesus monkeys.[8] These cute little grayish brown monkeys were in a study where they were separated from their mothers. He provided them with "mannequin mommy monkeys" in two forms:

1. A wire framed mannequin that had a feeding bottle strapped to it
2. A terrycloth towel-covered mannequin with no feeding function

Harlow and the staff found that the infant monkeys spent more time holding onto and snuggling with the terrycloth "mommies" than the feeding ones. The staff also set up a noisy clanging toy in front of the monkey cages. The baby monkeys freaked out! They ran squealing to the soft "mannequin mommies" when they were frightened, and especially clung to them in distress. From this study, researchers concluded that monkeys, and probably humans too, have an intrinsic need for touch and cuddling that is separate from their food appetites. Harlow labeled this as a need for "contact comfort." More than food, baby monkeys preferred touch and cuddling.

The babies turned to their cuddly safe place, especially in times of distress!

Humans have an intrinsic need for touch and cuddling—contact comfort.

This finding was groundbreaking because the widely held view at that time placed more emphasis on the role of oral gratification as being the agent that bonded infants to their mothers. Bowlby learned a lot from the primate studies.[9] He noted that humans needed to be cuddled and held, not only having their basic needs cared for in an institution.[10] Contact comfort was the thing that monkeys and humans needed in times of separation distress.

The Window of Time for Bonding

Bowlby guessed that the initial bonding phase between an infant and mother must occur during the first nine months of life. Infants are aware of being in the arms of a stranger by the age of 9 months. They protest strongly and have the most separation anxiety between the ages of 12 to 16 months. This suggests that infants are already bonded to their mother by then.

Bowlby felt that infants did best when they had one primary bond, one primary attachment figure. This attachment figure is responsible for the infant's survival; so of course the infant would protest being pulled away from her to the arms of a stranger.[11] We now know that an infant does not bond only to his or her mother. The infant may have several attachments in young life, with one attachment being primary.

Two researchers in Scotland, Rudolph Schaffer and Peggy Emerson, found that attachment to a primary person started to occur at around 7 months and lasted till 12 months of age. They found that it was normal for children to have multiple attachments from the age of 12 months onward, but one attachment was the primary of the group. For many children, attachment to the mother was at the top of the hierarchy; but for others, the main attachment was to the father. It's important to note that the strength of attachment between child and caregiver was not merely related to the length of time spent with the child. The bond was not just due to which basic care-taking functions were fulfilled, such as feeding.[12]

The quality and intensity of interaction between parent and child determine the strength of the attachment bond.

Later research has expanded on Bowlby's initial ideas, which is good news for fathers since it recognizes their role in the attachment process. The truth is that we have come a long way in the field of psychology in the past half-century. Psychology has advanced in many ways beyond those early studies of institutionalized infants, rhesus monkeys, and greylag geese. Studies today continue to confirm and build upon the findings and truths that Bowlby had discovered.

Attachment Theory

Bowlby pulled all these separate findings together and began to organize them into a cohesive whole, the beginnings of what we now call Attachment Theory. From these studies Bowlby determined that:

1. An essential bonding process occurs between an infant and a crucial caregiver. This process is called attachment.
2. Attachment is a process of seeking physical and emotional closeness with an attachment figure, especially during moments of distress, for the purpose of survival.
3. Infants become attached to adults who are sensitive and responsive to the infant with such a quality and intensity of interactions that a strong bond, a secure bond, is formed.
4. If a caregiver is consistent in providing this during the first six months to two years of life, then that caregiver will be the primary attachment figure for the infant.

With this platform in place, Bowlby began to look more specifically into the behaviors that take place when an attachment bond is interrupted. Bowlby believed that it would be important to look at what happens to children when they can't be in close physical contact with their primary caregiver. He was surmising that separation from a child's parents could be very stressful and that certain factors might lessen a child's stress. He also wanted to carefully look at what happens when a separated child is reunited with his or her parents. In other words, it heightened the focus on the importance of *separation* and *reunion* as key facets of development in the lives of infants.

Separation from a parent is a critical moment in the life of a child, even in small doses. Separation from a loved one and reuniting with our beloved are important events throughout our entire lives. This includes adult marriage relationships!

Reactions to Separation: Protest, Despair, and Detachment

Children have a specific set of reactions when separated from their primary attachment figures. As you learn about those reactions, you may start to see similarities to your own responses when you feel separated or distant from your spouse. Let's take a look at this study that revealed those reaction patterns.

In the late 1940s and early 1950s, John Bowlby began to work closely with James Robertson at the Tavistock Clinic for children in London. The two of them developed a unique way of assessing children's behaviors that included direct observation and filming at multiple points over time. These guys were some of the first "reality TV" pioneers as they filmed real human reactions to stressful events.

James Robertson and John Bowlby wanted to examine the short-term effects of maternal separation on young children.[13] The children in this study were between the ages of 1 and 4 years. They were separated from their mothers due to being hospitalized themselves or having their mothers hospitalized. So the observations took place in residential nurseries and hospitals.

Robertson and Bowlby began to notice a predictable pattern when a child was separated from his or her mother. It could be broken down into three phases: *protest, despair, and detachment,* with each phase flowing into the next.

Protest

The initial phase of protest could begin immediately after the mother leaves, or it might be delayed. In this phase the children showed great distress, calling for mother, crying, shaking their hospital cot, and looking eagerly for their mother's return. The children would reject anyone other than Mom who offered care and solace, clearly communicating that they expected their mother would return. The period of protest could last from a few hours to a week or more.

Despair

In the second phase, despair, children were still preoccupied with their missing mother, but their behaviors suggested an increasing state of hopelessness. They were less physically active, and more withdrawn. Children displayed apathy and diminished interest in their surroundings; it appeared that they were in a deep state of mourning. Though calm on the outside, self-soothing behaviors, such as thumb sucking and rocking, indicated that they were still experiencing a great deal of internal distress. This stage could last for a few days and was followed by detachment.

Detachment

In detachment, the children appeared to be coping better with the separation since they showed more interest in their surroundings. They accepted the care of nurses, and might even smile or be sociable. However, all was not well, for the children were strangely aloof when their mothers would visit them. Rather than clinging to their mothers again, they might stay far away. Instead of tears, they could display a listless indifference, appearing to have lost interest in their mothers.

These behaviors seemed to suggest that the children had been so hurt by the separation from their mothers that they had given up on being bonded to her. However, good news was only a few weeks away. After children were reunited with their mothers for a few weeks, they gradually allowed themselves to trust in her again. Over the course of time, most children reestablished the relationship that they once had with their mother.

There were a few exceptions. If children were hospitalized or separated from their mothers for several months, they fared worse. They had the experience of getting their hopes up often, only to see them dashed. Such children often went through the entire cycle of protest, despair, and detachment several times. This could occur if a child became attached to one nurse, only to lose her after a month and then move on to another nurse. After a series of attempts in committing trust and affection to multiple mother figures, these children had less capacity to make such commitments. They became increasingly self-centered and focused on material objects like toys and treats for their solace and enjoyment. Though they might be interested in the gifts their parents brought on visiting day, they stopped being interested in their parents as special people.

On the outside, these children appeared sociable and unafraid, but on the inside they cared less and less for anyone besides themselves. They had put off caring in order to protect themselves from the multiple hurts they had experienced when they cared for someone, only to lose their connection all over again. Perhaps you might relate to these children.

Have you ever promised yourself that you would not risk it again in love?

On a milder scale, have you ever sworn off reaching out to others because you had been rejected repeatedly? If you have, you are a normal human being. All of us have had that inclination at one point or another in our lives. These ways of coping with separation and loss still play out in our lives as adults, especially in our marriages!

Bowlby and Robertson's work was extremely helpful because it demonstrated that these tendencies are hardwired into us when we are very young children. We so desperately need to be connected to others that we protest when we sense our loved one slipping away. We despair after the loved one fails to return, and we may detach ourselves from caring about others when we have gone for too long without the rewards and comforts of being connected to a significant other. This work punctuated the focus on human responses to loss and abandonment, and highlighted the need for a better understanding of the *strategies* that people use to cope with the enormous strain of separation in human relationships.

Research through the 1950s and 1960s helped to clarify that children become attached to a primary caregiver within the first two years of life, and that they are able to distinguish among a number of caregivers, including strangers.[14] These studies showed us that children experience separation from their primary attachment figure as distressing, and that they use a number of strategies to cope with this loss or to attempt to bring their caregiver back to them.

The Genius of Mary Ainsworth

Mary Ainsworth was an American developmental psychologist who had a significant influence on the creation of Attachment Theory. In the early 1950s, she moved to London and worked at the Tavistock Clinic with John Bowlby and James Robertson. Ainsworth went on from London to conduct years of research among African children and mothers in Uganda, and this gave her a perspective on how attachment and bonding take place in cultures around the world. In the 1960s, she developed her own experimental method for isolating and observing the effects of maternal separation on children called the Strange Situation.[15] This method was humane and could be used to do research with children, where some of the early methods (like keeping baby monkeys from their moms for months!) could never be used with children.

The Strange Situation

If you have taken an introductory class in psychology, you may have heard of the Strange Situation. In this procedure, a child aged 10 months to 5 years is observed for about twenty minutes interacting with a caregiver and a stranger. For the sake of ease in describing this procedure, I will generically refer to the caregiver as "Mom." A child's primary attachment figure could be a father, so bear that in mind as you read the following.

The procedure starts as the child and mother are introduced to the experiment room, which is equipped with toys and places to sit down. The mother allows the child to explore the room for a while, and then a stranger (often a female) enters the room. Mom leaves the room, while the stranger stays behind. Usually the child is distressed for a while, and the stranger tries to comfort or distract the child. In the next steps, Mom returns to the child and comforts the child before leaving again. At that point the child is alone for a period. The stranger returns to relate with the child, followed by the mother who picks up the child, and then the experiment is over.

Ainsworth and her colleagues came up with three categories to describe how the child copes and responds to the stress of being separated from Mom in this Strange Situation.[16] For ease of understanding, I am blending her terms with those of Robertson and Bowlby:[17]

1. Secure Attachment
2. Ambivalent Protesters
3. Detached Avoiders

As you may have already guessed from the first category title, the child with secure attachment is the one with the best ability to cope with the separation experience. In the other two categories, the children are having some real trouble dealing with the separation from their mothers. The other children are insecure, seemingly stuck inside two stages that children go through when they face separation: protest and detachment.

Style of Attachment	Description
Secure	The child is assured that mom is available and constant. The child feels free to branch out and explore the environment. The child turns to mom for comfort in times of distress. When mom leaves, the child cries for a brief period. When mom returns, the child is happy to see her.
Ambivalent Protesters	This child is anxious even when mom is close by. The child does not have assurance of her constant presence, and is reluctant to explore the environment. When mom leaves, this child is extremely distressed. When mom returns, the child does not know whether to draw close to mom or push away. This child is still angry with her for leaving.
Detached Avoiders	This child seems to have concluded that mom is not available. The child essentially avoids mom while she is in the room and turns away from her advances. This child does not explore the room. When mom leaves, the child is detached. The child avoids mom when she returns.

Adapted from Ainsworth and colleagues, *Patterns of Attachment*

Securely Attached Children

Securely attached children have a solid and stable foundation with the mother. These children branch out from that foundation to go and explore the room, but check back in periodically with Mom in times of need. They use their mother as a secure base from which they branch off to explore the world, but they come back to her when they are in distress. (Do you remember Harlow's monkeys clinging to the soft mannequin mommy when they were afraid?)

A securely attached child misses Mom when separated from her, and spends a brief period of time protesting her absence. But when Mom returns, the securely attached child is happy to see her and greets her warmly at the time of reunion. The secure child keeps the stranger at a distance, only interacting with the stranger when Mom is in the room, which gives a sense that it is safe to do so. The secure child clearly prefers Mom over the stranger, which seems to suggest that the primary bond has been formed with Mom and that this bond is stable.

The other two categories of children have excessive anxiety surrounding the time of separation, which seems to suggest that they have a less than secure attachment bond with their mother. We seem to observe a pattern of inconsolable and angry protest in the first group, and we observe a pattern of detachment in the second group.

Ambivalent Protesters

Ambivalent means that there is a "tug-of-war going on inside of the child, pulling the child in more than one direction." Ambivalent protesters show anxiety about exploring the room when mother is present. They remain anxious about interacting with the stranger even when Mom is present. When the mother leaves the room, these children are extremely distressed. Their distress level is somewhat reduced when Mom returns, but they appear to remain conflicted; they appear torn.

These children are not easily comforted when Mom returns, but they do make some attempts to remain close to her. They seem to have some resentment toward her for leaving, and they show resistance when she tries to connect with them by pushing away from her angrily. If these children could speak openly, they would probably say, *"I'm so anxious about you leaving, Mom. I don't really know if I've got you. I'm mad at you for making me feel so scared."*

Detached Avoiders

In the third category, detached avoiders, the children also have a higher level of anxiety. It is manifested in the form of avoidance, for these children are prone to essentially avoid or ignore their mother during the Strange Situation. They do this when she is in the room, when she leaves, and when she returns. Any welcoming behavior that they display toward their mom is also mixed with avoidance, such as turning away. Avoidant children do not explore the room much at any point in the experiment.

They display very little emotional range, regardless of who is in the room or whether they have been left all alone. These children seem to be stuck in a detachment sort of state. If these children could describe their experience it might sound something like this: *"Mom, I gave up counting on you a long time ago. It's just safer now to rely on myself instead of getting my hopes up and being let down again."*

As a result of Ainsworth's Strange Situation experiment, child development researchers have come up with ways to assess children's responses to maternal or paternal separation. They have developed a categorization system to denote three ways that children may respond to the stress of parental separation. This system starts to classify and qualitatively describe the strategies that children use to engage their fleeing parent and to reconnect with Mom when she returns. These categories stood the test of nearly two decades of research, and they captured the styles of most children all around the world. However, in

1990, two researchers, Mary Main and Judith Solomon, added a fourth category—disorganized.

Disorganized Attachment—No Way to Cope with Separation Distress

It took longer for the category of disorganized attachment to appear in the literature because it is so rare. In the disorganized category, the child appears dazed and confused, seeming to lack any organized way of dealing with separation and reunion. It is as though the child has no clue about what to do to be effective in coping with the separation from their mother. If you put yourself into this child's tiny shoes, you might imagine the following dialogue: *"I have no idea what to do to bring my mother back to me. I don't know if I should bring her back to me, or whether I would just be better off alone. Oh, I just don't know what to do!"*

Of course, these children don't have the kind of language and vocabulary yet to have such a dialogue, but their behaviors seem to suggest that this is exactly what is going on. Main and Solomon note that these children never formulated an effective strategy for connecting with their parent because their earliest months of life were filled with times of chaos or confusion.[18] Many of these children were traumatized by being victims of abuse, or by interacting with parents who were mentally ill.

Applying Attachment Theory to Your Life

If you are like me, it takes a couple of times to read through these categories we just examined to get a handle on the behavior pattern that is being described and what that looks like. Feel free to go back over them a few times, as we will be referring to them frequently during the course of this book. I ask you to look at your attachment style because it plays out in your marriage on a daily basis. So you need to understand what your attachment style is all about. Perhaps after having grasped a mental picture of each category, you are starting to ask yourself, *What makes the difference? Why do some children turn out to be securely attached to their parents, while others have such difficulty?*

The fourth category, disorganized attachment, starts to speak to this. Children who had no success in forming a secure bond with their parents and those who had successful experiences of attaching only to be shattered by abusive outbursts from parents will be confused about how to pursue their parents for closeness. In this extreme situation, it's easy to see why secure attachments never were developed. What about the others? How do those attachment styles form, become reinforced, and remain?

Bowlby believed the tendency to seek closeness with Mom is instinctive, placed into us at the time of birth by our Creator. Beyond that instinct, a child's specific attachment style is formed by numerous interactions between the mother and child.

In the next chapter we will zero in on the ways specific attachment styles are formed and examine how these styles, once learned, actually stay with us into our adult lives. These styles of attachment impact the type of relationship we will pursue in dating, our choice of a spouse, and the manner in which we parent our own children.

CHAPTER 2

Understanding Your Attachment Style

For You formed my inward parts; You wove me in my mother's womb. I will give thanks to You, for I am fearfully and wonderfully made; wonderful are Your works, and my soul knows it very well (Psalm 139:13-14).

At the moment of birth, an infant's first cry announces to the world that she is alive and that she needs attention. It is as if she were saying, "I am here! Comfort me; hold me. Take care of me, for I desperately need your help and to be close to you."

At birth, and in the first few weeks that follow, an infant is already equipped with some very basic strategies for drawing attention from the mother and father. An infant cries, coos, clings, and smiles. These bids for a parent's attention are designed to immediately bring a strong response of compassion or warmth from the heart of the parent. As the child gets older he may use behaviors like crawling, walking, following the parents, and talking to them as ways to stay close to his parents and to connect with them.

As any parent of more than one child will tell you, children seem to come out of the womb with differences in how they carry out their strategies. Some children are just more intense from the beginning and come across as "fussy babies." Other children are laid back from the moment of birth, cooing, napping frequently, and smiling often—these children might be called "easy babies."

I am intentionally making the point here that God endows children with a certain amount of temperament, or baby personality, from the day they are born. This temperament is genetically inherited from parents, and can also be influenced by prenatal conditions. It is from this starting platform of temperament that a baby launches her strategies to connect with and get the attention of her parents.

Each infant then, not only bids for the attention of parents, but also influences parental responses due to the intensity and frequency of the strategies the infant uses to connect with the parent. So, the quality of the bonding between the parent and infant is the result of the *interaction* between what the infant brings, what the parents brings, and the ways the two of them play off each other in the process.

Grace for Parents

Of course, the parent is still the responsible party in the interaction and has to be a grown-up whether the child is an "easy baby" or a "fussy baby." But I think it is important to extend parents a lot of grace at this point because some parents have a tougher job on their hands from the very beginning. Sometimes, through no fault of their own, they were just given a "fussy baby." In some cases, parents may have been ready for the challenges of parenting an "easy baby," but they were personally ill-equipped for the job of parenting that came to them through the gift of their strong-willed child.

Other parents were not fully equipped because they were overwhelmed with other factors in their lives at the time the child was an infant. This can include the overwhelming experience of caring for more than one young child during that time period. It's humanly impossible to meet all the needs of multiple children, even if you are a great parent and know how to bond well with your child. Some parents never had good bonding experiences themselves, so they are coming to the table without any kind of a map for how to be a responsive parent.

Parents are accountable for what they do with their feelings of being overwhelmed, and they should certainly seek help if they are not able to do their job effectively. However, as we sit back today and look objectively at the patterns of interaction between parents and infants, we can have compassion for what those overwhelmed parents were experiencing at the time. I want you to have access to this compassion so you don't get stuck in a blaming or victim mentality as we grapple with tough material ahead.

When we look at the dynamic interaction between infant and parent in these ways, it takes some of the blame away from parents who may have had a harder time being sensitive or responsive to their children. We can also start to examine the real impact of unresponsive parenting on child development without minimizing it. Let's begin to take a thoughtful look at how secure attachment bonds are formed, and what goes awry in the formation of insecure bonds.

Back and Forth: Building a Secure Bond

The bond between an infant and her parent is built through "back and forth" interactions between the two of them. The bonding process begins with the first cry from an infant, which signals parents to respond with lots of love and care to preserve this precious new life. It is up to a caregiver to be sensitive and responsive to those cries, so the infant knows that help is on the way and that the baby is not all alone in this strange new world. As the infant learns that his needs will be met within a reasonable amount of time, his fear subsides and a sense of security begins to form. This is especially important in the first year of life when a quick, comforting response to the infant's crying provides an important ingredient in the development of secure attachment.[19]

Bowlby states that the infant is an active participant in seeking interaction with parents, and the mother's behavior is reciprocal to the infant's attachment behavior. The development of the attachment is related to the sensitivity of the mother as she responds to the infant's signals. The quality of their bond is also forged through the amount and quality of their interaction. Better bonds are formed through high quality interactions. Bowlby describes it as follows:

> The baby initiates, and the parent responds. The response of the parent has an effect back on the baby. This back and forth process of bonding is a reciprocal interchange.[20]

The way that the two reflect back and respond to one another will help to define the nature of their bond together. If the parent responds in a consistent and sensitive manner to the baby's signals, then a secure bond will be formed. The infant comes to know that, "Someone is here for me when I need help. I'm not alone. It's going to be okay, no matter what happens!"

Building Emotional Intelligence

As we discuss these ideas, I want to talk about some added benefits that come to an infant when a caregiver is sensitive to the infant's signals. I am sharing this information with you because I want you to learn a bit more about how your brain developed as a child so that you can better appreciate your approach to relationships at the present time.

As discussed previously, the infant learns that her needs will be met within a reasonable amount of time when a caregiver is sensitive and responsive to her cues. There is also something more complex that takes place at the emotional processing level. First, it is important to understand that God gave us emotions as tools that signal to us what we need.

Emotions signal your needs and drive you to take care of your needs.

Emotions come to us rapidly through a blend of chemical and electrical signals from the limbic system within our brain. For example, we see a stranger nearby and are unsure what to make of him. Instantly our blood pressure is raised, our breathing rate increases, and we start to sweat as a way of cooling off the building intensity in our bodies. As adults, we have learned to process what these signals are telling us, "I'm scared or uncertain. I need to quickly gather more information about this stranger or remove myself from his presence soon." The signals come to us instinctively and without our immediate ability to put thoughts to them.

We have to sort through a number of thoughts before we decide exactly what is being said to us, and what we need to do about it. Well, part of the way that we learn how to make these types of inferences is based on that "reciprocal interchange" that Bowlby described so wisely. If we have a parent who took the time to comfort us when we were afraid and to help us make sense of our fears, then we develop a pretty accurate gauge on what is true danger and what is merely a false alarm. On the other hand, if our parent is unresponsive or is actually a source of fright, then our abilities to figure out and cope with threats are going to be impaired.

Let me give you another example. An infant starts an interaction by feeling something stirring in his belly. Nothing is being done to make that stirring subside and so he starts to softly whimper and babble. Then he begins to give a soft hunger cry. If Mom is sensitive and responsive, she might draw close to his crib. She may pick him up and hold him very close to her face and say, "There's my little fellow. You've not eaten for three whole hours. You must be hungry. Come on, Mommy's going to take care of you now." All the while she is calm, friendly, and reassuring in her vocal tone and in her facial expressions. She feeds him, and that strange stirring in his belly subsides.

This infant has just had an experience of tuning into his internal cues, expressing them to his mother, and having his needs met. As Mom intuits the baby's experience and reflects that back to him with calm reassurance, she is mirroring him. He receives so much comfort and also learns a great deal about how to respond to his own emotions through her mirroring.

Mirroring

Mirroring is a term that refers to the action that one person takes when she reflects back the experience of another. It is a reflection of emotion back to the child which captures the heart of the matter in a caring and knowing way. Mirroring is not mocking. It shows the initiating party that his needs are heard and are being taken seriously.

A sensitive parent is one who not only responds to the child but also mirrors him. The mirroring is a matched reflection of the infant's experience, and it adds a dimension of validating the infant and letting her know that everything is going to be okay. Mirroring can be done in happy situations, "There's my girl! How happy you are! I'm so happy too." It can be done in mastery situations, when an infant has tried something new and conquered it. "You're so brave and so strong too! That's my big, strong boy!"

Mirroring is also essential for situations where a child is frightened or sad: "My sweetie, you're hurt. You fell down and got a boo-boo. It was startling! But it's okay now. I'll kiss your elbow and make it better."

In this example, the parent is reflecting to the child that she is aware of the incident and that it must have hurt and been really startling. The parent also reassures the child that everything is going to be okay.

This interaction would have numerous back and forth signals and responses at the verbal and nonverbal level, many more than I could type out for you here. Through the parent's mirroring and the reciprocal interchange, the child will actually develop a sense for what her own body signals are telling her. In the skinned elbow situation, she would be trained to take her signals seriously and to communicate them to others right away. Her parent's calm response also trains her to not be overwhelmed by those emotions, even if they are strong. This wonderful mirroring and reciprocal interchange actually develop the child's emotional intelligence.

Emotional intelligence is the ability to perceive, interpret, make sense of, and act in a wise manner based on your emotions.

There is even a specific part of the brain, the orbital frontal cortex, which gets developed to do this task. A great deal of this development is the result of the sensitive response of the parent, through mirroring and the reciprocal interchange. It is clear how very important it is to have a sensitive parent for optimal development of the infant brain. The sensitivity of the parent has direct bearing on the type of attachment bond that is formed between the infant and parent.

Styles of Attachment

In Chapter 1 we discussed three main categories that are used to describe the attachment style of children: secure, ambivalent protesters, and detached avoiders.[21]

Secure Attachment

From our earlier discussion we noted that a securely attached child has a stable bond with Mom that persists even when the two are separated. The secure child branches out to explore the world from the basis of that bond. This child uses Mom as a secure base to venture out from, and returns to her in moments of distress to seek comfort. Each time the child receives help from Mom in times of need, it bolsters the child's sense of security. And each experience of receiving help seems to educate the child about how to cope with problems in the future.

This child knows who his primary caregiver is, and will not follow the lead of a stranger, unless Mom lets him know by her presence that it is okay. I am reminded of the way Jesus, the Good Shepherd, speaks about His bond with us as His sheep:

> *...He calls his own sheep by name and leads them out. When he puts forth all his own, he goes ahead of them, and the sheep follow him because they know his voice. A stranger they simply will not follow, but will flee from him, because they do not know the voice of strangers* (John 10:3-5).

A secure attachment bond is formed when a parent is sensitive and responsive to the infant's signals. Because the mother is available to meet the needs of the infant in an appropriate and responsive manner, the infant comes to trust Mom and rest securely in the knowledge that there is one who will meet his needs. You can immediately draw more spiritual parallels here, comparing a secure child with a believer who is secure in God. A secure Christian is one who trusts in his or her heavenly Father: *"And my God will supply all your needs according to His riches in glory in Christ Jesus"* (Philippians 4:19).

There are notable differences in the parenting styles of securely attached infants when compared to infants who are insecurely attached. Infants who are securely attached are more likely to have mothers who are more sensitive to the infant's cues, accepting, and expressive of affection toward them, in comparison with insecurely attached infants.[22]

Insecure Attachment Styles

In contrast to the secure children whose parents were sensitive and responsive to their cues, insecure children had parents who were inconsistent, distracted, or overwhelming. Too often they did not receive the reassurance and mirroring that they needed in order to be certain of their parents' physical and emotional presence in their lives. They have deep sorrow in their hearts or anxiety about whom they can count on. The following verse describes the result of their repeated disappointments: *"Hope deferred makes the heart sick"* (Proverbs 13:12).

Ambivalent Protesters

The ambivalent protester is caught in an internal tug-of-war, like the term ambivalent suggests. This child is extremely distressed when Mom leaves and is not fully comforted when she returns. The child seems angry with her for leaving and tries to keep her at a distance, while feeling torn in wanting to be close to her. The ambivalent child is anxious about exploring the world and about connecting with strangers.

This style of attachment seems to be associated with a parenting style which is *inconsistent*. Sometimes, the child's needs are ignored while the parent is completing another activity or is preoccupied. When Mom gives attention, it may be based on her own needs as opposed to what the child is signaling for. Mothers of ambivalent babies are insensitive in their interactions with their babies and are often low in affection.

Sometimes ambivalent children get positive attention, so they cling to hope that their needs will be met. However, it is confusing because the attention they get may be delayed or based more on their mother's needs, which makes them angry and unsure of what to expect. This uncertainty is what leads them to be constantly anxious, fretting about strangers and fussing a great deal when Mom leaves. They are not assured that when she returns she will be emotionally available. When they feel separated they think, *I better really turn up the volume to get my mom's attention! It makes me mad and anxious to be so unsure of her, but maybe this time I will get through?*

Detached Avoiders

Detached avoiders have had their hopes dashed one too many times. These children are pretty shut down, not exploring the world with Mom in the room or when she is gone. Avoiders ignore Mom, showing little emotion whether she comes or goes. They ignore Mom, avoid her gaze, and do not make attempts to seek closeness with her. Strangers are treated in much the same manner.

This avoidant style of attachment develops from a parenting style that is *disengaged*. Mothers of avoidant babies are frequently insensitive to their infant's signals and don't hold them close as often as they need. Instead of being affectionate with them, avoidant mothers may actually be angry or irritable with their children. As a result of this pattern of disengagement, the child's needs are seldom met, and the child learns that it makes little difference what is communicated to Mom. Mom is not going to respond.

This can take place even when the parent has been physically close with the child for most of the time. A parent's lack of emotional presence, as shown by insensitivity, irritability, and lack of holding the child, has much of the same effect as if the parent were physically absent. The avoidant child has been repeatedly reinforced with the message: *It doesn't matter what I do, even if Mom is in the room with me. I cannot get close to her; I cannot bring her near. I will protect myself from further rejection by not even showing her that I'm upset when she's gone.*

This pattern of thinking and responding on the part of the child is going to be hard to change or replace. You could make the argument that the effects are more enduring than if he had the mixed experiences of the ambivalent protester who sometimes got attention and sometimes did not.

Disorganized Attachment—No Set Way to Cope with Separation Distress

The disorganized category is rarer than the other three and was described by later researchers, Mary Main and Judith Solomon.[23] The disorganized child is dazed and confused when Mom leaves the room or returns. This child may attempt a number of strategies, such as pursuing closeness, pushing away from Mom, detaching altogether, and even attaching to strangers. This is a sad state to observe, and it often develops due to the effects of trauma.

Trauma occurs when a child senses that he is in imminent danger. The abuse, neglect, substance abuse, or mental illness of the parent make the child fearful for his well-being or even his life. The child may not truly be in danger of losing his life, but as a little kid he has no way to precisely gauge the level of danger in a situation. It is his perception of danger that matters the most in determining whether he is traumatized.

A child who is traumatized by a parent will also have some times when she is close to that same parent. There are occasions when the disorganized child receives contact and comfort from her parent. But in other situations, the one from whom she received comfort actually becomes her enemy—neglecting, terrifying, or hurting her. The very person who was supposed to comfort the child was the one who was frightening or hurtful!

So it makes sense that this child would be highly anxious. He would have a high degree of confusion, not knowing how to approach Mom for closeness or what to expect when he approaches Mom. Abusive parents, substance abusers, and mentally ill parents are unpredictable. The child has no way of guessing what the parent will do because sometimes the parent's responses just don't make sense or fit the situation.

As a result, the disorganized child becomes confused about what strategies will work. This child has not had any consistent reinforcement of one approach strategy or another. He does not know what to do in order to get his needs met. He struggles, *I don't know whether to come or go. If I get close to Mom, will she hug me or hurt me? Maybe I'll be really dependent and pleasing just to calm her down. Or I could reject her before she rejects me. I don't know what to do!*

In this example, I have given a voice to the thoughts that a young child might have in mind as he considers what will help him get close to and remain near to his or her mother. I also deliberately chose to include some internal dialogue about what the child might do in order to avoid getting rejected in attempts for closeness. While we know young children are not that verbal, the reality is the behavior patterns they display are consistent with such self-talk.

The truth is, most of us developed the strategies we use to pursue closeness or protect us from loss *long* before we learned to speak. We learned how to do relationships before we could ever put it into words! Child development researchers would say these lessons we learned about what works to bring closeness were "pre-verbal."

Your Map for Relationships

Bowlby was among the first to describe the map that gets built into us, the framework that we use to view relationships and to pursue closeness in them. Bowlby called this framework, an internal working model. Bowlby believed that a child begins to construct this model just as language is starting to develop and that the child lays many more pieces of the model as language blossoms. He believed that the child forms a:

> model of how the physical world may be expected to behave, how his mother and other significant persons may be expected to behave, how he himself may be expected to behave, and how each interacts with all the others. ...within the framework...he evaluates special aspects of his situation, and makes his attachment plans.[24]

What we are seeing is that a child develops her maps for how to do relationships within the same period of time that she acquires language. This map is so basic to her understanding of relationships and life that it may feel automatic or instinctive. Her map, whether secure, ambivalent protesting, or detached avoiding, was what she had to do in order to cope with the conditions she faced with parents. Her model was formed through lots of trial and error experiences.

> *Okay, that one didn't work…let's try another way of getting attention. Hooray! The new strategy was successful! I think I'll stick with that one for a while.*
>
> *Oops, that didn't go well, I better try something else that doesn't make Mom so angry. I'm really in trouble if Mom gets angry and ditches me!*

Through the rewards and pain of these attempts, a child develops his characteristic ways of approaching closeness in relationships. These models actually *become the lens* through which the child sees relationships, and it includes all of his strategies for trying to build secure attachment within those relationships. These experiences guide the child's feelings, thoughts, and expectations in later relationships.[25]

By the time the child has settled on a particular approach style for seeking closeness, she has already gone through the pain of ruling out many options, in order to be left with the final set of successful options. Based on the length and complexity of the learning process alone, we can see why a child's characteristic way of approaching closeness would be pretty firmly rooted. However, the pattern of approaching relationships is not only a learned behavior, it also becomes hardwired into the very fabric and structure of the child's developing brain.

Attachment Experiences Shape Your Brain Development

The infant's brain structures (essential working components of the brain) are developing at a time when two important things are happening in the life of the child from an attachment perspective. First, the brain is in its most active stage of growth and development at the time in which the secure or insecure bond is being formed with the primary caregiver. Second, the brain structures are also being formed at the time in which the infant is developing a working model through which she will view current attachment relationships and all future attachment relationships.

These structures include those associated with observation, planning, self-regulation, and higher level thinking. The structures also include key components of the emotional response system and the regulation of the brain chemicals that trigger and facilitate specific emotional states, such as happiness or fear.

Think about that for a second. At the very time when the infant's physical brain is developing in crucial areas, she is also having formative experiences in the area of learning how to attach to significant others!

Life experiences activate the brain at the structural and chemical level. The brain is responding to these attachment experiences with excitement, confusion, peace, or anxiety. These early attachment experiences actually help to determine which parts of her brain get utilized and strengthened, and which parts will be underdeveloped.

Have you heard the phrase "use it or lose it"? This is literally taking place in the child's brain in the first three years of life. Portions of the brain that are not activated or utilized are actually pruned away so that the active areas of the brain will receive the most resources. The result of this process is that only the most useful brain structures and communication pathways will endure. The remaining structures of the brain, once formed and locked in place, will determine a person's potential to analyze and respond to relationship situations in the future.

An infant's early life attachment experiences will also influence which brain chemicals get released in the context of human interactions, and in what quantities. The chemical regulation system of the brain, which forms during the child's early months and years, will also influence the way the child responds to attachment situations. If the child learned that attachment relationships are secure, then her brain will release peaceful and mellowing agents into her brain when she gets close to others.

The child who was abused when he got close to a parent will have a brain flooded with fear and hypervigilance brain chemicals during times when he tries to get close to others. As a result, it may be very physically overwhelming for the abused child to get close to others. His brain is literally trying to signal him to be hypervigilant for the prospect of danger right in the moment when he tries to draw close to someone else.

What I have stated about brain structures and brain chemicals is an oversimplification of the way in which the brain develops and functions in the early years. But I include it to give you a sense for how attachment styles and strategies become hardwired into our brains. Physiologically you can't help but have certain responses in attachment situations, because many of your brain's structures and chemical response systems were actually put together in the context of your earliest attachment experiences. Cognitively you can't help the way in which you automatically view relationship experiences. Your strategy map for how to do relationships was created at the very time that your brain was developing.

You can't help the way you think and feel about close relationships!

I do not want to sound fatalistic or to convey a sense of doom over the life of one who has experienced trauma or confusion during the early experiences of attachment. Modern research shows that God made our brains in wonderful and resilient ways. Our brains can recover from trauma, rebuild new brain tissue, and compensate for areas of damage and underdevelopment. We may also have new experiences in later childhood or even as adults that help to reprogram our brain and teach us healthier ways to connect. However, I think it is important to note that it is quite automatic for us to rely on the strategies for attachment that we learned during the earliest years of our experience.

When we look at it in this light, it makes sense that children's characteristic ways of perceiving and experiencing attachment relationships are so firmly rooted within them. It would follow then that this characteristic way, this internal working model, would stay with them for years to come. Research shows that our attachment styles remain with us from infancy, through later years of childhood, and into adulthood.[26]

We internalize our viewpoint about how relationships should be and what the best ways are to obtain closeness. This internal working model then guides us as we approach relationships in childhood, adolescence, dating, and into adulthood with marriage and parenting.

Attachment Map for Adults in Marriage

Now I'd like to ask you to read over the following chart that may help you see how your attachment style plays out with your spouse. Attachment styles are on the left, along with a description of what each person does in moments of distress.

Marital Style of Attachment	Description
Secure	You are assured that your spouse is available and constant. You feel free to explore and share your internal world with your spouse. You turn to your spouse for comfort in times of distress. You think fondly of your spouse when the two of you are apart, and you are glad to be reunited.
Ambivalent Protesters	Sometimes you are anxious, even when your spouse is close by. You do not have assurance of the constant presence of your spouse. You are unsure about whether you can explore/share your inner world with your spouse. You worry about your spouse when the two of you are apart. When you are reunited, you can't decide whether you are happy to see them or angry about all the times that you have felt distance.
Detached Avoiders	Due to repeated experiences in childhood and with your spouse you don't believe that your spouse is available for you. So you don't even try to share/explore your internal world with them. You keep some emotional distance from your spouse when the two of you are together. If you are apart, you don't often miss them and seem to be relieved that you have a break. You may feel anxious about getting close, especially during conflict.

Adapted from Hazan and Shaver, "Romantic Love Conceptualized as an Attachment Process" and Ainsworth, et al., *Patterns of Attachment.*

Adult Attachment Strategies Are Subtle and Flexible

It is important to note that the three main categories—secure, ambivalent protesters, and detached avoiders—are most descriptive of little children. These categories were developed to describe the way that infants and toddlers respond to separation from their parents. If you think about it, there is a lot at stake for the infant in the event that the primary caregiver leaves. The infant could be lonely, go hungry, develop serious emotional problems, or even die without the caregiver nearby. This is why the infant or young child protests so strongly when the caregiver leaves and is desperate to get the parent to return.

Remember that this was what started John Bowlby's entire journey of discovery into the attachment process in the first place. Of course, the infant's distress level is much higher in moments of abandonment than we would find in an adult. The infant's strategies to try to reunite with the parent are going to be much more pronounced and intense. In adulthood, isolation is not life threatening, but it is still damaging.

Adults still display traits related to their childhood attachment styles. However, they will likely have more subtle ways in which they display these traits.

For example, if a detached avoider husband is in a conflict with his wife where she is criticizing him, his avoidant behaviors may be pretty subtle. However, if his wife is threatening to leave him for good, this might lead him to protest immensely and then completely shut down. So the intensities of the attachment behaviors vary by situation.

In addition, an adult has a much more developed brain than the infant, a brain capable of reasoning things out in a way that calms the adult. As such, an adult may engage in self-talk that is soothing and keeps the adult from feeling quite so desperate. He or she may sort through a number of strategies to use in a situation where there is a threat of loss or abandonment. Research on adult attachment suggests to us that each adult will still have a propensity toward one style of approaching attachment. Other strategies would take more effort to use and practice over time. But it can be done.

Hope for Improving Your Attachment Style

A person does not have to be locked into one category, for example, detached avoider. An adult may show some traits of avoidance and also some traits of secure attachment. It makes a lot of sense to me that a person may predominantly lead off with avoidance in times of distress, but over time he may learn to rely on other strategies. This person may improve to the point that he or she only uses avoidant strategies in the time of highest distress. In addition, within the category of avoidant, there are people who are more extreme in their avoidance while others are milder. Allowing for this range of possibilities within a category and allowing for flexible movement across categories gives us hope that we can change. As adults there is hope!

We can learn to be more flexible in the way we draw close to others so that we have an entire array of strategies to choose from when connecting with them. We can develop new ways to manage our anxiety when we are faced with the threat of loss or abandonment. With practice and new experiences, we can grow to a point where we stop viewing each conflict as an event that threatens loss or abandonment. Conflict becomes a process where we learn more about ourselves and our spouses' unmet needs.

We may have been trained as infants to be insecure in our attachment style. We may have experienced rejection in our childhood, but God offers us hope in every aspect of our lives. If we were rejected in infancy, God says He will not forget us.

> *Can a woman forget her nursing child and have no compassion on the son of her womb? Even these may forget, but I will not forget you. Behold, I have inscribed you on the palms of My hands. Your walls are continually before Me* (Isaiah 49:15-16).

Even if you were abandoned by your mother when you were a baby, God says He will not forsake you. He says you are securely connected to Him. You are engraved in the palms of His nail-scarred hands, and He is always thinking of you. If you went through the pain of being forsaken as a child, the psalmist David offers this comfort:

> *Though my father and mother forsake me, the Lord will receive me. I remain confident of this: I will see the goodness of the Lord in the land of the living* (Psalm 27:10,13 NIV).

We have hope that God will bring restoration to us, even on this side of eternity. We can have hope in the Lord for this life and for the next, that we would have closeness with Him and a secure bond with our Maker.

We will never be completely devoid of the effects of the fall of the human race. At some level we will always have an empty place inside of us that yearns for more. The apostle Paul speaks about this, noting that "the whole creation has been groaning as in the pains of childbirth right up to the present time" awaiting the expectation of fulfillment (Romans 8:22 NIV). We long for perfect closeness and complete security. This stems from our awareness of our disconnection from God and our desperate longing, our groaning, to be restored to Him. It also stems from our incomplete attachment and whatever insecurity we have from our childhood.

We carry this expectation, this longing for fulfillment, as we approach our quest for a dating partner and a secure marriage. Our level of expectation for what marriage will do to fulfill our needs for attachment, or make up for the lack of attachment that we received in childhood, is largely dependent on how disturbed our attachment process was as children. *The more disrupted our attachment was, the more we are inclined look to marriage to fix the broken pieces or make up the difference.*

So as we enter into dating, we have a couple of factors driving us: 1) our healthy need for secure attachment and 2) our need to make up for the disruptions in our childhood attachment. If we pursue dating for the sake of finding a marriage partner, then we must assess the nature and potential of marriage before we even enter into this sacred union.

We know that marriage can be a glorious, wonderful, secure, and sanctifying union. However, it can never meet all our needs, make up for our past, or replace our need for a secure connection with our Creator. So losing our illusions of romance as the answer to all our loneliness and woes actually frees us to enjoy our marriages more.

There's just one problem, though. It is very difficult to ground yourself with these realistic appraisals of marriage as you enter into a dating relationship because most of us get a little silly, "punch drunk" with infatuation, blinded by love. That's why we have to understand the true power of intoxicating love.

CHAPTER 3

Intoxicating Love

God blessed them; and God said to them, "Be fruitful and multiply, and fill the earth, and subdue it; and rule over the fish of the sea and over the birds of the sky and over every living thing that moves on the earth" (Genesis 1:28).

"Be fruitful and multiply?" We are really talking about romance and sex! The first part of this passage only hints at the pleasures, intoxicating romance, and exhilaration that comes from the initial union of two lives who are enjoying God's plan for fruitfulness on the planet. As we obey God's command, we actually catch a deeper glimpse of who He is. We participate in the romance of His infinite love, and we become cocreators of life as He designed it to be. So, as with many portions of Scripture, the depth and beauty lie within a deeper exploration of the meanings of the passage.

When God told us to be "fruitful and multiply," He gave a command and also created a beautifully fascinating way to carry out His will. I am not merely referring to the act of sex or the miracle of conception. If you back up further in the process, you'll stand amazed at the many steps that God designed so that we humans might "be fruitful."

He provided us with a complex set of systems and subsystems that work together to ensure that a man and a woman will have the best possible chances to be fruitful and to multiply themselves. This carefully orchestrated process ensures that the couple will actually produce a child and that the child will live. When everything works together as it should, the process ensures that the child will be healthier and stronger than the parents who gave him or her life. And the whole process begins with attraction and the intoxicating experiences of romantic love.

Early Views on Infatuation

For thousands of years humans have known that something special and extraordinary takes place between a man and woman who have "fallen in love." So mysterious and powerful are the forces of this intoxicating love that earlier civilizations actually viewed them as coming from outside of us, through the intrusion of one of the "gods" into our lives and hearts. The Romans came up with Cupid, the god of erotic love and beauty, in their quest toward understanding this powerful force. He is still depicted today on the front of our Valentine's Day cards and in popular cartoons shooting his arrows at some unsuspecting person who was just smitten with love.

Lovesick, giddy, punch drunk, crazy in love, and head-over-heels are just a few of the phrases that we use today to describe the ecstatic roller coaster ride that we find ourselves on when we fall in love. It is a wonderful, emotional, sometimes painful experience, as anyone who has ever fallen can tell. You can't sleep because you are thinking of your beloved. In the daytime, you may be daydreaming because you cannot keep your mind off of the object of your affection. At times you lose your appetite, your pulse races, and you get sweaty palms. You may have seemingly boundless energy to be with your love, and may do zany things that you would never do under any other circumstance, like shouting to an entire amusement park or town square, "I LOVE THIS WOMAN!"

All of this takes place in the name of love. It truly is a special time in a person's life, an intoxicating experience that is referenced even in the

Bible. Solomon mingles kisses and wine in his love poems: *"...your mouth like the best wine. May the wine go straight to my beloved, flowing gently over lips and teeth"* (Song of Solomon 7:9 NIV). Solomon was describing romantic love in his Middle Eastern culture several thousand years ago. Literature and music from every culture and era describe the nature of this exhilarating experience.

Helen Fisher is an anthropologist and human behavior researcher at Rutgers University who has studied romantic love across cultures and around the world. She has integrated the findings of modern-day neuroscience with the cultural richness and lore that she has surveyed. Her findings help unravel the mysteries of intoxicating love and give us a deeper appreciation for its role in jumpstarting the attachment process of love that lasts a lifetime. These findings help us stand back in awe at the God who gave us all forms of love, and who is Love itself: *"God is love"* (1 John 4:8 NIV).

Lookin' Good to Me!

Attraction starts off in a surprisingly balanced sort of way. In examining cultures from around the world, there is a lot of variance in what constitutes beauty and good looks. Some cultures value blue eyes and blond hair, while for others the darkness and mystery of brown hair and eyes are the standard of choice. Certain cultures value height, to the extent that they will even elongate their necks to make this happen. But, across all cultures, there is one universal beauty trait, and that is symmetry. In other words, if one half of a person's body or face aligns nicely with the other half of their body, then we are inclined to find that person attractive.[27] It's our first clue about whether the attractive one might be a physically healthy and balanced sort of person.

Most men and women fall in love with people who are similar to themselves in terms of ethnicity, class, religion, level of education, comparable intelligence, values, and communication abilities. We may fall for a person because we find ourselves spending a lot of time with them, and "love sneaks up on us." This is the notion of proximity breeding attraction. At other times, we are more ready in our process of maturing to make a commitment to another, and so we allow ourselves to be open to feelings of romantic love. I have seen in many cases that a person who is cautious about getting hurt cannot "let go" and take the risk of falling in love. Such a person has a harder time being ready to "fall in love."

Each person approaches romantic love with a conscious and unconscious set of hopes and expectations about a future partner.

We gravitate toward people who seem to line up with our set of hopes and expectations and desires. Many factors enter into this mix, making up a person's love template or love map.[28] Key factors will include our awareness, both conscious and unconscious, of our attachment style and our need to find a partner who will recreate and add to our attachment experiences.

You Smell Good!

One surprising piece of the attraction process comes to us through our nose. Yes, that's right, the traveling salesmen and perfume counter attendants were actually on to something when they crafted potions and colognes to draw attention our way. Contrary to myth, there is no love potion that will magically draw others our way.[29] There is no "Love Potion Number Nine" that will make all the men swoon for some lucky girl. It's actually a good thing too that we have not created an elixir so powerful as to lock others in its wafting spell, as we will soon see. But God does use the magic of pheromones and the human sense of smell as an important piece of the process of romantic attraction.

In what has affectionately been called the "sweaty t-shirt study," a Swiss researcher named Claus Wedekind tapped into the mysteries of human pheromones.[30] Wedekind and his colleagues recruited about one hundred male and female college students from different campuses to participate in a research study on the human sense of smell. They asked the guys to wear the same cotton t-shirt for three days, without the added benefits of cologne or deodorant to mask their masculine scents.

They also asked them to stay away from spicy foods, alcohol, and smoking, which could also interfere with the scent of a man. The t-shirts were carefully stored in airtight plastic containers and then presented to the unsuspecting female college students.

Can you imagine the surprise of the women when the researchers opened up the containers of three-day-old sweaty t-shirts?

The women were asked to rate the t-shirts in terms of which scents they were most sexually attracted to. Their noses led them in the right direction; results indicated that women had a clear preference for the smells of certain guys. As it turned out, they preferred the smell of guys who would actually make better reproductive partners. Specifically, the women were most attracted to the smell of t-shirts that belonged to guys with an immune system profile that was different from their own.

This immune system profile is called major histocompatibility complex (MHC) and it reflects the array of diseases that a person can readily fend off during the course of life. If a woman pairs up with a man who has a profile different from her own, their resultant child will have the benefit of both profiles and the boosted power this affords in fending off illnesses. Isn't that ingenious? God instilled this remarkable capability into women as they search for a mate. They have the ability to literally sniff out a man who will be more likely to help them be "fruitful and multiply."

It is likely that women were endowed with this important facet of smell because they have a lot more invested in bringing life into this world than men do. If a woman is going to give up nine months of her life to pregnancy, and then many more months to follow, she had better make sure that the child will have a good immune system to survive the wiles and diseases of life. We will speak more about women's investment in childbirth and child rearing in the sex chapter, Naked and Unashamed, later in the book.

Who would have thought that a woman might fall in love with a man because he smells good? Who knew that the man and the woman could somehow tell from the symmetry and smell of the other whether their offspring would have a better chance to survive on the planet? Let us not forget the many unnamed and equally "mysterious" unconscious factors (factors that we are not immediately aware of) that lead us to one partner as opposed to another.

For example, a shy person is often attracted to a more outgoing person. A detail-oriented person goes for a partner who loses sight of the details while quickly gaining the big picture. Some combination of biology, symmetry, pheromones, personal hopes and dreams, and God's knowledge of what we each need to grow, all come together to set our affections on that special someone. And, once that process of attraction begins, we are off to the races. We find ourselves on the roller coaster of intoxicating love.

The Intoxicating Cocktail of Infatuation Chemicals

The roller coaster begins as our brain surges with new levels of specialized brain chemicals called neurotransmitters. It is truly a cocktail of these intoxicating substances that mix together when we find ourselves attracted to another. And the dosages of these substances come heavy, hard, and fast to ensure that we will focus all our time and courtship energies on one person, and one person alone.

Modern brain science has given us detailed insights into the chemical mix that takes place in our brain during the first year to two years of romantic love. Current brain imaging methods, such as functional magnetic resonance imaging (fMRI), give scientists the ability to look at what parts of the brain are active at any given point in time. Those parts of the brain literally "light up" with color on a TV monitor if they are active while the scientists are viewing and studying them.

A View of the "Fallen in Love" Brain

Helen Fisher and colleagues conducted functional magnetic resonance imaging (fMRI) studies of the brains of ten women and seven men who had been in love for an average of about 7 months.[31] So, think about it. They were taking a peek into the brains of people who had just fallen in love. Participants were asked to look at a photograph of his or her beloved while the fMRI mapped out the regions that were activated in their brains. The casual observer would note how a broad smile might come across the face of the lover, coupled with a deep sigh. But the brain imaging results go much deeper and speak to the functional and chemical changes that take place in that moment of viewing the photo of the beloved.

Several specific regions of the brain were highly activated during the moments that the lovers gazed at the photos. These regions included the "reward center" of the brain and regions responsible for producing the chemical called dopamine.

Think of dopamine as "human cocaine," because it is associated with feeling high, a sense of ecstasy, intense energy, sleeplessness, elevated mood, clinging, and craving. Dopamine is also linked to drive, goal seeking, and motivation. Areas that produce and respond to dopamine were activated in the brains of these people who were newly in love. Results suggest that dopamine is one of the chemicals that contributes to all those aspects of romantic love.

This makes intuitive sense when we observe or recall the high feeling that lovers get just by being in the presence of their beloved, and their drive to go to any lengths to be with the one they love. Dopamine would also account then for that driven, almost obsessive, focus that we have on our new lover. We can't get them out of our minds.

Rosy Red Cheeks—The Blushing Power of Norepinephrine

Helen Fisher believes that norepinephrine is another chemical that is heavily involved during the romantic phase of love.[32] It acts more generally within the nervous system and is key to the "fight or flight response" of the brain physiology. Think of a pounding heart, elevated blood pressure, flushed skin, sweaty palms, and breathless sensations and you'll get a clear picture of the effects of norepinephrine on the human body.

Doesn't that fit exactly with some of your own memories of what it is like to fall in love? In fact, we so often associate this type of physiological arousal with attraction that we can even be faked out by these same sensations, if they are artificially created. A study, taught in introductory psychology courses, illustrates this point in a clever manner.

Donald G. Dutton and Arthur P. Aron were two psychologists who were curious about the various ways in which people make sense of their arousal feelings.[33] Their most famous study has been dubbed, "The Love Bridge." In this experiment the psychologists had an attractive female graduate student stand at the end of a long suspension bridge that stretched over a deep gorge. They had this same female graduate student stand at the end of a standard and tamer sort of bridge.

Male participants were randomly assigned to walk across either of the bridges where they were met by the female student who asked them to fill out a survey. She also provided all of them with a phone number where she might be reached. As it turns out, a lot more of the guys who walked across the scary suspension bridge made a phone call to the female student. Hardly any of the tame bridge guys put forth the effort to initiate contact with the woman.

The scared, flushed, and breathless guys got tricked by their own body cues. They thought they were weak in the knees from the beauty of the female student! The psychologists concluded that the suspension bridge guys felt like they must have been attracted to the female student, when they arrived in front of her already breathless and flushed. These fellows, under the influence of norepinephrine, were tricked into believing that they might have some sort of "chemistry" with the female student. Funny or sad, depending on how you look at it, this study appears to confirm the presence of norepinephrine in the cocktail that we experience during infatuation.

Searching for Serotonin

There is one more chemical for us to think about in our experience of romantic love, and that is serotonin. Serotonin is the "feel good chemical" of the human brain, that puts us at ease, makes us mellow, and helps us feel upbeat. Think of the relaxed euphoric feeling that you get after a turkey dinner on Thanksgiving Day while you are sitting around with your family on the sofa, just about ready to take a nap.

Fisher says that romantic love is paired up with a decrease in serotonin activity in the body.[34] She noted a study that compared twenty people with severe, unmedicated Obsessive Compulsive Disorder (OCD) with twenty people who had fallen in love in the past six months. Twenty normal people were included in the study to provide a group for comparison. The serotonin levels in the people with OCD and those who had fallen in love were significantly lower than what the researchers found in the normal participants.[35] In other words, the brains of the love-struck people in this study looked a lot like folks with Obsessive Compulsive Disorder.

Love-struck people have a lot in common with people with OCD!

So it is likely that reduced serotonin contributes to the obsessive focus that lovers have on their beloved, and to the impulsive things done for their love objects. This is the wonderful chemical cocktail that floods our brains as we fall in love with another person. The mixed drink of love makes us obsess on our lover, do anything to be with them, go without sleep, and crave their presence.

Intoxicating Chemicals Kick Us into High Gear

Intoxicating chemicals affect our judgment, causing us to do things we would not ordinarily do. As with any high dose of a chemical substance, it also affects our ability to accurately perceive a situation. We literally can't see the whole picture because we are high at the time. This wonderful and wild ride ensures that we will attend to one love object at a time and not waste valuable time or energy chasing several people. It leads us to court and marry that one, and to eagerly pursue the actions of sex and procreation.

We see that the chemical cocktail of infatuation really shifts our attachment-building behaviors into high gear. We learned in the first two chapters about what it takes to build a close and secure attachment bond between a child and parent. Attachment styles and the building of attachment ties both carry into adulthood. Recall that a secure attachment bond is formed between two people through attentive and sensitive responding over time. The bond is formed through reciprocal interchange, where one person's action leads to the other person's reaction, and vice versa. Mirroring is involved too, which is the responsive connection invoked in face-to-face communication.

You can see how two doting lovers, under the influence of infatuation, are able to attend to one another, respond quickly, gaze deeply into the other's eyes, and form an attachment bond rapidly. They are chemically driven to do all of the behaviors necessary to form an attachment bond and to do it very quickly. Infatuation creates "attachment behaviors on steroids" so that the behaviors we need to form an attachment with another person are coming at a fast and furious pace.

When we fall in love, these bonding behaviors just seem to gush out of us. Under the influence of infatuation, we can't see straight because we are intoxicated. We are not looking out for potential harm or weighing all the risks. Instead, we throw caution to the wind and open ourselves to our beloved in the most expressive and vulnerable ways.

Impaired Judgment: Infatuation Clouds Your View

Infatuation is a wonderful ride, but there are a couple implications to consider in the aftermath of this fast and furious bonding process. First, the chemical influence on our brain makes us blind to most of the inherent character flaws in our beloved partners. These flaws include things they do defensively to protect themselves from loss and abandonment. Our beloved is hardly showing any of those characteristic protective strategies, though, because our lover is high too! Our beloved is throwing caution to the wind and acting vulnerable and undefended. There ought to be a "Surgeon General's Warning" about the cocktail of infatuation:

DANGER! INFATUATION IMPAIRS YOUR JUDGMENT AND ABILITY TO SEE ANYTHING BUT THE GOOD QUALITIES IN YOUR PARTNER.

The fine print would state: "Slow down and take in the opinions of your friends and family, who are not high at this time like you. The more you pursue the physical side of dating, the blurrier your vision will be. You could end up with a person who has a lot more difficulty with getting close to others than you ever realized."

Second, infatuation makes relationship building and connecting appear to be easy. You both were vulnerable, and you both were motivated to build closeness in the relationship during that time. I have heard many people in marital therapy say to me:

> *Jesse, I just wish we could go back to the way it was when we first fell in love. It was so easy then, and this feels like so much work.*

> *He never acted like this when we were dating. This feels like he was playing a trick on me about who he really was.*

Depth beyond Infatuation

I have some hopeful things to say about both of these concerns. Regarding blindness to our lovers' flaws, the hope is that even people with baggage (we all have baggage) can be healed and set free by being in partnership with someone who is building a secure marriage with them. We can unlearn former ways of relating and connecting and replace them with healthier and more fulfilling connection strategies. In fact, I personally believe that God ordained marriage to bring about emotional and relational healing in our lives. *"God sets the lonely in families…"* (Psalm 68:6 NIV).

Second, about the hard work that it takes to build a marriage, I'm not convinced that some hard work is a bad thing. We know that hard work makes us value something more than if it comes with ease. The sense of security we gain from our loving labor together in building a bond is far greater than what we attain from a quick flight into love in the early days of bonding. Each step of building the marriage relationship takes time and effort, and gives us a chance to know our spouse in deeper ways.

It is true that marriage building takes work after infatuation wears off. After that phase in our relationship, we have to be intentional about taking those steps that will build security in the marriage. The end result is a bond that has been strengthened, a relationship that has been deepened, and a love that has grown in felt security. This is far more stable and valuable than a relationship strictly based on infatuation.

I have more good news. Each intentional step we take in building security has its own immediate rewards. Each labor of love brings understanding, comfort, healing, and greater freedom right in that moment.

We will be learning more about how to take these steps through our discovery together of the Seven Keys to a Secure Marriage. The keys are framed as ways to break free from insecure patterns of attempting to relate—and replacing them with new and life-giving sources of connection. First we will have to understand where we are getting stuck, so we can learn how to return to our face-to-face stance toward one another.

CHAPTER 4

Locked in a Struggle, Locked Out of Your Heart

...the willing is present in me, but the doing of the good is not. For the good that I want, I do not do, but I practice the very evil that I do not want (Romans 7:18-19).

When we first learned to dance with our spouses, it was all so easy. He took the lead, and she followed. Both of us wanted to be on the dance floor, and most of the time we were standing face-to-face. We even had a little chemical help through infatuation that drove us, compelled us, swept us into the dance, and often carried us away together.

For most of us, that fluid dance was continuing on the day we took our vows. Our hearts were filled with love and a desire to connect to our spouses, a desire to cherish, protect, and stand together through thick and thin. It all started with such promise and such hope. We pledged our whole selves to one another, standing face-to-face once again. We made ourselves available, opening our hearts fully to the ones we loved.

If you are a married person, you have by now had the experience of those moments when your spouse did something that hurt you. It may have been intentional, but most times it was not. Yet you found yourself pulling away from an open posture toward your spouse. You stopped dancing with your spouse. You retreated, or you put on protective armor in order to defend your heart from emotional pain.

Wired for Protection: Fight or Flight

The strategies we use to protect ourselves from pain are relatively simple. They line up clearly with our God-given protection mechanisms, which are programmed into us so that we might survive on the planet. The "Fight or Flight Response" is a fascinating hardwired mechanism that all humans possess.

Think of what would happen inside your body if you were to suddenly see a tiger leaping into the room where you are now sitting! Your mind and body would spring into action to prepare you to deal with your striped guest. A whole series of circulatory, respiratory, digestive, and cognitive changes would launch within your body in a fraction of a second. When there is a threat to our well-being, our bodies instantly launch into the fight or flight response as follows:

1. The blood leaves our brain and flows to our major muscle groups, to ready us to run away or to fight the source of threat.
2. Our lungs begin to breathe rapidly to oxygenate that blood, which prevents us from having muscle cramps.
3. The cooling system, also known as human sweat, kicks on so we won't overheat and fall prey to the source of threat.
4. Our stomach tries to empty itself, out one end or the other, so that we will be lightweight and not waste valuable energy on digestion when we should be fighting or running.
5. Last, our brain shuts down most of its functioning in order to hyper-focus on just one thing. The brain narrows its focus to dealing only with the threat so we won't be distracted from the survival task at hand.

So, under the threat of harm, we literally cannot help ourselves from kicking into a fight or flight posture. This posture is opposite from standing face-to-face with an open heart toward our spouse. It should be noted that there is a third survival response, in addition to fighting or fleeing from the threat. That third response is called "Freeze," and it literally makes the human freeze up in the moment of stress. Freeze occurs when the person is too overwhelmed or the threat so great that he cannot escape. It is pointless to fight, and so we freeze. Despite the frozen appearance, the person is still enduring tremendous physiological strain internally as he is torn between fight and flight, yet he can't move.

We don't typically face life-threatening circumstances in our daily lives. There are no wild tigers walking through the woods of North America. There are very few bears in our neighborhoods. In fact, driving on the highway is about the only time that we really need the huge surges of adrenaline, energy, and the narrowed cognitive focus that our fight or flight response affords. Yet, fight or flight kicks in at a mild or even full blown level for all of us each and every day. In most situations it is overkill and actually detracts from using our full brain power to deal with the problem at hand.

Danger at Jesse's Favorite Store

I remember that April, my wife, and I were driving through the parking lot of the Lowe's Home Improvement Store (my favorite store) one afternoon. As I came to a stop sign, my shoe slipped off the brake pedal. I had to instantly recover and slam on the brakes, so I would not crash into the car that was already in the intersection! My fight or flight kicked in as it should, leaving me breathless and with a pounding heart.

Prior to that moment, April and I had been having a nice conversation. After "slamming the brakes," I took a few seconds to get breathing again. We kept driving, and I looked over at her and said, "You've got to just give me a minute here before we keep talking. My fight or flight is turned on, and I can't listen right now." She knew immediately what I was talking about and gave me a breather to recompose myself.

This is a nice example because I knew clearly what the source of threat was, and it wasn't a perception that April was being hurtful. So I could talk about it with her and grant myself permission to settle down and regain my full brain power. However, most of the time in conflict with our spouses, we are viewing them as the source of threat—emotional or other. In those moments, it is pretty hard to ask their permission to settle down so that we can listen to them and resume an open-hearted posture. That is the last thing we instinctively feel like doing.

If you have a series of experiences with your spouse when you stopped dancing and started fighting, then you start to assume a more alert and vigilant posture over time. It's only natural. Your brain is simply trying to protect you from getting hurt again in a fight. The hurt comes because your spouse has stopped meeting your attachment needs.

During conflicts, your attachment needs are not being met.

In conflict moments with your spouse, you are hurting because your attachment needs are not being met by the one you look to for closeness and security. When we have repeated experiences of finding our spouses unavailable in the time of need, it is only normal that we start to close our hearts to them. We stop looking to them with hope and trust and gradually view them as sources of potential pain!

You can get into the habit of locking them out of your heart, which only raises their anxiety. Your spouse gets anxious, sensing that you are pulling away from the relationship. This only serves to make your spouse less available. A locked out struggle repeats itself and, before you know it, a pattern is formed. The following diagram illustrates this pattern. I have listed the "Husband" as being in flight mode in this particular diagram, but the flight member varies from marriage to marriage.

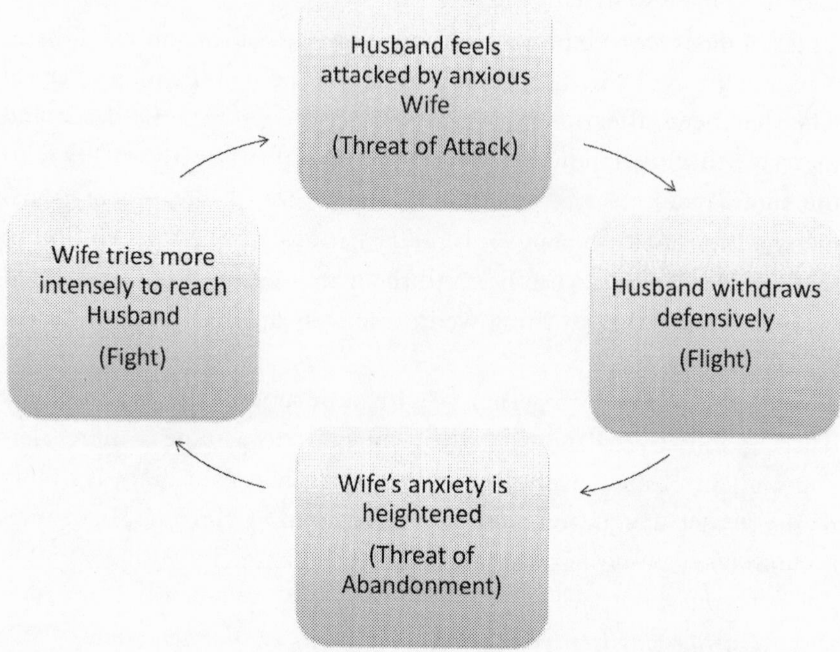

How tragic! Two lovers who once stood with an open posture toward each other are now locking their beloved out of their heart. It is not intentional. It is instinctive.

Often the husband and wife are not even conscious of what they are doing. They are so focused on responding to their spouse's aggressive or defensive fight or flight maneuvers that they cannot tune into or begin to change themselves. Each one focuses on the ways they are being hurt and on their need to defend from hurt. This leads each one to respond in increasingly protective ways.

Most times when I sit down with a couple to begin marital therapy, their dialogue and way of describing the problem reflects this tendency to hyper-focus on what the other spouse is doing wrong. Each one tells me what the other spouse is doing wrong and blames the other for the problem. The following is an example of what this sounds like.

Roger: "I have to tune her out and flip on the TV. She is so critical! It's unbearable for me."

Cloe: "He is so irritating…with his total inability to listen to me. He deserves to be criticized!"

This has been affectionately dubbed the "Blame Game" by many marriage therapists. The spouses are not able to pull back and look at the bigger picture. They can't see how they keep the struggle going by locking horns or locking out. The bigger picture includes our awareness that *the pattern* of fight versus flight response is really the most important thing to focus on in our work together. It's not about what either spouse is doing individually. It's the way they play off of each other!

The pattern is the problem!

As a younger marriage therapist, I often got caught up in the fray of accusations from one spouse to the other. I could clearly see why each one was angry, but I wanted each spouse to try to be more reasonable and understanding in how they handled things. It was like a ping pong match, and I just tried to be a referee and to remember to wear extra deodorant on the days when I saw this couple. This changed for me when I started to grasp some of the wisdom of the great marriage and family therapists who have been in the trenches for years.

First Glimpses at Fight or Flight Cycles

Salvador Minuchin is a Jewish psychiatrist who was born and raised in Argentina. He is one of the patriarchs of family therapy. Family therapy is a compassionate attempt to change the patterns of how families relate so that they will be more effective and functional. In other words, family therapy pulls back from the ping pong match and looks at the overall ways each person is locking the other out of their heart.

Minuchin and his colleague Charles Fishman were among the first to identify the interactive pattern where one spouse's fight response triggers the other spouse into flight, and vice versa.[36] Specifically, the more the fighter presses in, the more the flight-oriented spouse pulls away. The more the fleeing spouse retreats, the more intense the fighter gets to gain attention. We're going to call this the "protester-avoider pattern" in our talks throughout this book. It will help you understand your marriage distress in a totally new light.

What they are telling us is that the problem lies in the interaction pattern between the spouses. It is not about the husband being irritating or the wife being critical. The problem is that *when* the wife feels irritated, she fights and presses in by being critical. *When* the husband feels criticized, he pulls back in flight and does things that irritate the wife like living in front of the TV. The more she fights, the more he flees. The more he flees, the more she fights to get his attention. Round and round the couple goes. The pattern is the problem.

Minuchin and Fishman gave us hope because, through their new lens, we could see what was really going on. We could see where the problem lies, and that the couple needs to change their pattern to reconnect. A few years later, two other researchers constructed a marriage therapy approach to reverse the pattern of fight and flight. Leslie Greenberg and Susan Johnson put together a rich, beautiful, and caring approach to reverse the patterns that lock couples out from the heart of the other.[37] Johnson further enriched this approach and continues to actively expand the research base for the field of marital therapy.[38] Much of this book was inspired by her work.

Johnson outlined three patterns that lock couples out from one another. These patterns follow all the possible combinations and interactions of fight or flight between two people. The following table is adapted from her work and maps out these patterns to give you a picture of what is taking place in your marriage.

Name of the Pattern	Description of the Struggle
Protest—Avoid (Fight—Flight)	One spouse tries to restore the marriage connection with too much protest. The other spouse pulls away and detaches.
Protest—Protest (Fight—Fight)	Both spouses are desperately trying to be heard. Neither is listening to the other. The best defense is a strong offense.
Avoid—Avoid (Flight—Flight)	The original Protester has given up and is now pulled back in detachment too. Both spouses are detached.

Three Patterns that Push Us Apart

The first and most common pattern is protest-avoid. In this pattern, one spouse is fighting by pursuing the other one and intensely protesting because attachment needs are not being met. The other spouse is in flight, detaching and avoiding the pain, feeling inadequate or not cared for by the one to whom he looks for love.

The second pattern is protest-protest. This takes place when both spouses are fighting and protesting. They both want to be heard and are increasingly anxious because neither is being listened to or heeded. This ratchets up in intensity very quickly, decreasing the chances that either spouse will ever hear the other.

The final pattern is avoid-avoid. This is a sad state of affairs where both spouses are in flight, feeling hopeless about ever connecting. This usually takes place when the original protester has given up hope and is now in a state of detachment too.

Protest-Avoid

Let's take a look at the protest-avoid pattern first, since it is the most common pattern found among married couples. The pattern often includes a spouse who has a detached-avoider attachment style as we discussed in Chapter 2. This partner slips into the avoidant mode of dealing with conflict and assumes the avoid stance too often in conflict. The protest-avoid pattern usually includes a spouse who has an ambivalent-protester attachment style (see Chapter 2). This spouse falls quickly into the protest part of the interlocked cycle and protests the fact that attachment needs are not being met. These can include feeling unimportant, insignificant, or lonely.

Sonda and Larry

Sonda and Larry are a married couple who illustrated this pattern. Larry was a quiet, gentle, and kind sort of fellow who had a subtle sense of sadness about him. I knew that it would take some time to get to know him due to his quiet and cautious way of approaching relationships. Sonda was more vocal and spoke quickly. Her eyes flashed with anxiety and a sense of desperation that she was losing something precious. She felt terrible about herself when Larry could not engage with her. She was prone to criticize him, demand his love, and insist on attention.

Topics of conflict ranged from their lack of sexual intimacy to whether the couple actually spent any quality time together. Whenever Sonda would start intensely talking to Larry, he would get really quiet. She would get anxious that he was not responding and would turn up the volume and pace of her speech toward him. Then he felt even more helpless to speak to her needs, inclining him to shut down more or pull away in frustration. Larry had needs too, but he did not know how to tell Sonda what was going on for him.

Larry and the Pine Trees

Larry came from a home that was simple and cared for his basic needs. He spent many hours playing alone. Sadly, neither of his parents seemed to have the capacity to really tune into him or show him much affection. He recalled doing some gardening with his father on occasion, and that was his most vivid recollection of being connected to either parent. Other than that, no one asked him about his day. No one took interest in his inner life, and seldom if ever did he hear the words "I love you." I got the image of his family as a group of solitary pine trees. They all dwelled together in the same forest but seldom touched branches. Larry was fairly detached from emotional connection—a detached-avoider.

Sonda and the Vines

Sonda's family was very different. Her father abused alcohol, which led to unpredictable mood swings. Sonda remembers approaching her father to see if he was okay, only to come across his angry temper. He was not trying to be mean, and he would end up apologizing profusely with tears and lots of affection when he sobered up the next day. Sonda's mom got overly involved with her one and only daughter, and she blurred boundaries in her style of parenting. Sonda did not know what to expect or on whom to count. I saw her family as a group of climbing vines, all intertwined with one another. This left Sonda anxious and insecure—an ambivalent-protester—in her attachment style with others.

You can clearly see how the stage was set for Sonda to protest and for Larry to avoid when it came to conflict in their marriage. You can see how Sonda would be primed to protest with anger and anxiety in trying to reach her spouse. Larry would cocreate a disconnected dance by detaching due to his own fear and felt inadequacy. Much brokenness, loneliness, and pain followed in this example of the protest-avoid pattern.

Gender Differences in Protester-Avoider Patterns

Elements of Larry and Sonda's story are very similar to many married couples that I see. For example, the avoider partner is often a male, while the protester partner is often a woman. There are biological and physiological reasons for this stereotypical breakdown in communication between the sexes. When this impasse in connection takes place, there are biological reasons why it is particularly grievous and frustrating too.

I'll never forget about a research study I heard of in the early 1990s by John Gottman.[39] He is a famous and innovative marriage therapy researcher who has written many journal articles and books on marriage. In a research study that took place in the late 1980s and early 1990s, Gottman set up an apartment that he called the "Love Lab." He wired up males and females in a high tech apartment research setting. There were cameras and microphones placed strategically throughout the apartment. The males and females were wearing monitors that recorded their blood pressure and other indicators of physical functioning.

You can imagine that he learned some very valuable things, including information about gender trends in the protester-avoider pattern. Gottman found that there were gender differences in how the spouses experienced conflict. As he measured blood pressure readings, he noted that women were slow to get elevated as they approached conflict with their spouse. He found that they settled into a "slow simmer," so to speak, as they were having intense discussion with their spouses. Gottman also noted that men's blood pressure readings spiked very quickly in the interactions with their wives. They reached a "rapid boil" in no time at all when compared with their wives. While wives were just starting to get warmed up in a discussion, the husbands had already reached a very uncomfortable boiling point!

During heated discussions, wives simmer slowly while husbands boil quickly.

The implications are clear. Husbands have a lower physiological tolerance for verbal conflict with their wives. This means they will be more likely to avoid conflict than wives will be when we look at the averages. This sets husbands up to be the ones in the avoider position in the face of intense protest from their wives. It speaks to the need for husbands to stay connected enough so their wives won't get intensely anxious. It is helpful for their own cardiac health to attend to wives, and not cocreate the protester-avoider pattern with them. The findings tell us that women ought to generally be calm and deliberate in approaching their husbands in order to increase the likelihood that they will be heard and still have an audience.

There was one set of irregularities in the Love Lab data. Gottman found a very small percentage of men whose blood pressure went down in the face of conflict. They actually came into a normal range when their wives were distressed. These men would be classified as sociopaths who don't have the same wiring for conscience and attachment as normal humans possess. Recall Bowlby's original study of the "Forty Thieves" who were abandoned by their mothers as children and had "affectionless psychopathy." Such men would need to be measured by their long-term behaviors in relationships to determine whether they could be trusted or whether they were engaging in a con man exercise for their own selfish ends.

Protest-Avoid is Biologically Backward

Outliers aside, I have been provoked to a lot of thinking about conflict between marriage partners since hearing of Gottman's work. I was recently pondering how a protesting female-avoiding male pattern is biologically abnormal. Let me explain what I mean. Of course there are variations in the pattern, but in broad terms it is usually the male who pursues the female at the start of a dating relationship. The male is not pulling back and in a state of retreat from the female.

Empowered by a mandate to be "fruitful and multiply" and energized by the chemical cocktail of infatuation, most men are the ones to pursue their wives in the early stages of courtship. Arguably, many women have stated that they don't wish to be the one who has to pursue the guy, or at least to be pursuing the guy without him pursuing her back for any length of time. Subjectively, many women feel valued and prized when their men pursue them and initiate contact, beginning a life of closeness and adventure together. Most men feel respected and good about themselves when they are seen as strong by their wives. They feel confident, even affirmed in their pursuits of their wives.

Of course this all has to be done within a balanced framework, but the trends are pretty strong in our culture. In fact, two very popular books resonated with thousands of Christian readers as they advocated these types of roles for the genders in our modern-day society. John Eldredge's book *Wild at Heart*[40] describes the male desire to be courageous, strong, pursuing, and adventurous in reclaiming authentic masculinity. John and Stasi Eldredge cowrote *Captivating*[41] to describe the woman's desire to be pursued, treasured, and valued as an essential part of femininity.

Gender Roles

An earlier theorist spoke of gender roles as part of our normal biological development in childhood, as we acquire and form our gender roles. Erik Erikson was one of the great theorists in the field of developmental psychology. He mapped out the stages that a human must go through from infancy to old age. At each stage of life there are important developmental tasks that must be accomplished in order to enter the next stage with maturity and grace.

Erikson describes the task of beginning to understand our gender roles just as we enter grade school.[42] He notes that boys are literally wired to be "phallic and intrusive," while girls are wired to be "catching" and receptive.

Erikson describes the need for boys to develop the ability to be undertaking, planning, and "being on the make." Girls must develop an ability to make themselves catching, fetching, attractive, and endearing. One can immediately see the biological and reproductive necessity of developing these traits in order to "be fruitful and multiply." It is biologically hardwired into males to be pursuing and to put themselves forward. For females, it is biologically necessary that they be receptive and open to pursuit.

You can see this even at the level of the nonverbal signals that men and women send to one another in the course of courtship. She tussles her hair and pulls it back with a flourish, indicating interest and availability. He leans forward and sticks his jaw out squarely to show that he wants to be with her. He strides with a confident motion, indicating that he would like to hold her hand. She gently responds with hands and wrists that signal complementary movement with his and not resistance.

For most of us, this is the way that our dating relationship began. By some point in the early stages the guy was assuming his biological role, moving forward, taking interest, and showing himself to be strong. The woman was being receptive, flirtatious, and responding to his overtures. There was a sense of adventure, belonging, and security, that all was as it should be emotionally and biologically. The couple was bonding and forming a connection, and there was every indication that they had what it takes to make it together to "be fruitful and multiply" on the planet.

Biological Tragedy

It seems to me that in addition to the loneliness and shame, one of the great tragedies of the couple locked into the protest-avoid pattern is the loss of biological normalcy for each of them. When the woman is protesting the loss of connection with her mate, as opposed to being pursued, this would elevate survival anxiety in every sense. She says to herself, *I'm alone, and our family has little chance of surviving and thriving on the planet!* Her anxiety takes on an almost primal panic state in that moment.

The male is withdrawing, instead of assuming his confident, respectable, and strong role of letting his wife know that he has what it takes. He should be strong for her and for them both. He needs to be available and ready to make her feel secure. Instead, he is feeling shamed, inadequate, and lonely.

I have witnessed several cases where the wife experienced this state of primal panic at times where she was desperate to get her husband's attention. These women have been physically abusive on occasion, and they have also levied scathing remarks against their husbands in their efforts to "wake the sleeping husband." In essence, they used whatever was at their disposal to try to get their husbands to notice them.

The husbands have had a variety of very significant distancing behaviors that fueled the intense protest of their wives. These included workaholism, substance abuse, retreat into the basement, sarcasm, irritability, and defensiveness. These men appeared indifferent, but inside they were hurting, sad, and scared. The more aggressive their wives became, the more they wanted to stay away from home. Even when they were physically present at their homes, they were often emotionally absent.

Admittedly, these are extreme examples of the protest-avoid pattern. I am selecting salient examples because they clearly illustrate the pattern and may help you to begin to identify your own pattern of distress in your marriage. I am also choosing these strong examples to give you a sense that you are not alone. Other couples have felt great pain and are dealing with the same things as you in their quest to get and maintain healthier marriages. Many of them have had to overcome significant hurdles in order to achieve closeness once again.

Protest-Protest

The second pattern that we will examine is protest-protest. This tends to be the most animated of the patterns in which couples find themselves. Essentially, both partners are protesting against something that the other has done and they are raising the volume in order to be heard. Both partners are in the fight mode. One of them is the original protester who is protesting the loss of closeness in the marriage. But the other is responding with a defensive protest. Defensive protesters are not retreating; they are fighting to make the case that they are adequate and are not going to be controlled.

Defensive protesters fight for their honor and to not be consumed!

You can quickly see that the protest-protest pattern is at elevated risk for violence since both parties are going into the conflict full steam ahead. With both partners in the fight mode, you can imagine that neither of them is actually listening to the other one. They are talking *at* each other, instead of talking *to* one another. Even when they say important things about their pain, it simply goes right over the head of their loved one.

Dan and Flo

I am reminded of a couple who we'll call Dan and Flo. The week before Dan and Flo came to see me they had been in a huge fight that involved physical violence. This was not "domestic violence" where one partner had a pattern of abusing the other. This was a situation where two hurting people both acted with force to the extent that police were involved. It was a huge upheaval for them, setting the stage for us to begin our marital work.

Dan—"My best defense is a strong offense!"

During our session, Dan had a habit of talking very fast in response to Flo. He even spoke very fast when he was initiating a topic in session. He did not yell, but he had a certain intensity to his voice and pace of speech. He sounded like he was a lawyer arguing his case, and he only had a minute to make his closing remarks. Though he was very active in his analysis and own defense, he was not very emotionally present during these monologues.

He was actually inclined to withdraw and to fear being smothered. But what he showed was a strong offense. He seldom spoke about how he felt criticized, not good enough, or controlled. He was too busy being on the loud defensive. His displays were very intense but actually superficial in terms of any disclosures about himself.

Dan was only 5 years old when his mother lost her parental rights to care for him due to her involvement with the legal system. He was placed in the home of his uncle who was ill-equipped to handle the needs of Dan and his two siblings. His uncle tried to exercise control over the situation through yelling and violent discipline. All of this made it difficult for Dan to trust others, and it gave him a strong aversion to any sense that others were controlling him. Dan had a real tug of war inside of him, as he wanted closeness with Flo, but was not about to let himself be controlled ever again. She was the one person he had allowed into his heart years ago—when they first started dating and were like two carefree kids. It was freeing to him to find that kind of love, and it was very unsettling for him to start to perceive that his sweet freedom was giving way to the threat of control again.

Dan's best defense was a strong offense. Whenever he felt threatened by Flo's way of saying that she wanted to be closer to him, he would jump right into an active argument with her. Essentially, he was telling her that he would not allow himself to be controlled. Nothing and no one was going to take him back to that place of pain. She did not really want to control him. All she wanted was to be with him and know that he wanted the same things.

Flo—Terrified of Losing Her Friend

Flo was different in her approach toward Dan. She often got anxious and jumped to conclusions about what she saw in him at home. It seemed that he only cared about his own rights, and that he did not place her as a priority. What she was seeing in arguments with him only confirmed her greatest fears, that he was looking out for himself and had lost sight of her needs.

Flo was more engaged emotionally, with an earnest petition that Dan draw close and spend time with her. She got angry at him when she thought that he was only focused on himself. Flo would often show tears in the session during moments of sadness and frustration. Neither of them could hear the other as they talked loudly, getting more frustrated and frightened at every step.

As long as they were locked into the protest-protest dance, neither of them could see that they both missed each other and just wanted things to go back to that place of being two carefree kids. They needed to pull back and see the big picture. They needed to take a deep breath and be silent long enough to let the words of the other sink into their hearts. I will share a story of one key moment when that occurred between Dan and Flo in Chapter 8.

Avoid-Avoid

The final pattern that couples find themselves in is avoid-avoid. This is the pattern where for some period of time both partners are pulling away from the fray of conflict, along with the pursuit of connection. Unfortunately, this represents a very serious state of affairs for the marriage.

If neither spouse is fighting for the marriage, it's hard to make things better!

A pattern of marital discord does not start this way. The relationship would never have gotten started in the first place if both spouses were avoiding one another. Usually the pattern of avoid-avoid occurs when the spouse who once was protesting the loss of closeness has now run out of steam and started to shut down. She or he has become discouraged or hardened in heart after so many failed attempts to reach the other. A sense of futility and self-preservation has set in.

Often there is a complete avoidance of conflict. It is just easier that way, and they have stopped looking to the other one as a source of strength and comfort due to the repeated disappointments that took place. Couples in avoid-avoid patterns will sometimes tell me, "It just feels like I am living with a roommate these days. We just pass by each other, but we don't connect anymore."

John and Patsy

John and Patsy slid into the pattern of avoid-avoid over the course of their thirty-four years of marriage. When they came to see me, John had decided to invest anew in the marriage as the couple entered retirement. Their children were grown, and he knew that he would have to improve his marriage or else face real loneliness in his retirement years. They both worked hard and had a deep faith in God that sustained them as they pulled through this situation.

John—The Very Busy Man

John grew up with eight siblings on a farm in Central Pennsylvania. His family was very hard working, but also very poor, and struggled to just put food on the table. Unfortunately, John's mother struggled and faltered under the strain of raising her nine children and helping run the farm. She loved her son but was too overwhelmed to devote individual attention to him. John developed a detached-avoider attachment style because of the neglect that he suffered. But he also was a hypervigilant sort of fellow too because of his impending sense that things were about to collapse when he was a child. So he was very active and busied himself on the tasks of short-term and long-term survival.

John was intelligent and did very well for himself in his career, but he focused on building his career to the detriment of his marriage. He was a loyal provider and committed to Patsy, but not very connected. He was always "on the go" even when he was not at work. It was hard to get John to slow down and settle for any length of time. John's excessive involvement in his career and activities had been so chronic that Patsy experienced decades of abandonment.

Patsy—The Burned-Out Protester

Patsy was a kind and gentle woman who was very nurturing. She was patient, fairly soft spoken, and she moved at a slower pace. She worked as a children's librarian for many years and was an avid reader. She preferred to be in her own home whenever she had leisure time, and could frequently be found curled up with a good book and a cup of tea in her hand. Patsy tried for years to get John to slow down and join her.

Patsy had a fairly stable and intact family environment during her own childhood. Her family had a tendency to internalize their feelings when conflict arose and to let out their anger in the form of sarcasm. Patsy was also intelligent, and she had clear opinions for how their marriage should function. Her sarcastic protests of John's absence were often crafty and hard to get around. The truth is that she was missing her husband, longing to spend time with him, and literally tired of being alone.

John had a hard time settling down in the first place and looking past his own immediate needs in the moment. So when he encountered

Patsy's sarcasm and criticism, it was very hard for him to draw close. He felt like he couldn't win and pulled further away. Patsy grieved their marriage connection in the second decade of their marriage, giving up hope that John would meet her needs. Were it not for her deep faith and John's fervent attempts to renew the marriage, I suspect they would have gotten a divorce. This is what happens to many avoid-avoid couples when their kids are grown.

There are a few situations where the couple never had much connection in the first place, after the infatuation phase came to an end. This can take place when two people with detached avoiders attachment styles pair up. Neither party was ever good at relying on the other for their needs to be met. So, a lack of connection can grow over time because there was never much infusion of gratitude or need fulfillment along the way.

In this situation, the lack of connection does not relate to one of them "giving up." It is more closely related to each one of them settling for the best type of relationship that they knew how to foster. The good news is that there can be more, a whole new world of depth beyond what either of them has ever known. This can also be the case for married couples who have gradually drifted into the avoid-avoid pattern.

Reengaging Two Avoiders

A couple in this pattern will have to patiently restore the intimacy that they once shared. In order to do that, they will have to dialogue once again about the hurts that drove them both into isolation. They will actually have to revisit the conflicts again, the conflicts that made them shut down. This must be a principled approach, where each one decides that the marriage is worth saving even if their emotions are far removed.

The couple has to hearken back to the reasons why they attached to one another in the first place. They must intentionally remember how good it was to have their needs met in the arms of their beloved. Along with that, the story must be told of the pain that came when those arms were no longer open and the heart was closed off. Then they must take risks with one another, perhaps for the first time in a long time, to find the satisfaction in being cared for by one who loves them.

When we stop dancing together, it is always due to conflict in which our basic attachment needs cease to be met. Susan Johnson notes that:

> From the cradle to the grave, humans desire a certain someone who will look out for them, notice and value them, soothe their wounds, reassure them in life's difficult places, and hold them in the dark.[43]

If our spouse is pulled away or is attacking us without awareness for our needs, then our basic needs have no chance of being met by that most important person. Now we know the patterns that lock us out from our spouses' hearts. These patterns, when left in place, will never allow us to have our attachment needs met. We must reverse these patterns so that each spouse will have a chance at being held securely in the heart of the other once again. The solution lies in meeting our spouses' needs for security and closeness, so they won't feel a need to kick into fight or flight anymore. The Seven Keys teach us how to unlock the cycle and to depend on one another like never before.

CHAPTER 5

FIRST KEY—IDENTIFY THE ENEMY

And you will know the truth, and the truth will make you free (John 8:32).

I am excited about this chapter as we now begin the active phase of working on your marriage. Solving problems, based on good sound theory, drives me and excites me. It grounds us in principles that we cling to when the storms hit us. I also love the part where we roll up our sleeves and start to shift the dynamics that are causing you pain. I have been eager to get to this point in the book with you. In the first four chapters we have covered a lot of ground:

1. We learned that attachment is the human bond that God created to meet our emotional and relational needs from infancy to adult married love.
2. We have learned about what secure attachment looks like, and what it looks like when attachment goes awry.
3. We learned that infatuation is God's design to put humans into hyper-attaching mode, so that we can quickly form the attachment bond with our love partner.
4. In the last chapter, we examined the ways that disconnected attachment patterns create frustration, distress, and loneliness as they lock us out of our spouse's heart.

If you have been in a state of marital distress for any length of time, then you are probably weary in the struggle. You are longing for solutions and longing for relief. In this chapter we will begin to apply what we have learned in order to reduce the pain and frustration that you have been feeling with your spouse.

If you are like most married people in distress, then you have an acute awareness of the things that your spouse is doing that cause you pain. In fact, you are an expert at talking about what your spouse does wrong and how it hurts you. God hardwired you, for survival purposes, to be able to tune into the things that are a threat to you. You literally get tunnel vision for the things that bother or threaten you. The net result is that the majority of your thoughts may pertain to negative things about your spouse at this time.

Each successive instance just confirms in your mind that your spouse is "a critical jerk," "an absent husband," or "an emotional cripple." Your brain is on the lookout for the hurtful things your spouse is doing. This is causing more and more damage to your view of your spouse. It is also bad for your soul and sense of worth. After all, what kind of person would knowingly marry "a critical jerk" or "an emotional cripple"? That can be pretty hard to swallow. The only way you can preserve your own sense of self at this point is to devalue your spouse further.

As long as your brain is on the lookout for the bad things your spouse is doing, it will be hard for your brain to actually see the positive things. The culprit is that fight or flight response that we spoke of in the last chapter. It is narrowing your view, and you literally can't help it. Your spouse *has* done painful things that hurt you. I am not denying or minimizing that fact. I am simply noting that your brain is somewhat stuck now on the negatives, and can't see the positives or any other explanation for what is taking place.

We've got to help your brain get unstuck. We must have a paradigm shift that explains and validates the pain but also points toward a solution. We have to pull back from the narrowed focus on what your spouse is doing. We need to pull back far enough to see *your* contribution to the things that your spouse is doing. We've got to give you access to something that you actually can control instead of focusing on your spouse's behaviors. You can't control those.

You need to focus on something you can control.

If we pull back even further, we begin to see the pattern of interactions between you and your spouse. We start to look at the ways that each one's behaviors play off the other. This expanded view, this new paradigm, actually looks at both sides of the relationship. It sees the way that your defensive actions play off of your spouse's defensive actions, and vice versa.

The Truth that Sets You Free

We need to look at how the attacks of one person lead to the distancing of the other, and on it goes. The last chapter clearly outlined the patterns that couples get into that lock them away from the heart of their best friend and keep them locked into a struggle. In this chapter we are taking it one step further. The problem is not that you are married to "a critical jerk," "a distant husband," or "an emotional cripple." The problem is that the two of you are locked into a negative cycle. Further, the negative cycle is the problem.

The negative cycle is the enemy!

Your spouse is not the enemy, and you are not the enemy. The negative cycle is the enemy of your relationship. As long as you are stuck in one of the negative cycles, you will feel awful, remain alone, and have no chance of connecting securely with your spouse.

Psychologist Susan Johnson, mentioned previously, is the leading marital therapist who made this point clearly about the impact of the negative cycle on married couples. Johnson says that the central problem for a couple in distress is "the positions the couple take in the pattern of interactions...the negative cycles that have taken over their relationship, and the compelling emotions that organize each person's responses."[44] The cycle is the problem, and the negative emotions inside of it serve to perpetuate the pain.

When you start to grasp this truth, you have a perspective that gives you a chance to break free from the distress and pain that are plaguing your marriage. The negative cycle is imprisoning your marriage, choking the life out of it at every turn. You have to see this clearly, and focus on the cycle rather than focusing on your spouse's actions. As long as you are focusing on your spouse's problems, you will remain stuck.

We have identified the enemy of your marriage, and it is not your spouse. A new view of the problem has come to you—the negative cycle is the problem. It is the culprit, and it is the enemy. The negative cycle is what repeatedly damages your attachment bond with your spouse, and that is what causes you so much pain. Now you know the truth, and you have a chance at freeing yourself from the cycle of pain and distress.

Identify the Enemy

If I were working with you in marital therapy, this would be the point where I help you identify the enemy, your specific negative cycle. We would do this together as a team. I would be using examples from our conversations about how you and your spouse argue so that we could put together a model for the negative cycle that seems to fit your situation. It has to make sense to you and fit your marriage situation, or else you will never be able to catch the cycle in the heat of battle with your spouse. In the heat of conflict, it is quite hard to catch the cycle. Remember that every survival fiber of your being is trying to defend you from the threat of pain.

So, in marital therapy, I would help you identify your negative cycle. Then I would talk to you about your cycle dozens of times in sessions to follow. You might even get tired of hearing me repeat my observations about the negative cycle. But I know how important it is to blame the cycle. Repetition helps to change our thought patterns. It literally reprograms our brain circuits, the immediate "response highways" that we so commonly travel down in moments of distress. This helps us to change our view and even our reactions.

It is especially important to change our reactions in the heat of the moment. In a fraction of a second our brain's limbic system gets activated into fight or flight, and then we have begun our side of the negative cycle. The practice and skill of being able to spot the cycle pulls us out of the narrowed range of functioning of the limbic system, and it engages our rational brain.

Power Play

There is so much more power in our rational brain to cope with difficult situations than we realize. Think of the difference between the coping skills of a toddler and those of a 25-year-old adult. The range of difference is huge! That is because the toddler is operating predominantly out of the limited resources of the limbic system, while the young adult is at an age where the rational brain, the prefrontal cortex, is fully developed. It's the difference between the power of a bicycle compared to a dump truck. Huge!

The practice and skill of identifying the negative cycle and blaming it for your problems is the quickest way for you to engage your rational brain. This incorporates some of the most effective tools of individual therapy, including "externalizing," where you label the problem as an outside observer instead of getting caught up within it.[45] It also incorporates the power of acceptance for my brain's automatic reactions instead of shaming myself for the fact that they so often get triggered down these tragic highways.

The net effect of verbally identifying the negative cycle is that it serves to settle down the emotional reactivity of the limbic system so that you can see straight again. And it points you in the direction of needed change, which is changing your cycle so that you two can be face-to-face once again. This is so much better than continuing to protest or withdraw from your spouse during moments of need. So let's do it. Let's get a clear read on what the negative cycle looks like for you and your spouse.

I am including the table from Chapter 4 again. I want you and your spouse (if possible), to look over this table again to determine which cycle best fits the distress pattern in your marriage. I want to encourage you to start looking for the negative cycle. Start to reflect on how this pattern comes up for you almost every time that you get into trouble together. It does not matter what the argument topic is. The two of you will end up approaching it via the negative cycle. We want to be able to spot the cycle so that we can change it and return to the face-to-face pattern of connection that we all had when we first fell in love.

Name of the Negative Cycle	Description of the Struggle
Protest—Avoid (Fight—Flight)	One spouse tries to restore connection with the other with too much protest. The other pulls away and detaches, feeling criticized or hopeless.
Protest—Protest (Fight—Fight)	Both spouses are desperately trying to be heard. Neither is listening to the other. The best defense is a strong offense.
Avoid—Avoid (Flight—Flight)	The original Protester has given up and is now pulled back in detachment too. Both spouses are detached.

Where do you see yourself in the descriptions? Are you more often the one who pursues your spouse, anxiously trying to get more time together or demanding that a certain behavior should change? Perhaps you are more likely to pull back in frustration, "clam up," and withdraw after feeling criticized by your spouse. You are going to have to clearly identify your own contribution to the negative cycle. You must find out what your automatic responses are so that you can see where you need to change.

Jenn and Joe

Let me give you an example from a married couple I saw recently. We'll call them Jenn and Joe. Jenn just accepted a new job and is really struggling to replace the friendships she used to have with her former coworkers. She looks to Joe for sympathy by complaining about how hard it is at the new job, but he feels blamed for her sadness. He gets fed up with her and says that she is difficult to please. The following is a portion of our session discussion:

Joe: You are never happy with friends! You are so picky. And that doesn't only happen at your new job, you were like that at your old job too.

Jenn: That's not fair. I liked plenty of people back then. I just have a hard time with whiners and complainers. Remember when we went on vacation with your sister Janet and her new boyfriend Robb? Remember how Robb fussed and whined like a spoiled child? Anyone with two eyes could see what a brat he was! It was miserable.

Joe: I agree with you, Robb was a big baby…

Jenn: So we got back from vacation and I told you, "That was awful! Don't ever make me go on vacation with them again!" But Joe, you didn't care. You didn't listen. You just told me that it wasn't so bad and to leave it alone.

Joe: Robb was a pain, and we wasted tons of vacation time…dealing with his drama. But you're not going to make me responsible for something that's not my fault…I have no control over him or the fact he's a spoiled brat!

Jenn: I was not blaming you for Robb's drama. I was trying to tell you that I just can't do that again. And you didn't give me any sympathy and understanding when I was trying to tell you that.

Joe: I didn't see you looking for understanding. All I got was anger. I thought you were mad at me.

Jenn: I know I get hysterical sometimes when I'm upset about things. I just want some sympathy from you.

Jesse (therapist): So Jenn, it wasn't about being angry at Joe. It wasn't like that at all for you. It sounds like you were just trying to reach him, trying to get him to understand. Joe, what happens for you when you hear that from Jenn?

Joe: Looking back, I can see I wasn't very understanding of her. I got defensive right away. I have this filter that comes down when she starts to go off like that. It's like a wall, and I get defensive.

Can you pick up on the pattern between this couple? I picked this example because they actually agree on the issue at hand. They both thought that Robb was a pain to deal with. But their problem was that they could not connect and share in their mutual frustration. Their negative cycle kept them from venting together, and it kept them from grieving together over the loss of enjoyment during their valuable vacation time together. In this example, Joe is the avoider and Jenn is the protester.

You could get stuck and think that this is a story about Jenn's social skills or her loneliness. While these are important factors, the most important thing to see is that Jenn gets even more sad and lonely when she can't get sympathy from Joe. When she is struggling the most, all she really wants is to find Joe as a source of comfort. Secure attachment means that we can find our loved one, especially when we are in distress. The negative cycle keeps this from happening for both of them. When I first spoke to Joe and Jenn about their cycle, it was a huge relief, for Jenn in particular.

Jesse: Can you see that Jenn just gets more anxious when she can't reach Joe? Jenn, you turn up the volume to reach him, and you can be pretty intense. Joe, it seems that you shut down…sort of feeling blamed and hopeless to help the situation. So when you withdraw it only makes Jenn get more upset. This cycle is what is keeping you from feeling connected, and makes you both endlessly frustrated.

Joe: I can see what you're saying there. It makes a lot of sense to me.

Jenn: It's nice to know that everything happening in our marriage is not my fault. I'm so tired of feeling blamed. It's exhausting. It's good to know that I don't have to keep blaming Joe for things. That's hard on me too.

I am sure that you can relate. We were not created to fight endlessly or struggle needlessly in our marriages. It is a tragic thing when we are going through pain alone, instead of being able to stand hand in hand with the one that God ordained to be by our side. We've known this since the beginning of creation when *"The Lord God said, 'It is not good for the man to be alone…'"* (Genesis 2:18 NIV).

Dan and Flo: My Favorite Show

I wonder if you can spot yourself yet in the negative cycle table? Let me give you one more example of a couple before I ask you to do some deeper self-assessment. You might remember Dan and Flo from the last chapter. I'll tip you off right away that they get caught in the protest-protest pattern, in case you forgot. I've picked an excerpt from a recent session that we'll call My Favorite Show. The couple had their first child a few months ago. Tune in to the ways that they are talking over top of one another, and neither one is getting through.

Dan: It's ridiculous. I get home from work after a hard day at the office, and all I want to do is sit down to watch some television in peace and quiet. You can't let me alone! You bring our daughter and sit on the sofa to nurse her while you make digs at my show.

Flo: I have to nurse her, and the sofa is the most comfortable place. I can't help it if your shows are boring!

Dan: I don't watch any TV all day when I am at work. Prime time is my chance to unwind and do what I want to do. You are just trying to wreck that for me!

Flo: It's not like I get any downtime being at home with the baby all day. I take care of her and never get a break. I figure if I have to nurse her one more time, I'm not going to be alone and miserable.

Dan: So you come downstairs and pick at my shows…is that it? So we're both miserable? I'm not going to let you control my TV watching! I'll just go watch Netflix on my cellphone!

Flo: That's perfect! You're going to look like a freak sitting there and squinting at that tiny little screen!

Dan: Well, I'd rather be a freak than be badgered to death!

The dialogue could go on and on, right? There are clear emotionally significant bids from each spouse to the other. Neither is picking up on them. Flo is feeling weary and lonely. Dan is feeling worn out and pestered.

In this particular example, Dan was bringing a need to the table. It was not a need for closeness, but a cry for help with how overwhelmed he feels. He will eventually withdraw, but not after having said many hurtful things. Flo will feel worthless and alone before the day is over. It's very sad, and sometimes downright dangerous.

Neither of them hears the other, as they are both wrapped up in their own pain and fear. In contrast to protest-avoid, this couple keeps going at it. They are both anxiously or angrily pursuing the other in attempts to get through. I guess there's an element of hope in that relentless protest. Each one still believes at some level that they will get through. At least they have not shut down yet or quit trying.

Self-Assessment: Your Attachment Style Fuels the Negative Cycle

I invite you now to take a careful look at your own attachment style. This is going to help you to better understand what fuels your side of the negative cycle. This may help you to have more compassion for yourself and also more compassion for your spouse. It's also going to guide you toward what you will eventually need to correct your side of the cycle.

To keep it simple, we really only have to assess what the main strategy is you that use as you are approaching threats to closeness in your marriage. As adults, we typically approach threats to intimacy in a characteristic manner. Each of us has to grapple with our fear of being left alone versus our fear of being smothered or controlled. But our childhood and adult attachment experiences cause us to be more sensitive to one fear in contrast to the other. For starters please ask yourself these two questions:

Do I fear abandonment in my marriage?
Do I fear engulfment?

Fear of Abandonment

Fear of abandonment is the great fear that if my partner moves too far away from me, then I will fall apart. If my partner pulls away, then I have lost my value as a person. If my partner pulls away, I have lost my identity and can't cope. People who were rejected or neglected as children are more likely to have an exaggerated fear of abandonment. Fear of abandonment is fueling you if you feel anxious and terribly lonely when not with your spouse. But when the two of you are together, it really isn't all that great. There's little bond when the abandonment anxiety subsides.[46]

Fear of abandonment can lead us to panic and display strong protest behaviors at times. If this seems to fit you, then you would more likely be in the protest side of the negative cycle in your marriage.

Fear of Engulfment

Contrast fear of abandonment with the fear of engulfment, which is the fear that if my spouse gets too close, then I will be overwhelmed, exposed, and open to being hurt. My spouse might control me or wipe out who I am and what I want. Children who are abused or dominated, along with those who were not loved for who they really are, can have a heightened fear of engulfment, thinking, *If loved ones get too close to me, then I could get hurt or overwhelmed.* Fear of engulfment is present if you can't wait to get away from the other person, but when that person is really gone, you feel lonely.[47]

Fear of engulfment is commonly linked to a strong desire to not be criticized. There's a sense that if I get too close, you might see me as "not good enough." A person who fears engulfment is much less anxious when he simply takes care of matters by himself, rather than relying on others and opening himself to the possible hurts of criticism and inadequacy. Avoiders typically struggle with this type of fear.

At one point or another we have all grappled with the fear of abandonment or engulfment. The universal nature of this struggle, coupled with the intense emotions that follow, is what lends to its expression in popular music. We are more attuned to one fear or the other, based on our childhood experiences. This leads us to specific patterns of attachment in our closest relationships as adults. If we fear abandonment, we are more likely to pursue closeness with intensity. If we fear engulfment, we are likely to withdraw from our spouse in moments of distress.

The Love Quiz

Take the second step now in your self-assessment by seeing how these two fears play out in your adult attachment style. Attachment researchers Cindy Hazan and Phillip Shaver created the first questionnaire to measure attachment in adults.[48] The following questionnaire is based on their work and consists of three sets of statements describing an attachment style. Please take a moment to honestly rate yourself.

1. Secure - I find it relatively easy to get close to others and am comfortable depending on them and having them depend on me. I don't often worry about being abandoned or about someone getting too close to me.
2. Ambivalent Protesters - I find that others are reluctant to get as close as I would like. I often worry that my partner doesn't really love me or won't want to stay with me. I want to merge completely with another person, and this desire sometimes scares people away.
3. Detached Avoiders - I am somewhat uncomfortable being close to others; I find it difficult to trust them completely, difficult to allow myself to depend on them. I am nervous when anyone gets too close, and often, love partners want me to be more intimate than I feel comfortable being.

Where would you rank yourself now in the negative cycle with your spouse? Do you lean toward the ambivalent protester side of the cycle? Do you find yourself too often in the detached avoider side of things? Can you see how the fear of abandonment fuels the protest side of the negative cycle? Does it make sense that the fear of engulfment leads a person to avoid?

I sincerely hope that these questions and examples are helping you identify your attachment style so you can determine your side of the negative cycle. Maybe you can also predict your spouse's complementary response to your actions in times of distress.

What you need to remember is that you are not bad or defective if you have an insecure attachment style. Many people in marital distress have an insecure attachment style to start with. Others have become insecure in their bond with their spouse as a result of the negative cycle. The more your negative cycle rages on, the less secure you feel. If you are abandoned, you protest the loss of your spouse. If you feel criticized by the protest, you withdraw to get away from it, perhaps with a few parting defensive shots while you retreat. It doesn't matter where it all starts. The problem is that the cycle is happening and it takes on a life of its own. The following diagram illustrates this for you.

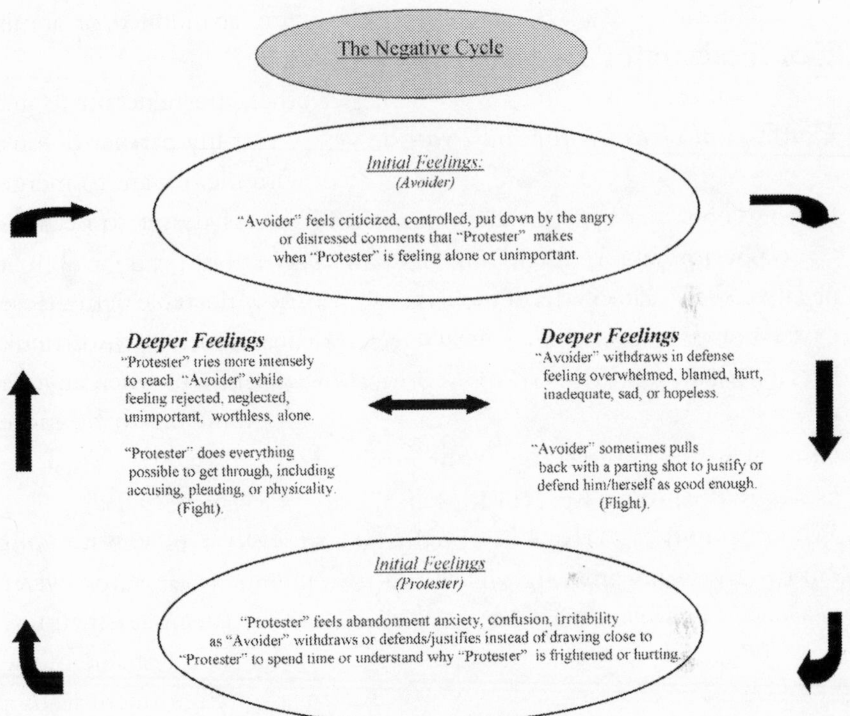

Each spouse is playing off the other in a reactive manner. Round and round it goes, and it is difficult to get off. The more it spins, the more you feel abandoned, or the more you feel criticized or inadequate. It can be very discouraging, and it can reinforce old beliefs that you have about yourself. Avoiders often wrestle with deep-seated fears of being overwhelmed in conflict and the fear of being made to feel "no good." Protesters usually fear abandonment and being left alone to care for themselves.

But there is hope. It is possible to pull out of the negative cycle. The first step is realizing that *the cycle is the enemy.*

I am including some confessions of faith at this point to aid you in integrating these newfound discoveries about yourself with truth from Scripture. You may want to say them honestly and prayerfully, inviting God to strengthen you for the journey ahead.

Confessions of Faith

Confession of Faith for the Protester

I realize now that my spouse is not the problem. He or she is actually a good person who is hurting just like me. We are both caught up in a negative cycle that robs us of the fellowship and joy that God created for us. In moments when I am feeling rejected or abandoned by my spouse, I realize that I can come across as critical or controlling.

God, help me to remember Your promise: *"I will never leave you nor forsake you"* (Joshua 1:5 NIV). Help me to *"Be strong and courageous"* (Joshua 1:6 NIV) so that I can boldly take the next steps You have for me to restore my marriage. I choose to remember that *"Though my father and mother forsake me, the Lord will receive me"* (Psalm 27:10 NIV).

Confession of Faith for the Avoider

I realize now that my spouse is not the problem. He or she is actually a good person who is hurting just like me. We are both caught up in a negative cycle that robs us of the fellowship and joy that God created for us. In moments when I am feeling criticized or overwhelmed, I realize that I tend to pull away. I know that this just makes my spouse feel more abandoned and rejected.

God, help me to stand strong and remember Your promise: *"When you pass through the waters, I will be with you; and when you pass through the rivers, they will not sweep over you. When you walk through the fire, you will not be burned..."* (Isaiah 43:2 NIV). God, help me to take healthy steps in conflict knowing that You are my *"light and my salvation—whom shall I fear? The Lord is the stronghold of my life—of whom shall I be afraid?"* (Psalm 27:1 NIV).

Ready to Make a Change?

In examining your own attachment style, it has started to become apparent to you that you have developed a protective approach style in your marriage to protect yourself and "play it safe." These are the ways that you defend yourself against further pain or loss. These will be the very areas in which you will have to take risks in the days ahead. You will have to learn to take some risks so that you can recreate and cultivate those feelings of love you once had. Susan Johnson says that *"Love can only be known when we take risks."*[49]

Anything in life that is worth having requires that you take a risk to achieve it. In the next chapter I will be sharing with you the specific steps of faith and growth that you must take, whether you are an avoider or a protester. We'll be strategic and incremental about crafting these steps. I have no desire to open you up blindly to the possibility of worse pain. You'll see from your spouse's response whether or not you can continue to take further risks.

A final note seems to be in order before we go to the next key. Perhaps you look at your marriage, and you are quite contented with things the way they are. You feel that you can go to your spouse with your needs, and you will receive comfort and help. You don't discern a negative cycle for you and your spouse. Congratulations! This would suggest that you have a secure pattern of attachment in your marriage.

You might then reflect on times when you leaned toward one side or the other, pursuing or distancing. You may still identify difficult times in the past where a negative cycle was in place. If you find yourself in a place of secure attachment to your spouse, your work in the rest of this book will be much easier. The remaining six keys will serve to enrich your existing bond. And, you may become a person who shares these keys with others who are struggling.

CHAPTER 6

Second Key—Vulnerable Language Changes Everything

"I see how much you're hurting. I wish I could take your pain from you."

Have you ever heard a parent say the above comments to a child? The parent is conveying deep appreciation for the pain and dilemma of the child. A father wants to ease his child's suffering. A mother wants her child to not be alone in the dark hour of need. When you see your child struggling so much, this is your desire.

You want to take the load off your child's shoulders by taking the pain that is weighing her down. But it is not physically possible to take some of your child's pain, is it? I cannot literally extract some of my child's pain to bear it myself, no matter how much I would want to alleviate the suffering.

The best we can do is to have them share their pain with us, verbally and nonverbally. The best we can hope for is that our children will let us in, and that we will be present with them in their pain. And that is of great value! That is precious when it takes place. Just knowing that a parent cares this much for you somehow eases your pain. As a child, I know then that I am not alone, and I know someone cares for me. The parent cannot physically remove the pain from the child, but when sharing takes place, the emotional burden of the pain is now carried by two. The load is somewhat lighter.

Brain science shows that the very act of verbalizing our painful experiences to another person helps us to better integrate the distress of those experiences. We are better able to make sense of them. Our confusion levels go down, along with our initial sense of anxiety about facing the pain alone.

We hurt less after we talk about our pain with a trusted person.

Easing pain is what every attuned parent wants to do for a child in need. I am inclined to believe that this is the same desire of every spouse in early marriage. We don't want our beloved spouses to hurt. We want to be *with* them in their moments of need. I actually think that it takes a very long time for this level of caring to be diminished.

Even in more advanced stages of conflict, the listening spouse still wants to take the pain of her beloved. The husband wants to be able to do something to ease his wife's pain. In my opinion, it is not so much a difficulty with listening that takes place within a distressed couple, it is a difficulty in being able to convey pain in *vulnerable* ways that would draw our spouses to us versus pushing them away.

When we are hurting, our entire nervous system is wired to fight or flee away from the pain. This makes it very difficult to draw close to our spouses during those times when we get hurt in the marriage. We defend ourselves with an attack, even before we get started on the approach toward letting them in. We brace ourselves for rejection and inadvertently sabotage ourselves, pulling away from ones who want nothing more than to help us.

In this chapter, we are going to take a look at ways that we can use the gift of vulnerable language to bring healing and hope to the areas of our marriage that have been damaged by the negative cycle. We will be challenged to use language in very specific ways to take risks with one another again, to melt our defenses, and to bring down the protective walls that we built in our frightened moments. As you speak in vulnerable and committed ways to your spouse, you will have power to draw them close and build emotional security once again.

The Gift of Language

Language truly is a gift to us as humans. It lifts us into a realm above all the other creatures on earth. It helps us richly communicate our joys, our longings, and our sorrows. It binds us together and helps us connect to one another throughout our lives. As any parent can tell you, the advent of language in your infant child comes with eager anticipation, great welcome, and joy. You long to fellowship with your child, and you rejoice when the door opens to new depths of communing and new depths of knowing.

When first we fall in love, there is such language! Oh, the poetry that flows from the lips of one lover to the other. How we croon our devotion! How we extol the virtues and beauty of our beloved one. We compliment, make promises, and dream aloud of all the ways that we will be together, ways that we will be one. Language links us and binds us, and it is the precursor to physical affection.

My maternal grandparents fell in love through the course of many letters written while he was miles away in college. This was long before the days of cell phones and Skype. Language shared between those two dear ones, led to a great romance and a legacy of love. I am a recipient of that legacy today.

Language is limited at times in what it can convey to us about the deeper truths of life and the essence of divinity. Sometimes there are no words to express what is profound or transcendent. However, language is a gift that we finite human beings have for our understanding of God and one another.

God's Words Reassure Us

God uses language to tell us something of who He is. In Exodus chapter 3, God reveals to us His constancy and His ever-present nature through the story of Moses at the burning bush. God tells Moses, "I will be with you" and reveals that His constant presence is part of His name, "I am."[50] This is His very nature, an *"ever-present help in trouble"* (Psalm 46:1 NIV).

"I will be with you." What comfort that promise brings to us humans who are wired with needs for security and hardwired with fears of the future and uncertainty about the unknown. God's promise, conveyed through language, soothes our fears and provides deep reassurance of His presence with us, His guidance for us along our journey.

We understand and are known through our use of language. The primary way people can know about our internal experience is through our use of expressive language. Language is the means by which we tell other people what we are going through, what we are thinking, and what we need.

I am so thankful that God communicates to us in a way that we can understand! Language has its limitations in conveying to us the vastness of God's nature, His love, and His faithfulness. Yet we receive so much assurance and wealth, as God expresses Himself to us through His words in Scripture and His promises to us in our daily lives.

God stoops to our level to impart His truth to our minds. His messages bring us light, comfort, and guidance. We internalize these words and make mental pictures of them whenever we hear them. Sometimes they are stored more deeply in ways that anchor us, bolster us, and connect us to Him. When we go through difficult times, we rehearse His promises in our minds. This gives us strength to keep going and connects us to Him along the way.

His expressed promises assure us that He is with us, will never forsake us, and that He has a purpose for our lives. In this same manner, we can use language to build security in our marriage relationships! We can even use language to break out of the negative cycles that lock us into so much intrapersonal and interpersonal pain. Estelle Frankel is a Jewish psychologist who speaks of language as sacred and instrumental in the "Exodus" of breaking free within our souls. Frankel tells us, "It is through the act of articulation that we break through the walls that separate us from ourselves and each other."[51]

In the following sections we will consider specific ways that we can build security in our marriage relationships through the gift of vulnerable language. We will carefully tailor our language to enable us to break out of negative cycles and bind us once again in covenant unity.

Vulnerable language allows you to share your needs in new ways.

This is not just about communicating differently or using "I statements." Vulnerable language is the way we posture ourselves to share our needs in new ways. We want to frame to our spouses that at the core of all our marriage distress is our deep need to be connected to them. We are positioning ourselves to share needs, longings, and the hurts that come when we can't find our loved ones at those key times when we are reaching for them.

Negative Cycle Language

We learned in the last chapter that the negative cycle is the enemy of security in our marriages. When the negative cycle is spinning, each spouse is getting hammered, shamed, isolated, and abandoned. The language of the cycle only serves to heat up these raw emotions that further fuels the distance between spouses. It's punctuated by defensiveness, accusations, and blaming the other. The following statements are examples of how I might speak to you as my spouse in the throes of the negative cycle:

> "You're punishing me with your words! You pound me, and I run away from you."
>
> "I'm disgusted with you! You never make time for me! Everything else is more important to you than me."
>
> "I don't know what to do to make you happy. You're never satisfied, no matter how hard I try."
>
> "You don't know how to play. You're frigid and cold!"

Notice the defensive and protected stance taken in the language of the negative cycle. It's replete with projections of pain onto the other. There's no owning that my pain stems from a failure in our ability to connect in the ways that I want to be connected to you. In the negative cycle, I don't acknowledge that my pain is due to a lack of connection with the person that I care most about in the whole world. I am too busy in my fear instincts, jabbing and ducking, to tell you that it's only a fight because of how much you mean to me.

If I didn't care about your opinion of me, then I would not retreat from your criticism. If I did not want to spend my close moments with you, then I would not be outraged that you pull away from me. It follows clearly that the negative cycle is always painful because of how much I care for you and want to be close to you.

The only reason we fight is because we care so deeply. I want to be close to you because you are my most important person! I don't want to feel criticized by you because I value your opinion of me, more than any other person in the world.

Yet, those personal and vulnerable words seldom cross my lips in moments of conflict and pain. Perhaps longings for closeness and caring have not been expressed since I was infatuated with you and pledged to be yours forever. It may have been ages since that way of speaking came through to you. But, that is what the struggle is always about. Any pain that we experience stems from the breach of that all important attachment bond with our loved one.

I duck from your attack so that I won't have to feel one more reminder that I am no good to you or that I am letting you down. I jab and poke because I am trying to get you to come back to me, to be present with me in any possible way that I can. The following statements reveal the heart of what I am truly saying to you as my spouse during a fight:

> "You are my most important person. I want you to like me and accept me more than anything in the world. I want to take care of you and to feel good about myself for the ways that I get that job done. I got married so that I could be with you. I just want to be close to you because you matter to me. I get scared when I can't reach you. I feel sad when we don't connect because I like spending time with you."

It makes perfect sense that the fight we're having is always about trying to get back to a place of connection. It's all about my attachment to you.

> "You are my most important person, and I want to be good for you, and to be seen as good by you. You are my person, and I like being with you. I must be able to reach you when I need you. Can't you see? Please be there for me."

The negative cycle takes place because things are all out of alignment, and it *keeps* us out of alignment. We used to be close and connected. We used to say the types of things that built each other up. Now we only tear each other down. I used to be stuck to you like glue, but now I can't even find you when I need you.

The first key is recognizing this negative cycle and pinning the blame on it while we recognize the fear and shame that fuel it. *The second key* is to begin to use vulnerable language to mend fences and sew up the fabric of our hearts.

Vulnerable language powerfully shifts us out of the cycle and starts to place us face-to-face once again. It is like a manual override on the rapid cycling of raw emotions that we race through in our fight or flight mode. Vulnerable language is soothing to our ears and our raw emotions. It slows and softens the intensity of the defensive emotions that fuel the negative cycle.

Reframing: A Picture with New Words

One of my jobs in marriage therapy is to be an "expert reframer." I get to translate the negative cycle speak into language of connection and belonging. It's one of the most satisfying parts of my job. I get to literally slow it down for the couple and get to the heartfelt desires that are at the core of the conflict.

> "You are the most important person to me, and that is why I…"
>
> "I count on you to be the one who has got my back and so I was…"
>
> "I care about how you see me, so I was crushed when I thought that…"

When I say these phrases to most couples they chuckle at me, and say "I would never talk like that." But they don't dislike hearing it. Their warm smiles tell me how good it feels to hear someone say that to them.

The process of reframing language must start with you.

We have to start with vulnerable ways of reframing what is really going on. Susan Johnson speaks about this crucial process of stepping out from the negative cycle and rebuilding connection between spouses. To break the cycle and step toward a face-to-face connection, we must begin to speak to our spouse about our attachment longings and desires.

Johnson states that the avoider must use language that clearly reframes his withdrawing behavior as stemming from an "unfulfilled need and longing for acceptance." The protester must use new language that describes her sense of abandonment panic and her need for contact and closeness with her most important person.[52]

The new frame is pretty simple to understand. We want to connect attachment significance to the things that we say to our spouses. It's all about our connection to them. We have to start framing any pain that we experience as stemming from the breach of that all-important attachment bond between us.

Vulnerable Language for Avoiders

If you are often in the position of being the avoider in your negative cycle, then we have to begin by talking to you. I am not saying that you are the problem. It's just that we're going to have a hard time conducting the dialogue if you are not even in the room to have it with your spouse.

Avoiders, we have to start with you. We have to hear from you first!

It makes sense, right? We have to get you back to the table so that we can begin to change the negative cycle. So we have to talk about the reasons why you left, why you are pulling away on a regular basis. Nothing will really change until we have you back in the game.

If you are typically in the position of being the avoider, then you may have the detached avoider attachment style that we spoke about in the past two chapters. Such a person is less afraid of being abandoned, and more afraid of engulfment. This is the fear of being criticized, inadequate, made to feel "less than," swallowed up, or consumed.

In times of conflict you may have the strong desire to "end the discussion," just to avoid dealing with the pain. This can take the form of retreat, or defending yourself as being worthwhile or good enough. In your efforts to be a good spouse, you get the sense that you are being accused of coming up short. You may feel that no matter what you do, it is not good enough. And every conflict with your protesting spouse seems to confirm that you are failing. You may retreat into work, screen time, pornography, or even into the arms of someone else where you feel good about yourself.

Story of an Avoider: The Man Who Viewed Too Much

I am reminded of a painful story involving a couple I worked with. You may remember them from Chapter 4: Larry and Sonda. They began therapy because Larry had a problem with viewing pornography while he was away on work-related travel. His job required him to travel and be away for extended periods of time; and when he went away, he would often view X-rated films on the hotel TV.

Sonda was angry and hurt by what Larry had done. Her eyes and entire face flushed with emotion whenever she would talk to Larry about their marriage. In the sessions, she did most of the talking, in rapid and animated ways. Sonda grew up in a very volatile family with a father who had a substance abuse problem. The whole family was involved in one another's business, like tangled vines squeezing and reaching into the space and emotions of the others. Her father's volatility caused her to fear abandonment.

Larry grew up in a disconnected family, like solitary pine trees in a forest. They did not celebrate birthdays to any degree. His basic needs were met, but that was about it. He had no clue about how to relate in a conflict. He was gentle and quiet, and prone to shutting down. He had never had those after-school talks with his mom where she says, "Hi Larry. How was your day?" No one listened to his experiences to give him a sense that what he was going through was real and valid. I believe that he used pornography to fill the void when he felt lonely in his adult years.

In our work together, Sonda was trying to get back on solid ground after learning of Larry's addiction. What she wanted from him was for him to check in over the phone while he was traveling. She wanted him to reassure her that she was still in his thoughts. It was the longing of her heart and would help her to be less scared.

But the way she presented her needs to him was overwhelming. She came across as critical of him, controlling, and angry. However, Larry could barely get a word in edgewise. On top of that she was just beginning her lifelong dream of starting a small business. It required most of their savings, right at a time when she was unsure of their future. So her security needs were heightened at the time of our working together. Larry sat there like a whipped hound, squirming uncomfortably and trying to appease Sonda to get her to calm down.

I was stunned when a more passive aggressive side of Larry surfaced just at the time of Sonda's business grand opening. He completely missed the grand opening ceremony because he went out to an adult club that night and got very drunk. Staggering! How could this avoider have come to such a tragic place?

This was an extreme case of a negative cycle. He was the avoider, and she was the protester. He felt criticized, inadequate to even speak to her, and he felt badly about himself. He never got to deal with that or reengage, and she sensed it. So she kept scrambling to get him back, with her protests and her demands. She could sense that he was far away, and was desperate to get him back. But she was so intense that she pushed him further. The stress of starting her own business threw them into crisis mode. She was desperate to know that she would not be abandoned. He was afraid of never being heard or noticed by Sonda, like his last chances were slipping away.

Three Strategies for Avoiders

I have three strategies that I like to share with folks who get stuck in the avoider side of the cycle. These strategies are designed to help you share your side of the struggle for emotional connection. They are less of a formula, and more of a way to help you frame your needs for closeness and to be valued by your spouse. The first sounds like a country music song, the second is a soul music song, and the third is the Million Dollar Question for any situation with your spouse.

Strategy 1: "I want to talk about me!"

A number of years back there was a country music song by an artist named Toby Keith. Toby is on a date with a very talkative woman, and he gets an earful. He stands up and loudly asserts, "I want to talk about me!" To my knowledge, Toby does not struggle with assertiveness or stepping up in moments of conflict. I use this song as a funny and memorable anchor for avoiders to hold on to.

The first time that you step forward to talk about what is going on for you, it can be incredibly stressful. That is where this bold cowboy song may provide a funny but bold image of strength to press forward and begin to change the negative cycle.

If we would plug this in for Larry in the story just shared, the following are some of the words that he would need to say. They are all "I statements." They talk about "me." They use vulnerable language to describe the effects of the protester's actions on Larry. "I want to talk about me!" is the opposite of staying silent with our spouses. We step forward and lovingly challenge them to see that their actions are hurtful to us. And we ask them to change their approach.

Larry: Sonda, you have got to tone it back. I know that you are upset, but when you talk so fast and intense, I can't even think straight. I feel like bolting.

Larry: Sonda, when you yell at me, I feel terrible about myself. I am trying here, and I feel like I am all bad to you. I can't stand feeling like I'm a failure to you.

Larry: I may as well just get out of your way. It hurts less that way, than to take the constant criticism.

Larry: I see the fight coming, and I just pull back. I try to keep things from getting worse between us. I do damage control by pulling away.

Larry: Your opinion of me matters more than anybody else's. If I can't get it right for you, I'm really messed up.

Notice that Larry is stepping forward to talk about his feelings and his experience. He is not calling Sonda names. He is talking about the effect that her behaviors have on his emotional experience. He is letting her know that he is in pain because he still has a stake in the marriage. He gets hurt while trying to do the right things. He cares about her opinion of him. He is actually trying to protect the marriage. In sharing these things, Larry is letting Sonda know that he is affected by her. He is not numb or uncaring.

He has a lot going on behind the scenes, things that she may not have been aware of based on his retreat. He is tipping her off that her actions are having an effect on his ability to stay connected to her. It's all about the connection and the things that threaten it for him. She is the most important person to him. How she sees him can either hurt him badly, or make him feel like a king.

Strategy 2: "You've really got a hold on me!"

The next strategy for avoiders takes us a step deeper in the journey of vulnerability. "You've really got a hold on me!" When I hear this phrase in my head, I remember the 1962 smash Motown hit by Smokey Robinson with the same title. The singer is deep and passionate in letting you know the way you hold his heart. In his own heartfelt way he is saying, "You are my world, and I need you."

It takes a tremendous amount of courage as the avoider to step forward and open up in this way. Everything inside us tells us to flee the potential conflict or rejection when we have been wired to avoid. It can make us shake in our boots to be this vulnerable, but it is the very thing that our spouses want to hear from us. They are longing to know that we care.

So, we have to rouse ourselves to share the deeper meaning within, "You've really got a hold on me!" It is taking the risk to let your spouse know who you long to be for yourself, and where you are struggling. It is telling our spouses all that we want to be for them and to them. It lets them know how much they mean to us.

"You've really got a hold on me!" tells your spouse how much you need him or her to feel good about yourself.

If they believe in us, then we can face any challenge. When we take care of them, we feel good. We want to be connected, more than anything. Our spouses are so important to us, and we speak to them about the deeper wishes that we have for our connection together. Let's take a look at how Larry could have told Sonda, "You've really got a hold on me!"

Larry: Sonda, when you complain, I feel bad about myself. But it's the worst because I want to be good for you. I want to satisfy you. I wish I could hear something that I did right for you.

Larry: Sonda, I can't believe how badly I hurt you by viewing porn. It's hard for me to see the pain on your face. I freeze up because I don't know what to do for you. I just wish I knew how to fix it.

Larry: Sonda, I got scared when you were starting your new business… that you'd have even less time for me. So I pulled away first, so that it wouldn't hurt as badly. It's hard to admit it, but I need your attention.

Larry: Sonda, sometimes I see how successful and driven you are. I wonder if you even need me. I feel pathetic. I want to feel needed by you.

In "You've really got a hold on me!" Larry speaks about his shame and feelings of failure to his wife. Larry speaks about his desire to have her think highly of him. He wants to satisfy her, and take care of her. He feels inadequate when he can't seem to do that. More than anything, her opinion of him counts. He speaks about his fear of being lost in the hustle of her new business, no longer a priority. He tells her that he wants to be her "go-to guy" in order to take care of her, and to feel good about himself. He's telling her his view of himself, and of his longings for her. More than just wanting an end to conflict, he longs to hear her say she needs him and to feel like he is good for her.

Confessing that "You've really got a hold on me!" is quite a risk, and you may need to wait until your beloved protester has taken a first step and softened the pursuit of you before you feel comfortable to attempt this. You may wish to see that your protester has made progress in reducing the blaming statements, and is better at speaking about deeper needs too.

I am not telling you to hold back on sharing. I am just bracing you for what lies ahead. Your protester may still be frightened and angry from all the times you were far away. Summon up your courage, while you move in slowly and with low, soft tones. Like a stealth bomb lover, you are coming back to home base.

Low and slow. Let 'em know how much you care and want to be the go-to person.

As avoiders open up and share, "You've really got a hold on me!" the protesters get to hear and view their spouses in a totally new light. This type of communication reinterprets the avoider's actions so that protesters will have compassion on them. It reassures protesters of their important place and that avoiders want more than anything to be connected to them, to be valued by them, and to care for them.

Strategy 3: The Million Dollar Question

The first two strategies for avoiders were geared at helping you open up and talk about what is really going on. This third strategy is to help you listen and stay engaged when it is your protester's turn to speak.

Most spouses who are in the avoider position have arrived at that place because they had endless experiences of feeling like they failed or were not good enough for their spouse. They tried and tried, but nothing seemed to work to satisfy their protesting spouse. They always came up short.

This was devastating because they were fully invested in being good news for their spouse, not a problem or perpetual failure to their spouse. I have affectionately dubbed this strategy the Million Dollar Question, because it is a simple anchoring phrase to help you stay engaged, even when the going gets tough. The exact wording of the question itself is not the key, but it reflects the right stance that you will need. It anchors you to the goal of staying engaged and gives you a picture of what that looks like.

For most avoiders, there is a keen focus on hearing what they are doing wrong. They feel blamed. The protester is accidentally helping that along by throwing out a series of critical or blaming phrases. But you are in a new place now. You are aware of the negative cycle. You have been honest with the protester about how "I want to talk about me" and how your protester's comments threaten your ability to stay connected. You have spoken about your deeper longings for connection and what you *need* from your protester to stay engaged. Now you are ready to listen to your protester's side of things and to look for your chance to use the Million Dollar Question.

The Million Dollar Question helps me stay engaged, even if my protester is not doing such a great job of speaking about how much she or he needs me. Ultimately, I know my protester is talking to me *because* he or she needs me. It's when she stops talking to me and pursuing me that I am in trouble.

So here it is, the Million Dollar Question. Look for a key point in the conversation to ask this, after you have listened to your protester and heard as best you can what the concerns and needs are. You reflect those back to the protester, knowing that the protester is coming to you because you are important and needed. You kindly offer these engaged, inviting, and clarifying words: "Is there anything you need from me right now?"

This question means that you have stayed engaged long enough to get to the heart of the matter. It lets the protester know that you see her, you hear her, you care about her, and you want to be the one who meets her needs. She can ask you for what she need. We'll together explore what that is and do what we can to meet those needs. She is not alone in her time of need because you are with her.

"Is there anything you need from me right now?"

This question helps you stay focused on where this conversation must go. It gives you something to say when you are unclear or unsure of exactly what the problem is. You can get clarity and sort through the noise. You may not even be able to solve this problem for your protester. But you can say, "I would like to be able to do that for you. I care."

Do you want to know something surprising? Most of the time, protesters just want you to listen or say something affirming to them. I know that there are times when specific requests are going to be made. But so many times, your protester just wants to be heard by you.

At this point we have made huge steps to reengage the avoider. He or she has spoken about feeling blamed or not good enough for the protester, the one who matters most (Strategy 1: "I want to talk about me!"). The avoider has told the protester the surprising truth that, "You've really got a hold on me!" (Strategy 2). The avoider has taken the posture of the one who is the solution to the needs of the protester by asking, "What do you need from me?" (Strategy 3: The Million Dollar Question).

We now turn our focus to the vulnerable language of the protester.

Vulnerable Language for Protesters

If you are typically in the position of being the protester in your negative cycle, then this next section is for you. Also, this section is for you if you used to be the protester, but now you have pulled back in total frustration with never being able to get your spouse to engage with you. So, at this point, you might look more like an avoider due to burnout, but that is not historically the essence of you.

If you typically are in the position of the protester, or if you used to be in that position, this will likely describe your dilemma. You may lean toward having the ambivalent protester attachment style that we spoke of in the past two chapters. You would not be a person who fears too much closeness. In moments of uncertainty in relationship, you are more concerned about being left alone. This is the fear of abandonment that we have spoken about previously.

Fear of abandonment comes at times when you are not sure that your spouse is going to be there for you. It comes at times when you don't believe that your spouse cares about you, or that you really are important to your spouse. You want to matter, to be important, and to have him or her pay attention to you.

In times of conflict, you may have tendencies to turn up the volume in order to get your spouse's attention. When you feel afraid that you don't matter to your spouse, you can end up accusing her of not caring about you. In moments when you are afraid of losing closeness, you may say many critical things about your spouse's distancing behaviors. You may even criticize your spouse.

The more your spouse pulls away, the more you turn up the volume trying to reach your avoider. You may nag, yell, criticize, call names, or even throw things, all in an effort to rouse your avoider from slumber and to get the sense that you are important once again.

Before I give you an example of a protester, I want to discuss a couple of possible differences between male protesters and female protesters, in the ways that they express their needs. Central themes for most female protesters include an expressed desire to be important, noticed, cared for, and to have more time with their husbands. It is a bit more rare for men to be in the protester role, but it does take place.

When husbands are in the protester role, they are apt to express the same needs to feel that they are a priority and to feel important. They may speak about a desire to be admired by their wife. "I want you to be my biggest fan." Their desire to spend time together often takes the form of sharing in activities, as opposed to just "sitting and talking."

Finally, protester husbands often are in the role of asking their wives for sexual connection. There is a subtle distinction between avoider husbands who ask for sex and protester husbands who ask for sex. For all husbands, there is a significant physical and emotional component to sex, which we will discuss further in the sex chapter of this book, Naked and Unashamed. But for the protester husbands, there is a stronger leading emphasis on the emotional side. You might not get that as the wife because all you hear are demands or criticisms of your "lack of sex drive." But protesting husbands are longing to be adored. When their spouses connect with them sexually, they feel worthwhile and more whole.

Story of a Protester: "Once You Say it, You Can't Take it back."

Vividly, I recall a couple whom we'll call Kent and Angie. Kent commuted to his job in a nearby city where he stayed Monday through Thursday nights. The couple seldom saw one another. They would see each other on the weekend, but this was pretty miserable for them. Arguments got intense as Angie yelled at Kent for working so much, and not caring at all about the marriage. Kent periodically fought back and swore in his own defense that he was not a bum. He was a "hard working husband and not out cheating or anything. It's your depression that's the problem!"

During the week, Angie would try to phone or text Kent on his cell phone. But, depending on his job situation, he was not always able to take her call. I remember one situation where he did not respond to her messages or texts for twenty-four hours. She was livid! When they were both at home, Angie reached a fever pitch several times, and slapped Kent. The truth is that her demeaning words toward Kent hurt much more than any of the times she slapped him. Kent just retreated further.

Of course Angie was depressed. She did not see her husband for days at a time. Then their occasional weekend time was filled with the ravages of a negative cycle. Angie grew up in a home where conflict was intense. Her dad died when she was little, and her mother was depressed for years to follow. Angie and her brothers had intense yelling conflicts replete with horrible name-calling on a regular basis. Angie was abandoned, but she had to be tough in order to make it as a little girl.

Kent's mom left his dad when he was in grade school, and they moved in with Kent's grandparents. Dad worked long hours, so he was not there for Kent. His grandparents were somewhat inept emotionally and placed all their emphasis on what a person achieves. As a result, all of Kent's efforts were spent on trying to impress his grandparents even though he had much more going on internally. Inside, he was really a sad boy who missed his mother terribly.

This story illustrates another extreme case of a negative cycle where neither party got what they needed. Angie felt desperately alone and completely powerless to get Kent to spend time with her. The more he withdrew, the more worthless she felt. She slashed him with her words in attempts to get him to stop making her feel that way. He felt less and less adequate. He retreated in hopelessness and felt like a failure.

Three Strategies for Protesters

I offer three strategies to protesters to better communicate the heart of the matter for them. These strategies are designed to help draw your avoider to you in your moment of need, instead of pushing him or her away. These strategies are crafted to help you better express your needs, your fears, and your longings. They are less of a technique and more geared toward helping you center your words on the heart of the matter. The heart of the matter is that you want to spend more time with your avoider and know that he or she cares.

Strategy 1: "You're the hero, not the bum!" and Strategy 2: "You gave me a scare!" will help reframe your dilemma in ways that engender compassion from your avoider. Strategy 3: "The Power of What" will help redirect you when blaming words come off your lips.

Strategy 1: "You're the hero, not the bum!"

This strategy gets to the heart of the matter for you and for your avoider. The entire reason that you are coming forward is because of your need for your spouse. Your spouse is the solution, not the problem. Your distress is because you can't find him when you need him. It's not because your avoider is a bum! He's the hero in this story, the one to listen to you, stand by your side, and let you know that you are not alone.

Somehow there has been a horrible misunderstanding that you think your spouse is defective or inept, the source of the problem. The truth is that your spouse's presence is the solution to what you need. The very fact that you are coming forward attests that you see your avoider as having what you need to get better and feel better. Your spouse is the one you are still looking to, still looking for, and still longing for.

In so many words you want to communicate, "You're the one I'm looking to because I believe you have what it takes. I need you with me because I can't do it alone. Your presence is the solution. You are the hero in my story, not the bum!"

If we would plug this strategy into the story of Angie and Kent, we'd listen to her say the following words. Her "I statements" are about her need for him. Her "You statements" stop blaming him and point to his value as the problem solver.

Angie: Kent, I feel so lonely during the week when I don't see you. I want to see you. I can't stand missing you so much.

Angie: Kent, I feel like I don't matter to you when you are gone like you are. I want to matter to you more than anything. Time together shows me that I matter.

Angie: I got married to you because I like being with you. It's awful being apart from you so much. Sometimes I yell to get you to come back to me.

Angie: I just need to know that you care. When you notice me, or talk with me, everything is okay. You make it all better.

Angie: When you see me or choose me, I feel wonderful. When you pull away, I feel worthless.

Angie's statements clearly define the problem as one of longing for Kent. She needs his presence in her life. She can't stand being without him. She has to know that he cares, or else she gets very upset. These statements tell him that his presence is comforting and give her a sense of value. It's all about wanting more of Kent because he is good in her eyes. She's telling him that she needs him, and she is telling him that he is the solution just by being there.

It's all about the connection and how their distance is bad for her sense of self. He is the most important person to her. He's the one that she wants to be with more than anyone else. When he disengages it hurts her badly, but when he is present it makes her feel like a queen.

Strategy 2: "You gave me a scare!"

I find that anger is one of the toughest emotions for most of avoiders to deal with. If their spouse is angry, then they must be screwing it up. I also find that protesters don't do a particularly good job of speaking about the real reasons why they are angry. That's partly because they don't often have an engaged partner to really hear them out.

But it's also due to the way that anger organizes the brain in moments of threat and danger. Anger is a protective emotion. Something is wrong, and I am going to stand up to it and make it change! There's a threat to me, and I won't stand for it any longer! In marriage, the threat for protesters is that they can't find their spouse when they need them. This can generate a lot of anger!

The attachment significance gets lost in the anger. The avoiders don't get even the slightest hint that they are needed or desired. They just get the angry signal that they did something wrong and bad.

I have a brief story that crystallized this in my own mind. My wife and I have a friend whom we'll call Mindy for this story. Mindy adores her pet cat, and he is a huge part of her life. This cat is super important to Mindy. We'll call this cat Jim.

About six months ago, I was doing a plumbing repair job on the sink in Mindy's upstairs bathroom. I was the only one at Mindy's house that day. Or, I should say, the only human. Jim the cat was also at home, sunning himself, taking naps, and periodically trying to dash out the front door.

I was loading up my tools in the car at the end of the project and suddenly realized that the front door was ajar for several minutes. I looked around for Jim but could not find him anywhere. Imagine my terror and panic! I bolted back out the front door and made a thorough search of the surrounding meadow and gully by the stream. (I felt something like the Good Shepherd searching for the lost sheep in Matthew 18:12).

I called my wife on my cell phone and she appreciated immediately the gravity of the situation. She consoled me and said a prayer that I would find Jim. She often reminds me to pray when I get stressed. After canvassing the woodlands a bit more, I returned to the front door of Mindy's house. Jim greeted me with a yawn from the sofa. I was glad to see Jim, very glad.

But I was also quite angry! I scooped him up and carried him back upstairs to his "cat room." *Bad kitty! You gave me a scare! I thought I lost you.* I was also angry at him because he had not communicated with me when I was searching for him around the house. It was as though he did not care that I was in distress about possibly losing him.

The rational part of my brain realizes that I had spooked him into some cranny or crevice of the house in my frantic search for him, but the scared part of my brain still wishes that he would have told me where he was. I set him back down in his cat room and carefully closed the door, making sure that it was latched shut.

Although this story pertains to a cat named Jim, you can quickly see the ways that it relates to any protester's dilemma with a spouse. The protester is feeling left alone in moments when she needs her spouse. When she can't reach him, she is frightened.

"You gave me a scare!"

The "scare" is twofold. One piece is that she can't reach him and may feel like she has temporarily lost him. The other piece is that she may fear that he does not truly care about her or care enough to be available to her.

Let's plug this back in to the story of Angie and Kent. Let's look at language that she could use to express her desire for connection with him, along with her fear that she had lost him or that he did not care.

Angie: Kent, I left you texts and messages for an entire day, and I got really scared that something bad had happened to you.

Angie: When you didn't call me back, I was so ticked at you for putting me in a position where I had to wonder if you were okay. I didn't like having to worry for even a second whether you were okay.

Angie: You're my guy, the one I want to go to. I got mad when I couldn't find you. I need you in my life. I don't want to lose you.

Angie: When I found out you were okay, I was relieved…but also mad that you hadn't called me sooner. I thought you didn't care about what I was going through.

Angie: I have to know that you care about what I'm going through. Calling me or texting back lets me know that I'm important to you.

As you look over Angie's statements, you can clearly see how she is working carefully on language that clarifies that Kent is the "hero, not the bum." She is also sharing with him that she was scared of losing him. She does not want to be without him. Angie gives him clear feedback about what he did that gave her a scare about losing him. She does it in a way that affirms how much she needs him. She does not sugarcoat her anger, but she lets Kent know that it stems from a fear of losing him and the sense that he did not care.

It all comes from her normal desire to be with him and to know that he cares. It is scary when her most important person is not accessible to her in a time of need. She does not like to live in that shaky place. She just longs to know that he is with her, and to know that he cares. This is a critical reframe of the anger toward her spouse.

Strategy 3: "The Power of What"

When you are feeling alone or afraid that you are going to be alone, it is very common to scramble to try to prevent it from happening again. When you are angry and scared with a feeling that your spouse does not care, you want him to stop doing the things that make you feel those painful emotions. "Where is your head, Kent? Why didn't you call me? Why are you doing these painful things to me?"

It's normal to try to understand the reasons why you are experiencing pain so that you can make it stop. And this approach works just fine when you are doing self-reflection, or if you are in a clinical setting where a neutral party is helping you diagnose the causes of your ailment and pain. But there's a hitch when it comes to trying this approach with your spouse. It doesn't work well, and often backfires when you lead off with this approach.

Remember, he is already feeling defensive and blamed. Language that leads off with "why" does not serve to build the connection that you want with your avoider. Unfortunately, "Why" language seems to have the opposite effect. It kicks your avoider into a defensive mode, and it keeps avoiders arguing instead of connecting them with their emotional experience.

Avoiders' emotional experience is the most valuable information that protesters can receive. Avoiders do care, but there is either some misunderstanding or the negative cycle itself that puts them in a position of pulling away from their spouses.

I am not trying to split hairs in this section or play with semantics. I firmly believe that you will get a much different result in your conversations with your avoider if you reduce your usage of "Why" questions. Instead, replace them with "What" questions. These are more likely to draw out your avoider and connect both of you with the attachment significance for what is taking place in moments of misunderstanding.

"What" questions give you more immediate access to your spouse's feelings. They give you awareness of your avoider's experience and circumstances surrounding key misunderstandings between the two of you. Examples include:

> "What was going on for you at that time?"
> "What was that like for you?"
> "What happened for you then? What happened to you?"
> "What is going on for you right now?"
> "What are you feeling as we talk about this?"

As you read these "What" questions, you can begin to appreciate the possibility of the deeper answers you might receive. As you read them, you can see how they convey a sense of caring about your avoider's felt experience and perspective. Yet they are pointed at getting to the heart of the matter.

"What" questions are not shying away from addressing the misunderstanding or painful circumstance that took place between the two of you. However, a "What" question is going to give you much more solid background information to address the problem. What was at work in that moment? What was getting in the way? What is it that needs to be understood, and what needs to change?

These types of questions will be less likely to put your avoider on the defensive because they are not blaming or seeming to point out character flaws in your beloved. Your avoider is not defective, inept, or a hopeless cause. Your avoider is human, with struggles and dilemmas at key moments in the relationship. In essence, the "What" question humanizes the avoider and gives him the benefit of the doubt.

Giving your avoider the benefit of the doubt is so hard to do when you are feeling alone, scared, and neglected. Yet I want you to use this "What" mindset as an anchoring tool in the middle of your emotional storm. Hold fast to this mindset—your avoider has a human and caring side to the story, which you need to know.

"What happened for you that day? What did you feel, and what did you do?" This can draw him out and draw him back into connection with you. It could make a huge difference for you, by reversing the negative cycle and drawing your avoider to you. It could make a huge difference for him by reinforcing that his experience is worth sharing instead of shutting down.

I know this is a stretch, but you and your spouse could actually come to view misunderstandings as opportunities to be known better by each other. Wouldn't that be a change? A misunderstanding, when shared in a vulnerable way, could give you both insights into your spouses' feelings and thoughts. That is our destination as we use vulnerable language. That is our goal in the next chapter, Embrace Conflict.

Summary and Practice Exercise

I am grateful for God's profound gift of vulnerable language. Language can be used to build connection and to share needs with ones who care deeply for us. In the negative cycle our language is defensive, blaming, and hurtful. In this chapter we got to the heart of the matter. Conflict is always a fight for a better emotional connection.

Avoiders have been given three strategies to strengthen them to move beyond the places where they are stuck. These strategies are not a formula; you have to find your own words to convey your needs. Rather, they are setting you up with vulnerable language geared at connection instead of withdrawal: Strategy 1: "I want to talk about me!"; Strategy 2: "You've really got a hold on me!"; and Strategy 3: The Million Dollar Question, "Is there anything you need from me right now?"

Protesters received three strategies to help them draw close to their spouses and share needs. These help you share anger without blaming and build a connection instead of pushing the avoider away. Strategy 1: "You're the hero, not the bum!"; Strategy 2: "You gave me a scare!"; and Strategy 3: "The Power of What."

Avoider Exercise

Take a moment as an avoider to remember a recent conflict you had with your spouse. Think about what you felt and what you needed to know from your spouse.

- Rehearse aloud how you would convey your side of it and your dilemma in the relationship ("I want to talk about me!").
- Remember to always frame it in terms of how much you *need* your spouse's approval to know that you are good and adequate ("You've really got a hold on me!").
- Try to remember what your spouse was saying about her or his pain at that time. Say aloud, "Is there anything you need from me right now?"
- If you are able, share all three of these steps with your spouse as they related to the recent conflict.

Protester Exercise

As a protester, please recall a recent conflict with your spouse. What were you feeling? How were you hurting? And what did you need to know from your spouse?

- Rehearse aloud how you felt pain because of a loss of closeness with your most important person, and how your spouse was the solution to your problem ("You're the hero, not the bum!").
- Remember to frame any anger as stemming from fear that you lost your avoider or that your spouse did not care ("You gave me a scare!").
- Try to remember what your spouse was saying about her or his pain at that time.
- Say aloud, "What was going on for you? What was that like for you?"
- If you are able, share all three of these steps with your spouse as they related to the recent conflict.

CHAPTER 7

Third Key—Embrace Conflict

Embrace conflict. You may be thinking that I am crazy for saying something like this. After all, your negative cycle of painful conflict might have been slamming you for years. You may only associate conflict with feeling blamed, belittled, rejected, or abandoned. How can conflict be good in a situation like that?

Frankly, in the midst of the negative cycle, there is very little that is good or productive about conflict. But we are in the process of changing that. You may not have had any positive experiences with conflict, even prior to marriage. So conflict is altogether a bad thing in your mind.

Conflict creates, for many of us, an unbearable feeling of anxiety and dread. This is especially true if the family we grew up in modeled conflict for us in violent, destructive, or unpredictable ways. Emotional violence, including name calling, threats, and manipulations, can be just as damaging as physical violence in the midst of conflict.

Ironically, it is also possible to have high anxiety about conflict when we grew up in families that avoided conflict altogether or never showed conflict in front of us. It was always conducted "behind closed doors."

The sad outcome of this in our marriages is that we lose sight of the essential function of conflict in a marriage. Productive conflict is a fight to improve your marriage. My mentor and friend, Dr. Tegan Blackbird, was one of the first to share this with me:

"Conflict is not a bad thing! Conflict is simply a sign that something is wrong and needs to be fixed. Of course, it must be done in a healthy way."

Conflict arises because something has gone wrong and needs to be addressed. It is an opportunity for growth, and it is a sign that one or both partners are still fighting to make the marriage healthier and stronger. The real danger occurs when neither spouse still cares enough about the marriage to complain or protest when something has been done to damage the emotional connection in the marriage.

When your spouse stops caring about things going wrong, your marriage is in real trouble!

Conflict is not a bad thing. It is essential for growth in learning how to better care for your spouse. It is essential to help you understand what you can do to prevent further pain to your spouse. Conflict affords you the chance to do prevention, maintenance, and enrichment in your marriage.

Prevention means that you may learn valuable insights about how to keep your spouse from feeling blamed, disconnected, unwanted, or alone. Maintenance means that through mild episodes of conflict you can stay on top of your growth areas in the marriage and not backslide into old patterns. Enrichment means that through conflict, you may learn about facets of your spouse that you were never aware of before. Perhaps your spouse was not fully aware of those facets until a twinge of pain brought it to awareness. Knowing that place of vulnerability is essential to true intimacy in marriage.

An April and Jesse Quarrel

I'll give you an example that took place recently in my own marriage. April asked me a question that immediately put me on edge. I got defensive and started pulling away because I am inclined toward being the avoider in our marriage. April invited me back, and I opened up to tell her how her question had reminded me of something painful. "Ouch, you just struck a painful place from my past!" This conflict moment gave her the chance to learn more about my past and gave me a chance to share it.

She would never have known this about me and cared for this if I had run away from the conflict. We are instinctively wired to run away from pain through our survival mechanism, the fight or flight response. However, if we live by this instinct alone, we will never have a deep connection with our spouse. We will never know the security of having a new experience with someone who loves us and cares that we got hurt.

In this recent conflict with April, I felt like pulling away. And, admittedly, my tone was not especially vulnerable as I spoke about the reasons why I had been feeling pain and was feeling afraid. It was an internal struggle to press through and tell her the whole story. Part of me was saying "Protect yourself, Jesse, and brace yourself for the worst." This was my survival instinct.

The other part of me has had so many experiences of connection and understanding with April, that I knew that I had to risk it with her once more. She was persevering and also kind to me. She challenged me about shutting down in a way that made us both laugh at the foolishness of running away from intimacy. That is another of the reasons why I married her because she challenges me toward greater intimacy.

Yesterday's conflict was fairly brief. That is because of all the work that we have put into our connection and our efforts to use conflict to grow us closer. I don't always want to press in and do the work of being vulnerable with my pain, and it is still scary sometimes to bring those places to her. It is a risk and a sacrifice to do this.

Dying to Self

Sacrificial love is required in marriage—from both spouses. In Ephesians, God speaks to the husband and asks him to lay down his life for his wife *"just as Christ loved the church and gave himself up for her"* (Ephesians 5:25 NIV). This sacrifice for husbands has many meanings. But in the context of reversing the negative cycle, it could look like what I had to do during our recent quarrel. Sacrifice meant laying down my survival instinct to run away from April and instead telling her, "You've really got a hold on me!"

Both men and women are instructed to honor one another and *"submit to one another"* (Ephesians 5:21 NIV). Then Paul goes on to specially emphasize that wives are to honor and respect their husbands. Again, this has different levels of meaning. But, in the context of reversing the negative cycle in marriage, honoring a husband may look very much like telling him, "You're the hero, not the bum."

Every time we run into pain in our marriage and we bring it to our spouses in a vulnerable way, we make our marriage stronger. Being able to turn to your partner, especially in times of distress, redefines the relationship as secure. God wants us to be secure in our marriage connection. He wants us to be secure in Him.

He wants us to be like a securely attached child in our relationships with one another so that we can fully demonstrate His love in marriage and to the world. Listen to this description about secure attachment and love as a pleasing aroma to God.

> *Therefore be imitators of God, as beloved children; and walk in love, just as Christ also loved you and gave Himself up for us, an offering and a sacrifice to God as a fragrant aroma* (Ephesians 5:1-2).

We are called to sacrificial love from a place of security in our relationship with God as a much loved child. We are to imitate Christ's love in this way. The beautiful thing in marriage is that our mutual sacrificial love just makes the bond stronger.

It is not a sacrifice to love when things are going easily. Love demonstrated in the midst of conflict, where there was pain or misunderstanding, is what brings growth and deeper connection. Conflict without the negative cycle is an opportunity for greater intimacy. When we do it in a connected and affirming manner, conflict becomes rewarding and fruitful. We may even view it as a chance to grow in our marriage bond.

Embracing Conflict for Growth

God even designed marriage to help us outgrow our old habits and unhealthy ways as individuals. Marriage is a relational vehicle of change. Through the ebb and flow of forging an increasingly secure attachment bond, we have a chance to grow and change. We may break off inflexible, outdated, and maladaptive patterns—our insecure attachment styles and negative cycles—and create the possibility for new patterns.

I have witnessed and personally experienced this. It is possible to grow up with an insecure attachment style and also to outgrow that through building a secure bond in your marriage. I have seen folks who were consistently caught up into negative cycles of relating in all their key relationships. As they learned how to break out of that cycle in their marriage, they learned how to relate in secure confident ways with other key relationships. But this only came through their hard work of embracing constructive feedback from conflict and directing that feedback in vulnerable ways.

Similarly, in our relationship with God, we grow over time through strain, sometimes through absence (ours), and often through pain. We grow and become more of what we are supposed to be. Through this journey of growth and redemption, we are drawn into life more *"abundantly"* (John 10:10), filled with a vast horizon of possible ways to approach and respond to life's situations and opportunities.

God wants us to grow into places of greater maturity within ourselves, in relationship with others, and in relationship with Him. Paul challenges us into this.

> *As a result, we are no longer to be children, tossed here and there by waves and carried about by every wind of doctrine, by the trickery of men, by craftiness in deceitful scheming; but speaking the truth in love, we are to grow up in all aspects into Him who is the head, even Christ"* (Ephesians 4:14-15).

Speaking the truth in love is something that mature people do. It is a vehicle for growth and for promoting greater levels of maturity. Sacrificial love in conflict with our spouse means that we pull out of our survival-based reactions that fuel the negative cycle. We have to be mindful of those reaction patterns, and that takes a lot of work.

But the more we do this work, the better our bond will be. We will also be quicker to interrupt defensive patterns and embrace vulnerable ways of sharing ourselves. We will be touched and blessed each time our spouses do the same.

A New Lens on Conflict

It's a whole new way to look at conflict, right? My spouse is coming to me to address something that grieved her or made her feel insecure in her bond with me. I am honored that she is talking to me about this. I would really be in trouble if she were not talking to me about this and were harboring silent resentment about it along the way. This very dialogue between us has the potential to grow us in our bond with one another. It may even help me to grow into more of the mature person God intends me to be.

Embracing conflict means that I start to develop an awareness that every conflict is a breakdown in the marital connection. It is a fight to restore it. There is an opportunity presenting itself to me for growth, prevention, and restoration. I could actually come out of this *more* connected with my spouse than I was before.

Most married people have had this experience, at least a couple times. They have worked through a conflict in a successful way. They have stayed out of the negative cycle or at least worked past it. They reached a deeper place of knowing their spouse at the end of it. They felt connected at a deeper level, and they may have even felt amorous.

That's where this phrase comes from: "Make-up sex is great after a fight." Did you ever think about the reasons why that is? First, dopamine is released during conflict, which is one of the arousing chemicals in the brain. That's part of the reason why you feel amorous after a successfully reconnected conflict.

The other big reason you feel like becoming "one flesh" with the other person is because of the depth of emotional intimacy that you have reached. He knows her, and she knows him. She embraces the places that he got hurt, and he accepts all that she is. You feel "as one" with your spouse emotionally. It may feel like a natural extension of that to embrace in sex.

When we talk about the pain of conflict, I want to be very clear. I am not asking you to be a masochist. No one likes pain, not even people who become skilled at navigating their way through conflict. But the people who learn this skill of embracing conflict will find their way to the truth and the deeper meanings behind withdrawing actions or protesting behaviors.

It's worth the fight for a deeper level of emotional connection!

Those who embrace conflict are connecting with the thinking part of their brains, the part that can identify the negative cycle. That part of the brain can also hold on to this new reality that "This is painful, but there is a reason behind this pain. I'm going to press through it to connect at a deeper level with my spouse."

In the next sections of this chapter, I want to speak to you about the process for embracing conflict. We'll start with a crucial first step: beware of the negative cycle. We're going to map that out. We'll then walk through the steps that demonstrate how each spouse can use the gift of vulnerable language to convey the key issues that are coming into play. The pain is always based on how important you are to your spouse. The way you see your spouse and treat her or him has a deep effect, because you matter your spouse. The conflict is always a fight to let you know what got hurt and to restore your spouse's connection with you.

Beware of the Negative Cycle!

I'm sure you have seen signs on a fence or a front door saying: "Beware of Dog." The owners are telling you to stay away from their property if you have evil or thieving intentions. They are telling you that there is a ferocious beast that will bite at you and make you regret the day that you ever stepped foot on the property. Occasionally the owners of the dog are actually not too afraid of burglars, they are just warning you that they have an ill-tempered dog. Either way you slice it, the sign is a warning of something that is going to mess you up and cause you harm.

What if you posted a sign in your kitchen that said: Beware of the Negative Cycle. What if you put one up in the bathroom too. It would be a reminder to you that the negative cycle is often lurking, ready to sabotage any productive dialogue between you and your spouse. It would be a reminder that your negative cycle is the enemy—not your spouse. It may help you to catch the cycle before it spins too far.

Beware of the negative cycle! It's your cue to pull back and look at the big picture. It's your chance to stop the sabotage and turn the conflict into something good. The negative cycle is destructive. It must be stopped. It is throwing you off track.

Conflict can be turned into a good thing when it is constructive. Conflict that is carried out in the throes of the negative cycle is painful and unproductive. Rather than letting your spouse know the true nature of your hurt, which is how you feel disconnected, the cycle blames your beloved and distances you from your connection.

Exercise 1 for Embracing Conflict

- Write out the words: "Beware of the Negative Cycle" at the top of a sheet of paper. You are welcome to fill out the negative cycle example on the next page, or to fill it out and copy it.
- Fill in the blanks as seen below each step in the negative cycle with the unique ingredients of your negative cycle with your spouse. Remember that each side plays off the other, so it does not matter whether you start writing the information at the bottom of the diagram or at the top. Neither person is to blame. The cycle is the problem.
- Circle the words that fit for you or write your own words in the spaces provided.
- At the top and bottom of the diagram, I have left space to map out your initial feelings. These are more superficial and reactive. We're not tapping into your deeper view of self, or the way you wish your spouse could see you.
- On the sides of the diagram, I have left space for you to write out your deeper feelings. These cut to the core of who you are, how you want to be and what's at stake for you with your spouse

in that moment. These feelings are about you and your own fears, desires, and insecurities. If you find yourself leading off with "You should not do this," "You are so…," then we aren't going deep enough. It's still focused on your spouse's actions and not your deepest attachment needs.

- Please look back at Chapter 4, Locked in a Struggle, for a review of attachment needs. Note the language of Larry and Angie in Chapter 6, Gift of Vulnerable Language, if you need help connecting with what is really at stake for you.

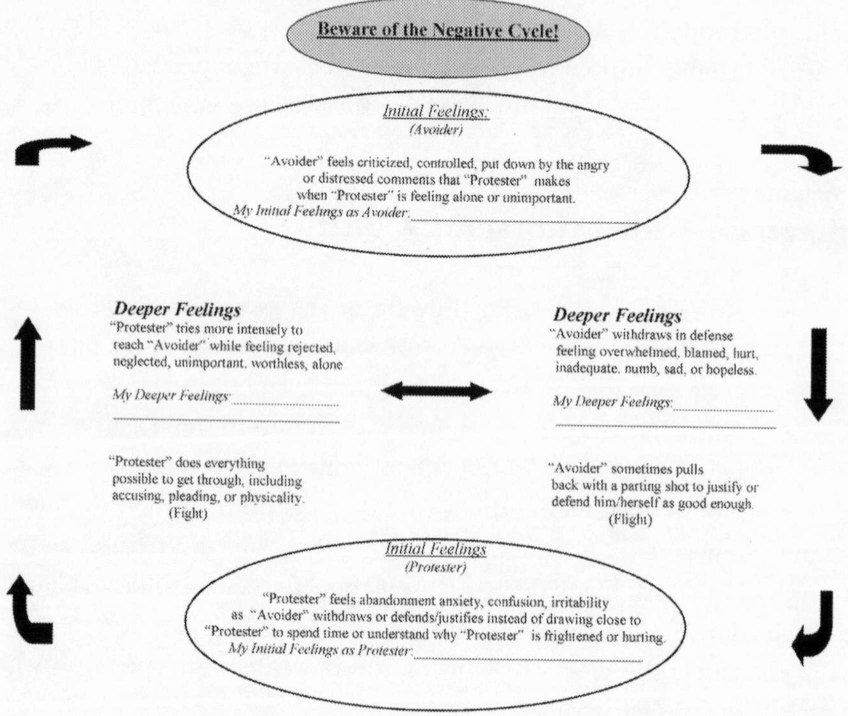

This diagram is designed to help serve as a warning to you to cue your awareness to the times that the negative cycle is spinning. It was also an exercise for you to understand some of the more vulnerable emotions that are in play for you while the cycle is spinning. They are always tied to how important your spouse is to you. We seldom talk about that in the midst of conflict.

We have to be trained to identify the negative cycle. It takes a lot of work since it begins so quickly. We also have to be trained to look for the signs of it, even signs within our physical body. What are some signs that the cycle is spinning?

Signs to the protester that the cycle has started:

- Am I getting flustered, frustrated, or irritated?
- Am I clenching my hands or my jaw?
- Do I notice my pulse rate going up rapidly and my movements getting agitated?
- Am I repeating myself over and over again but not getting through?
- Am I starting to raise my voice or call my spouse names?
- Am I feeling a sense of desperation, panic, or disgust?

Signs to the avoider that the cycle has started:

- Am I getting anxious and tense?
- Am I getting a sinking feeling in the pit of my stomach?
- Do I notice my pulse rate going up rapidly, or my hands starting to sweat?
- Is my jaw clenching or my shoulders tightening up?
- Am I putting my head in my hands?
- Do I feel an urge to bolt from the room?
- Do I find myself arguing, defending, and explaining myself repeatedly?

If you find yourself saying yes to two or more of these questions, then the chances are high that you are starting to spiral into your negative cycle. Get familiar with some of the ones that come up most frequently, as they are key markers for you personally.

When you notice that these signs are starting to occur, it's very important to tell your spouse, "I think that we are getting caught in our cycle." Don't blame your spouse for this, but speak to your need to slow things down and pull back from the cycle. This is your first step to pull back from your destructive cycle so that you can produce a benefit from this conflict.

Beware of the negative cycle! It's your first step toward connecting at a deeper level in this moment of pain.

Using Vulnerable Language to Embrace Conflict

Remember that your language can be used to blame or defend in the negative cycle. But it can also be used to clearly state how important your spouse is to you, and how much you look to him or her to feel good, safe, and valued. Let's join Kent and Angie in a recent marital therapy session. You will remember this couple as the one where he worked many long hours. When she would miss him and need him, she did not tell him in vulnerable ways. There were times in their conflicts when she had thrown things.

New Language for the Avoider in Conflict

Kent: She's not getting it, Jesse. She just keeps pounding me at home when we get into fights. Pounding me. She never learned how to fight fair in her house.

Jesse (therapist): How do you mean?

Kent: The things she says are awful. I don't like it when she has slapped me, but the things she says are worse. You can never take those things back.

Jesse: What happens to you when she talks like that?

Kent: I hurt. I feel really bad about myself, like I'm only two inches tall. I can't stand it, and I have to get away!

Jesse: So you get hurt, and it hurts so badly that you have to get away. You have to retreat from the pain, feeling badly about yourself. What would happen if you stayed in there?

Kent: I'm afraid I might say things that I'd regret too. And that is no good for anyone.

Jesse: Is there anything else that you are afraid of, Kent?

Kent: At this point, we have been stuck in our negative cycle so long. I'm just hanging on by a thread. I'm afraid that she's gonna say something that I won't be able to recover from.

Jesse: And you don't want that?

Kent: No, of course not. I don't want to go away. I don't want to lose her. She's my whole world. But when she says those things, it could be the end.

Jesse: She's so important to you, and you know how much that type of fighting is hurting you. You don't want to go. She's your whole world. But you pull away to preserve the feelings you have left. Is that right?

Kent: That's right.

(Avoider Strategy 1: "I want to talk about me!")

Jesse: Can you turn to Angie and tell her how this type of fighting is affecting you?

Kent: Angie, you've got to watch the things you say in our fights. They hurt really bad! I hurt really bad, when you say them.

(Avoider Strategy 2: "You've really got a hold on me!")

Jesse: Can you let her know that you don't want to feel small in her eyes, and you are holding on to every last strand of hope? You'd be devastated if you lost even that too. She's your whole world.

Kent: Angie, those things you say hurt so bad, because you mean everything to me. I can't stand feeling small in your eyes. I'm just holding on by a thread here, and I don't want to lose that by getting hurt any worse.

Can you see how Kent is dialoguing with Angie about their negative cycle? He is talking about what happens when they fight. He is being courageous and not giving in to the instinct that he usually has to retreat.

There is so much at stake for him, and he is stepping forward to confront her. He is embracing conflict without dipping back into their negative cycle. Rather than shutting down or pulling away, he is coming directly to her. He is sharing with her the unintended effects of her protest behaviors on him. He is telling her of the toll that her no-holds-barred approach to fighting is having on him and on their relationship.

He is speaking in the first person, and is in touch with his own feelings about the situation. He is employing the first avoider strategy, "I want to talk about me!" He's letting her know that she affects him. It's a myth to say that he doesn't care.

He goes deeper to tell her the "You've really got a hold on me!" about how hurt he feels. He lets her know that she means the world to him, and that her view of him is critical to his sense of self. He also sheds new light on the reason for his retreat. He is trying to preserve his remaining feelings. He does not want to give up. He wants to still have hope, but there have to be some changes to the ways that they talk about what is important to the two of them.

Let's listen in to Angie's response to Kent's statements. She is hearing his perspective in a clear way for the first time. He may have said these things before in the throes of the negative cycle, but they did not register. Our earnest statements can't register when the negative cycle is spinning out of control.

Angie: Kent, so you're telling me that I make you feel bad about yourself when I yell?

Kent: Your tongue is razor sharp when you get going.

Angie: It's hard to believe that you are so sensitive to what I say. You always seem so annoyed. I just yell at you to get you to listen to me.

Jesse: You're not trying to hurt him like that?

Angie: Sometimes…sure, I get vindictive. But most of the time I'm just trying to get his attention.

Jesse: You need his attention and you are trying to reach him, is that it?

Angie: Yes, that's right. But he's been pulled back for so long, and I get angry at him for making me feel so alone…so unimportant.

Jesse: You are angry because you need him so much. When you can't reach him, you feel alone and unimportant.

Angie: I don't mean to make him feel small. I don't want to force him even further away.

(Protester Strategy 1: "You're the hero, not the bum!")

Jesse: Can you tell him that? Can you tell him that he is the one you need and that you don't want him to feel badly about himself?

Angie: I didn't know how much my words are hurting you. I just need you, and I am trying anything I can to reach you.

Jesse: You don't want him to feel small?

Angie: No, I want him to feel confident…big enough to stand in and be there for me. I don't want to hurt him.

Jesse: You're not trying to send him away. So what are you feeling when he starts to shut down?

Angie: I guess I get panicked, like he thinks I'm just a nag when he rolls his eyes and slouches back.

Jesse: You panic, afraid that you are just a bother to him and he is fed up with you.

Angie: I see myself slipping away from his view, like I'm losing him. Maybe I already have.

(Protester Strategy 2: "You gave me a scare!")

Jesse: Can you tell him that? Can you tell him that you get panicked at the thought that you are just a bother to him, that you don't matter to him?

Angie: Kent, I know that I panic when I see you rolling your eyes. It's like you don't care. I get scared that I don't matter enough for you to stay around, and then I really let you have it then. But I don't want to push you away. That's the last thing I want.

Can you see how Angie has stepped out of the negative cycle? She is talking about her internal experience in the context of those moments when she is most angry with Kent. She is letting him know that his withdrawal, even in the signals of eye rolling and slouching, have a profound impact on her.

She is acknowledging the effects that her angry and critical comments have on him. She embraces conflict by giving feedback and receiving feedback. It helps that the negative cycle is not slamming them so they can look within and examine their own emotions. Angie is aided by Kent's engagement with her, so she is not in panic mode.

She is able to tell him how much he means to her, and that she is sorry for the ways that her words hurt him in moments of panic. She is letting him know how much she needs him (You're the hero, not the bum!). She is letting him know how scared she gets when she feels like she does not matter to him or that she has lost him (You gave me a scare!). She softens, and tells him of her fear and of her need for him.

She resists her instinctive reaction to blast him and to draw him into the cycle when she is feeling worthless to him, or when she is afraid that she is losing him. She softens and lets him know that his presence and love make all the difference to her.

Understanding Disgust

I have deliberately omitted many of the things that Angie said to Kent in their fights. You can use your imagination if you wish. I figure you've heard enough negativity in your own life, you don't need to read more in this book. But in this section, I have selected one phrase as an illustration of disgust.

I am not picking on Angie here, or even protesters for that matter. However, I do see protesters as having more difficulty with this area than avoiders. I also see how avoiders, who are already sensitized to not being good enough for their spouses, can quickly be triggered by phrases of disgust. And here is the phrase I have selected: *"Kent, you are ridiculous. I can't believe I married such an emotionally crippled person!"*

It's a bit of a zinger, right? Kent, who already feels inadequate to meet Angie's needs and feels small in her eyes, is going to drop a few notches further when he hears this phrase coming across the airwaves. There would also be the look of disgust in Angie's eyes as she delivers this or other choice phrases.

Disgust is derived from one of the primary human emotions—shame. The function of shame is to shut us down and punish us internally for doing something that is reprehensible to our peer group. This painful emotion serves to teach us to never do these actions again, and thereby ensures that we will stay connected with our peer group or significant others for a longer period of time.

Disgust is a fusion of shame at my own actions and anger at another person for seemingly tricking me into being vulnerable with them. I may be angry at myself for taking a risk with you in the first place. I may be mad at myself for continuing to put myself out there to you, despite numerous times of being rebuffed or made to feel rejected. I am torn, a part of me still wants to reach for you, and the other part tells me I am foolish for trying. That's my disgust. It's anger at myself that in this cycle I kept trying and was left feeling lonely and ashamed.

This can contort my face in the midst of such anguish, and the words that typically come out of my mouth will be negative words about the person who is making me feel so rejected. In another recent marriage session, the protester shared that she often felt like "such a sucker" for getting her hopes up and reaching out to her husband. For she only seemed to find once again that he was not there. He was pulled back.

In Angie's case, she is hurting in the loneliness of being emotionally separated from her spouse. She regrets being in such a painful situation, and she traces it back to the choice to marry Kent. But she makes a statement or expression of disgust toward Kent instead of saying something more vulnerable like, "I keep hurting, time and again. I can't keep putting myself out there, only to be left alone. I'm mad at myself, that I keep doing this…keep getting set up (by the negative cycle) to be rejected and alone."

I can't blame her too much. After all, she has not had the experience of Kent being there for her to listen to her, or even to help her unpackage why she is so mad at herself in this regard. So the phrases and nonverbal signals flow out of her mouth: "Emotionally crippled! Ridiculous!" These comments are damaging and fan the flames of the negative cycle instantly into a raging inferno. While the concept of disgust is a bit more complex to understand than basic fear or sadness, the way through it is just the same.

Angie needs to have the experience of talking to Kent, engaging him with her more vulnerable words and expressions of need. Kent needs to let her know when she is coming across as critical, so he can stay engaged throughout.

At the end of a constructive dialogue, a healthy conflict, Kent may actually get to ask his Million Dollar Question, "What do you need from me?" Then Angie will have a new experience, one of being listened to and embraced in her pain.

No longer will her brain be telling her, "You are foolish for opening yourself up! It's disgusting!" Instead she'll be relieved that Kent cared, and relieved that he understood her. She'll have a new experience that reinforces her for opening up versus punishing herself and her avoider for the abandonment she feels.

Not only that, her relationship with Kent will begin to be defined in new ways. Being able to turn to your partner for support and comfort, especially in times of distress, redefines the relationship as secure. It increases the likelihood that you will continue to turn to your spouse for help with your needs.

Standing Face-to-Face

In the example, Kent and Angie have completely dismantled their negative cycle, and they are learning to speak to one another using the gift of vulnerable language. A new model for connecting is being forged that I like to call "Face to Face." Each spouse is secure in their bond with the other, and each successive instance of sharing vulnerable language with one another will only serve to strengthen this bond. The following diagram illustrates this model for connecting and using conflict as a moment to *embrace* the feelings and soothe the hurts of your beloved. Neither spouse is protesting nor avoiding in this model, for both are now standing face-to-face.

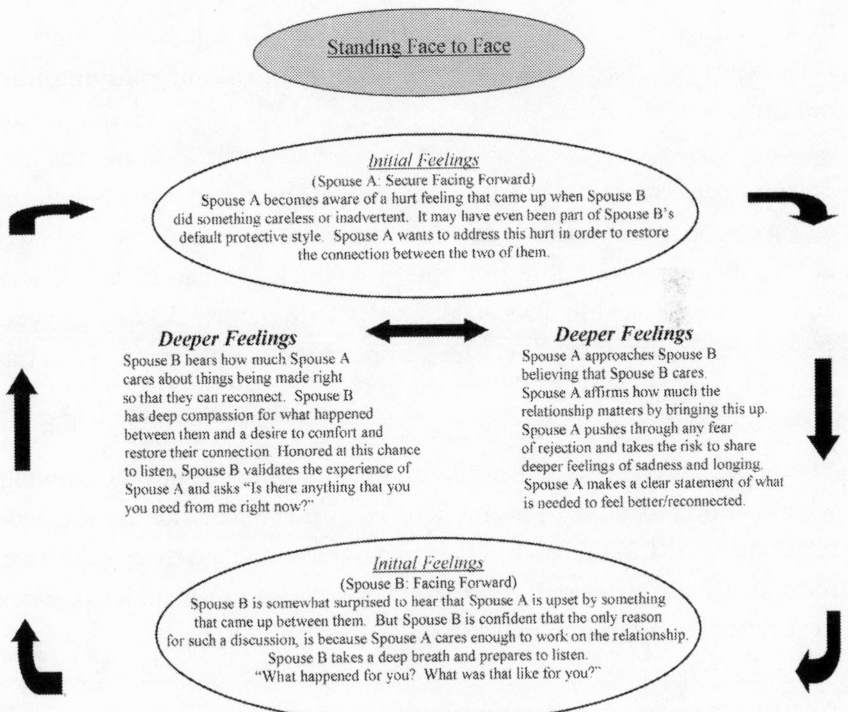

A Note about Triangles in Conflict

As we wrap up the chapter on embracing conflict, I want to share a final note about something that could very easily sabotage your efforts to deal with conflict effectively. These are called triangles. Triangles occur when either of the two people who are stuck in conflict turns to an outside third party. Instead of trying any longer to go to your spouse, one spouse turns to another person for comfort, understanding, or support.

Salvador Minuchin and H. Charles Fishman were the brilliant family therapists mentioned in Chapter 4, Locked in a Struggle. They were the first to coin the phrase "Triangles," and to note the various ways that they form.[53] They also noted how once a triangle is formed it makes it difficult to reconnect with the one you should be speaking to. It becomes safer to talk to the third party than risk jumping into the negative cycle once again.

Triangles are the result of an inability to connect with your spouse in moments of pain, *and* they fuel the disconnection between the two of you. Rather than addressing the things that need to be fixed, you circumvent the healthy process of conflict altogether. As a result, you are not able to fix things that need to be mended nor begin to put the relationship back on track.

Triangles can come as a meddlesome force from the outside as well, when a family member or friend (who is unfulfilled in a key attachment relationship of his/her own) butts into your marriage. It is important to be aware of this as well, for such a meddler can create a lot of stress in your marriage and foment your negative cycle.

As you are learning now about the ways to embrace conflict, I don't want there to be an ongoing triangle that will sap your efforts to reconnect with your spouse. If you are aware that you are turning to a person other than your spouse to meet your emotional needs, you must act swiftly if you want restore connection in your marriage. You must set new limits and boundaries on triangles and the extent that you turn to them for solace and support. In some cases, you may need to completely pull back from that third party for a period of time.

Act swiftly to restore connection in your marriage.

I know that it is scary to take a risk with your spouse once again. But the depth of intimacy will only come as you share your vulnerable side with your spouse in these new ways. When you bring your whole heart back into the marriage, it is a powerful force for change and connection. That is what I am encouraging you to do, and to be mindful of any triangles that are pulling you away from your spouse and keeping you from getting plugged back in.

Embracing conflict, without the negative cycle, is an embrace of your spouse once again. It is going to require courage and a bigger perspective, holding fast to hope and faith. Embracing conflict results from the ability to anchor yourself to the promise that you are fighting for something that is worth saving.

You are fighting for your connection with your spouse to be deepened, enriched, or even restored. You have to beware of the negative cycle though, and slow it down. The cycle spins so fast that it robs us of the deeper emotions that connect us—like longing for one another, the desire to be comforted, and grieving together for lost connection.

CHAPTER 8

Fourth Key—Grieve Your Losses Together

Surely our griefs He Himself bore, and our sorrows He carried... (Isaiah 53:4).

Back in the spring of 2006, I had a discussion with my good friend Dr. Ron Parks. He's a minister, and I am a psychologist. So along with the many things we talk about we are always reflecting on ways that people can be healed and brought to the Light. As he was reflecting on the root cause of brokenness in people's lives, he made a statement: "Jesse, when you think about it, everything boils down to grieving."

Ron's compassionate statement has caused me to ponder the effects and power of grieving upon the human heart. He speaks eloquently at funerals in ways that bring comfort and hope to the grieving. His view on grieving, so expansive and encompassing of the human condition, has shed light for me on the role of grieving in marriage.

Grieving encompasses much more than just the loss of a spouse through death, though that is the most clear cut case and example in our minds. We grieve in marriage when we do not have the connection that we once shared. We grieve when we have to work, and don't have time to play. When our spouse disappoints us or does not fulfill a promise to us, it is an occasion to grieve. We grieve when we lose jobs, promotions, friends, and sentimental reminders of our past. We may even grieve for something that we have hardly ever known.

Irma's Story of Longing

I am reminded of my former client, whom we'll call Irma. I am smiling as I write this and I see her kind and earnest face. Irma grew up in a solitary environment. Her mother left when she was young, and Dad did not remarry till she was nearly 9 years old.

Irma was something of an introvert as a girl. She had an active imagination, creating endless hours of play with her china doll collection that her grandmother had given her. She also fell in love with novels and spent hours tucked away in her room dreaming of families with mothers and what it would be like to have sisters someday.

Her new stepmother was a cranky sort of person who had very little patience for Dad or for his daughter either. Dad had his hands full with stepmother, and he did not have energy to play with Irma or to set up time for Irma to play with friends. Irma found it best to just stay in her room, imagining times of whimsy and friendship through the characters in her novels. She was shy and quite isolated.

However, Irma had several exquisitely happy moments in her childhood. I was privileged to hear of one of these experiences in a conversation that we had together. Irma's eyes lit up, and the corners of her mouth brightened with a smile as she told me the tale of her month-long trip to her aunt's cottage on the Great Lakes. Her aunt was a creative sort who had two daughters who flanked Irma in age. Irma reveled in the joys of playing with her cousins at the lakefront cottage.

Vividly, Irma recounted the excitement that she felt as she rode for hours to get to the cottage, past forests, farmland, and ultimately the grassy dunes that nestled the shores of the lake by the cottage. She and her cousins played for hours in the sand, sea, and tall grasses along the shore. At night they would clear the dishes, light the kerosene lantern, and sit with her aunt who regaled them with stories from her own imagination. Irma fell asleep with roommates and happiness in her heart.

Irma's eyes filled with tears as she told this joyful story to me, a story of days when she felt included and embraced by the warmth of family. These were days when she was not on the outside but was one of the bunch. Her supreme joy upon inclusion only contrasted with the loneliness that she felt in her own home.

Though she only had it in glimpses, Irma was grieving for the feeling of how it was supposed to be. It's like coming home when we experience it for the first time, even if we've never encountered such love before.

The Deepest Longing

How is it that we can grieve for a connection that we have never or seldom experienced before?

It is because God has woven the need for connection deep into our soul, the fabric of our being. When we feel closeness with a loved one or with a spouse, we are stepping into His perfect plan for our existence.

When we share an adventure, embrace in sorrow, or celebrate a moment of intimate happiness with one we trust, we are enriched and enlivened just by the virtue of having someone to share it with. We are comforted and no longer alone.

In the context of talking about the seasons of life, Solomon speaks about deep places in our hearts. *"He has made everything beautiful in its time. He has also set eternity in the human heart"* (Ecclesiastes 3:11 NIV). This passage speaks to me personally about the depth of the human longing for connection with God, a longing so great that it can only be satisfied over the course of eternity. It suggests to me that we will eternally be fulfilled in fellowship with the One who created us for connection.

> *Deep calls to deep at the sound of Your waterfalls; all Your breakers and Your waves have rolled over me* (Psalm 42:7).

God knows the depth of our soul's need for closeness. We were created for fellowship, not for isolation. This side of eternity though, we are abruptly confronted with the agonizing truth that we will lose those we love, those with whom we have connected on this frail journey of life.

Because the desire for intimacy is sewn into our hearts, we know of it even when we are not experiencing it. Here on earth we are acutely aware of the pain and sorrow we feel when we don't get to connect with the ones we long for, when we don't have loved ones who reach into our hearts to draw us out and share our experiences.

In those moments of loss, of things precious and things hoped for, we need to acknowledge to ourselves and another person what the sorrow is. When we are married we must be able to turn to our spouses at such times. It is for all these moments that we need our spouses to share our sorrows. And the bond is only strengthened between us when our spouse listens to us and validates our needs for connection and the legitimacy of our pain when those needs go unfulfilled.

The negative cycle drives us apart in moments of pain instead of binding us together to talk about what went wrong. The cycle keeps us from understanding the pain of our spouses when they feel disconnected from us, and it keeps us from grieving together. When this absence of sharing together takes place repeatedly over time, we find ourselves in greater and greater degrees of distress.

Grief in Marriage

A few years ago, I came to specifically understand that marital distress stems from unresolved grieving. This insight came through my conversations with my good friend, Pastor David Woolverton. David is a lover of people with a keen eye toward understanding patterns of behavior in church and family relationships. He has an extensive background in counseling and couple's work as well. During one of our talks together in the summer of 2007, David shared some of his thoughts about couple's counseling with me:

> Jesse, the biggest need that distressed couples have is the need to grieve their losses together. Marital therapy is a process of opening up a space so that couples can grieve together, instead of grieving alone.

In this chapter on grieving in marriage, our focus will be on cultivating ways that couples can hold on to one another when sorrows come. Rather than retreating or attacking in the negative cycle, they can be linked together in a comforting embrace. We will focus on how each member of the couple can be emotionally present to grieve disappointments, hurts, and losses. We are going deeper now, beyond the outer layers of friction and anxiety. We are heading for the core, being present when it matters the most.

A secure marriage is one where each spouse can turn to the other one at any time, *particularly* in moments of distress. When you find your spouse there for you, it strengthens the bond and defines the relationship as secure for whatever comes your way.

Three Categories of Grieving in Marriage

I am going to over-simplify this a bit, but I think it's helpful. In a marriage there are three main forms of grieving that arise:

1. Grieving that stems from something our spouses did or failed to do to.
2. Grieving that stems from losses we experience from sources outside the marriage.
3. Grieving for "old wounds" that were formed in us before marriage but are triggered by our spouses.

At many levels it is easier to deal with the losses inflicted by others on our spouses, as opposed to the losses that we accidentally inflict on them. Makes sense, right? If you are the source of loss, then you must nondefensively listen to what you did, validate your spouse's experience, own it, empathize with the pain you inflicted, and apologize.

When another source inflicted loss on your spouse, your job is important, but less demanding. We simply must validate and empathize with what happened, and let them know that they are not alone in their pain. But you don't have to wrestle internally with the struggle that takes place as you evaluate where you were coming from in an interaction, and the way that your spouse perceived that interaction.

It's important to remember that our spouses only have one way to perceive the situation prior to talking with us about it. They only have one vantage point. From that perspective, they see and know what happened. Prior to talking with us, our spouses' perceptions are the only reality they know.

Perception is reality.

It is hard to hold on to your perception of the situation and your good intentions while putting yourself into the shoes of your beloved. It's going to help tremendously if your spouse is able to offer the shoes in a nonaccusatory and nonblaming manner. That's why we have worked so hard to dismantle the negative cycle.

But there may still be times when your spouse is in a high state of distress as he or she is grappling with the anger, dismay, and sorrow of loss. It's going to be essential for you to implement the strategies we discussed in Chapter 6 about vulnerable language.

Use Vulnerable Language to Grieve Together

If you are an avoider, you know that you will especially need to work on staying engaged instead of retreating when your spouse has suffered loss. You will be viewing yourself as part of the solution and will need to stand in the gap with the Million Dollar Question: "Is there anything you need from me?" This will help you focus on the prize, so to speak, and tune into your spouse's need for you while in the midst of the pain of loss.

If you are a protester, it is easy to come across as critical of your avoider in moments when he is in pain and starting to shut down. I have offered you The Power of What as an anchor so that you can draw the avoider back to you with gentleness and patience. "What just happened to you? What are you going through right now? What was that like for you?" That way you will get to hear your beloved's true needs for you in "You've really got a hold on me" and be able to empathize with your avoider. The two of you will be able to share in the grieving. Your avoider will find you as a source of solace in moments of loss, rather than perceiving you as a source of criticism.

Whether you are a protester or an avoider, you will need to become something of an expert at using The Power of What and the Million Dollar Question as you join with your spouse in order to empathize and console. I have asked avoiders to particularly tune into the Million Dollar Question, because that helps them break out of the negative cycle. But avoiders will also be a strength and encouragement in listening to their spouses when they attempt to use The Power of What.

I have asked protesters to focus tenderly and patiently on The Power of What, because it helps them stay out of the criticizing posture and draw their spouses to them. However, protesters will be a source of strength and encouragement too when they compassionately say, "Is there anything you need from me?" (the Million Dollar Question). Remember, avoiders are not used to having another person help them in their pain. They are used to going it alone, so it can be very healing for them to have someone ask, "What is going on for you? Is there anything you need from me?"

First Category of Grieving: Grief over Something Your Spouse Did or Failed to Do

Allow me to start this discussion about grief by talking about a movie. Every now and then I watch a romance movie with my wife. I find that some of these movies touch on deeper themes about love, attachment, and human connection. I am thinking of one in particular that had powerful themes about forgiveness and moving forward from the pain of mistakes.

The movie is *Nights in Rodanthe* and costars Richard Gere and Diane Lane. It isn't a particularly good love story, but the way it dealt with grieving, confession, and forgiveness is quite powerful. I don't want to spoil this movie for you, but I have to describe one particular scene.

Richard Gere was a surgeon who accidentally killed a woman due to a mistake that he made in the operating room. He avoided his own grief about this tragedy along with the grief of the family who lost their wife and mother. Gere accidentally did something to this family by making a mistake in surgery. He *failed* to do something by avoiding the family after their mother died. However, he does not stay stuck in this distant and defended posture forever. Gere gets it right in the second half of the movie when he goes to the bereft husband and has a poignant exchange.

Gere looks deeply in the eyes of a man who lost his wife, his companion, his whole world. Gere's eyes show that he felt pain for what he had accidentally done, and that he was now truly joining in the sorrow of the grieving family. The grieving husband shifted and softened as he experienced validation of his pain in the terrible loss he was feeling.

This has become my gold standard for apology and reconciliation. It moves you when you look deeply into the eyes of the person who caused you pain, and see that he gets it. He grieves too. You suddenly lose part of your urge to carry out a vendetta against him or her.

Sharing your pain with the person who hurt you brings validation.

When you look deeply into the eyes of the person who hurt you and see that she or he is affected by your pain, it actually eases your pain. You are validated. For that brief moment, you are not alone in your pain. You are sharing it, and it does not weigh you down quite as much. The very person who caused you pain is remorseful and now stands with you in the midst of it all. That is a powerful thing!

It's a model for grieving together when you have done something that has been hurtful to your spouse. It's a way of responding when your spouse comes to you to tell you of a hurt or disappointment. It not only takes the wind out of the sails of unhealthy conflict and the negative cycle, but it bonds you together. We are both grieving this terrible thing that happened between us.

When we look deeply into the eyes of our spouses and see them feeling our pain, there is a release from our need to fight for their attention in protest any longer. There is a release of the pressure to withdraw.

To hear these words, "I would never have wanted you to feel that way," is such a powerful thing when we come to our spouses with a grievance about something hurtful that they did. This joins in the sorrow and the pain of feeling neglected, abandoned, or belittled. Ultimately, the sincere gaze of our beloved and these words of apology will free the hurting spouse to feel validated and to move forward.

It's not a guarantee that we will move forward toward reconnection. But it is certain that we can't move forward toward this if our spouses do not even own what they did to hurt us in the first place.

Let's listen in to this dialogue that took place between Kent and Angie in a recent marital therapy session. You will remember this couple as the one where Kent used to work very long hours, and Angie ended up throwing things in order to get his attention.

We're at a point in the work where Kent is talking about the damaging effects of Angie's words on him in the midst of conflict. Kent often looks away from Angie when they are in session. It is hard for him to make eye contact. This is especially true with the more vulnerable subject material.

Kent: She just doesn't get it, Jesse. The things that she says to me in our fights, you can never take them back! I would never say those things.

Jesse (therapist): What's that like for you, when she says those things?

Kent: It makes me feel terrible. It's hard for me to recover from how badly I feel about myself. It makes me want to just pull away.

Jesse: She's your most important person, and when she says those things…it's devastating for you.

Kent: Yes, that is how I feel.

(Angie is listening in, and she has a concerned look on her face. She is not defended.)

Jesse: Can I get you to talk to Angie about this today, Kent? Right now, could you look at her and tell her how her angry words make you feel so badly about yourself. It makes you just want to pull away from her.

Kent: (Turns and looks at Angie, who has a soft expression on her face) Angie, it's devastating for me, the things that you say when you are angry at me. I need you to be careful because I'm very sensitive to how you see me.

Angie: (Steadily gazing at Kent the whole time) Kent, I get it that the things I say are so hurtful. I don't want to hurt you. Deep down I do know that you are sensitive. Sometimes I just forget. I like that part of you. I don't want to lose that.

Jesse: What's going on for you, Kent, as you hear Angie?

Kent: I hear that she gets it, that I get hurt. But I'm still afraid that she's going to continue saying those things.

Angie: I don't know why I say such awful things. I know that it is how we argued in my house growing up. But I want to work on it, Kent. I really do.

As you look at this example, you can picture how the couple is making eye contact as they talk about Kent's pain. You probably don't know how hard this is for Kent, and how often he keeps looking away. But in the moment where he catches a glimpse at Angie's kind brown eyes, Kent relaxes a bit. He even smiles slightly with a look of relief. He's getting to talk about his needs. He is getting to talk about his longing for acceptance from Angie. She is touched by his pain. She sees him, and he is not alone in grieving for how devastated he feels.

As an avoider, Kent is learning, perhaps for the first time, how to bring his needs and his sorrows to his spouse. He has to take the risk that someone will patiently and gently empathize with him as he sorts out his feelings.

When protester Angie is less anxious about being abandoned herself, she is more able to tune in to what Kent is saying. She's no longer in survival panic mode, desperately reaching for him. She has seen him engage repeatedly. Now protester Angie can gently draw out avoider Kent with The Power of What. You'll notice in this example that I am in the role of using the Power of What to draw Kent out and to have him reflect on what he is experiencing.

At home, Angie would need to be in this role as the protester. She would no longer be trying to grasp at him or rouse him to life. She would gently draw him to talk about what got hurt, what was painful, so that they could grieve it together, asking:

"What's going on for you?"
"What's happening to you right now?"
"What's that like for you?"

These powerfully attuned questions convey that Angie sees Kent pulling back and hurting, and she cares about that. Even though she gets scared of losing him sometimes, she sees enough of Kent to reassure her that he isn't going anywhere. She is pausing for this moment to draw him out and tune in to his experience. It's safe. He can bring his needs and sorrows to her. This will work successfully for you and your spouse as well.

Let's take another look at grief work in a session with Sonda and Larry. You will remember this couple as the one where he missed her small business grand opening because he got intoxicated at an adult club. In prior chapters of this book, I gave you snippets of Larry talking to Sonda about how badly he felt when she complained about him. He spoke of how he had shame about his addictive behaviors. Larry also had started to talk about how he was scared that Sonda would not have any time for him after her business started.

In the session that follows, Sonda is talking to Larry about how she had become so anxious about his use of pornography when he traveled. Larry is more engaged at this point, having already shared his side of things. The avoider is reengaged and ready to listen to Sonda's experience.

Sonda: His porn use at hotels just put me over the edge with my anxiety. I panicked every time he had to travel for work. I would check up on him and make sure that he was behaving at night. Can you blame me?

Jesse (therapist): Of course it makes sense that you would be scared. You did not know where you stood with him.

Sonda: That's right, and he wasn't talking to me or telling me anything. So I had nothing to work with, nothing to go on to understand why all this was happening.

Jesse: So what did you tell yourself? How did you make sense of it all?

Sonda: I thought that he was not attracted to me, that there was something wrong with me. That was why he had pulled away. And I couldn't reach him.

Jesse: How did that make you feel?

Sonda: I felt so worthless, like Larry didn't want me. I felt so scared that I was losing him. I couldn't stand it, so I panicked. I just didn't know what else to do.

Jesse: Larry, I'm wondering what is going on for you as you hear Sonda speaking about what she went through during those months before her grand opening?

Larry: I just feel really sad. She was hurting. She was all alone, and I was too.

Jesse: Sonda, can you talk today with Larry about how frightening that time was for you, and how it made you feel about yourself?

Sonda: (Struck by how tuned in Larry was with his sadness, she turns to him on her own.) I didn't know what was going on, Larry. I felt so badly about myself. I had done something wrong and I couldn't get you to love me anymore. I was so scared… (her voice trails off).

Larry: (Tears in his eyes) Sonda, it wasn't anything wrong with you. I was a mess back then. But I know that I made you feel so badly about yourself. I know I did that. I'm so sorry.

Sonda: (Crying softly)

Jesse: Sonda, is there anything you need from Larry right now?

Sonda: (Nods) I just need him to hold me.

Larry reached over and held her. It was one of those moments where you know that something sacred is happening. Sometimes I wonder if I should even stay in the therapy room at that point. It's such an intimate space between the two spouses, a grief shared. It's a connection that is being restored. We recognize that this is God's plan for marriage—that the two should come together as one, especially in moments of grief.

I am inclined to believe that most people who hurt their spouses are not really trying to. There are exceptions, and we deal with those situations differently. But most people are trying to do the best with what they learned or were equipped with. The worst comes out in us when we are isolated or in a panicked mode because of the negative cycle in marriage. Our sin nature runs the show at those times, but we are changing that by looking at ourselves with a new perspective.

For a couple to grieve together, protesters have to learn how to personally share their grieving over feeling unimportant and left out in new ways. These are ways that don't blame but rather express a sad or frightened personal experience. As their avoiders are reengaged, they won't be so afraid of being left alone, so they can come openly and vulnerably.

When avoiders stand in the gap with their arms wide open instead of turning away, a new pattern is formed. When avoiders step forward with the mindset and the expression of the Million Dollar Question: "Is there anything that you need from me?" Protesters feel safe and secure. They are established once again in the security of their lovers' attention and embrace.

This is the power of grieving together. Our spouse bears witness to the ebb and flow of the journey of life. We don't have to go it alone. That is critical when they have done something or left something undone that made us feel neglected or ashamed. It is equally important for us to rest in the listening presence of our spouses in the midst of everyday stressors and also major losses that come to us from outside the marriage.

Second Category of Grieving: Losses that Come from Outside the Marriage

When your spouse is going through a difficult time, the greatest gift you can give is to be present. In your physical presence and your spoken words, you provide assurance that "Everything is going to be okay."

Now that we are standing face-to-face, it becomes a real possibility that our spouses will be there for us to bring validation and support. When the avoider no longer feels attacked and the protester no longer fears abandonment, a daily union of hearts can take place. It's reassuring to know that your spouse will be there for you at the end of each day.

> *…if two lie down together they keep warm, but how can one be warm alone?* (Ecclesiastes 4:11)

It warms our hearts to know that we don't have to go through life and all its challenges alone. We have a companion and friend who is on our side. It is comforting and strengthening to us at every level.

Take Me to a Better Place

I am reminded of John Steinbeck's 1937 novella, *Of Mice and Men.*[54] I am only slightly embarrassed to say that my first exposure to this work was through Looney Tunes Cartoons as a boy. Did you ever see the one where this brute of a man, with reduced intelligence, grabs Bugs Bunny by the ears and strokes him repeatedly? All the while he is stating with stammered and laboring vocabulary, "Uh, his name is George. And I will hug him, and pet him, and squeeze him and love him." Repeat.

I always chuckled at this as a boy, particularly at the uncomfortable expression on Bugs Bunny's face. Only as an adult did I learn the significance of the interaction between the giant and the reluctant bunny rabbit. It's actually quite touching.

Of Mice and Men is the story of a friendship between Lennie and George that takes place during the Great Depression in California. The two are migrant, displaced ranch workers on a quest to find and create a farm of their own. Lennie is this hulk of a man who is cognitively slow. George is the brains of the duo, a cynical man who is paradoxically the kind protector of the gentle giant, Lennie. Lennie is easily excitable, probably due to his neurological impairments. He soothes himself by stroking a piece of rabbit fur that he keeps in his pocket when he is in distress or bored. This is a nice example of "contact comfort" from Chapter 1.

Lennie has the dream of someday opening a rabbit farm with his good friend George. This would be paradise for Lennie, a virtual Eden, a land filled with abundance, comfort, and joy. The rabbit farm is quite the contrast to the daily hardships that the two encounter along their journey. During tough times Lennie often asks his friend, "George, tell me about the rabbit farm." Just the image and the dream of the rabbit farm is enough to comfort Lennie, motivate him, and give him hope.

The simple way of the giant man touches all our hearts, because deep inside we are all like him. At times when we get discouraged or become frightened, we long for someone who will tell us, "Everything's going to be okay."

"Everything's going to be okay."

These are words that we should bring to our spouses in sincere and tender moments of encouragement and holding. We can be physically present with our spouses in moments of need. And through our language we can take them to a better place. We can promise them our presence both now and in the future.

God promises us daily that He is with us: *"I will never desert you, nor will I ever forsake you"* (Hebrews 13:5). He has promised to give us His Holy Spirit as a Comforter and Guide:

> *I will ask the Father, and He will give you another Helper* [Comforter], *that He may be with you forever; that is the Spirit of truth, whom the world cannot receive…but you know Him because He abides with you and will be in you* (John 14:16-17).

By His grace and through His strength we can daily be a comfort and companion to our spouses through even the toughest of times. We can grieve with our spouses about the daily stresses of life, and even lament that we wish we had more time together.

Wishing for More Time Together

You may remember Dan and Flo, the Protest-Protest couple from Chapter 4, Locked in a Struggle. They had been so intense prior to coming to me that the police were called to mediate one of their more volatile conflicts.

I will never forget the eloquent way that Dan spoke to Flo one session about his longing for her and the return to their relationship prior to the days of the negative cycle.

They used to go to the Java Works coffeehouse near their college campus and talk for hours many nights of the week. These hours-long conversations continued as part of their bonding for years to follow. In dating and in their early years of marriage, she was his best friend, the only one who truly got him and understood him.

Dan said, "I still remember those days before things got crazy. It was you and me together all the time at the Java Works. Now, when I drive past it on my way home from work…I look over at the booth we used to sit in together. You're not there. It's empty where you once used to be. I miss you."

It was a rare and touching moment for Dan to soften and speak about his grieving for the loss of his connection with Flo. She was touched by this, and touched to know that he missed her. He really did value her. She mattered to him and still does today. His grieving gave a sense of value to her and let her know that he cared.

It's appropriate and good to grieve together over missing the time you once spent with your spouse before life got busy or before kids came into the picture. It's validating to hear our spouses say they miss us, wish they had more free time with us, or long to just get away from everything and be with us. What greater compliment can you give someone?

Saying, "I miss you. I know that your work schedule is crazy this month, but I really wish I had more time with you" is a good example of grieving a loss that occurred from sources outside the marriage. The hard-working spouse was not distancing intentionally when a busy work schedule was thrust upon him. Yet he can still mourn with his wife, that it resulted in less time for them together.

Daily Disappointments and Health Problems

What an honor it is when our spouses trust us enough to confide a disappointment that occurred that day. What a privilege it is for us to be the one who gets to listen and understand about a frustration that they had with a friend, coworker, or even with themselves. We get to be the one they come to, the one they rely upon.

You get to be the go-to person for your spouse!

Confiding in us is an affirmation of their trust in us and their confidence that our compassion will be there to comfort and to console. "What happened for you? What was that like for you? What is going on for you right now? Is there anything that you need from me?" This will help to lighten the load.

> *Bear one another's burdens, and thereby fulfill the law of Christ* (Galatians 6:2).

I have one more area to cover for losses stemming from outside the marriage—health problems. "In sickness and in health" is what we pledge at the beginning of our marriage. Yet when health problems come to one or both of us, we must find a way to cling to more than a resolution, more than a pledge. We must cling to our spouses and hold fast to them. We have to hold fast to Jesus, our Refuge, Healer, and Deliverer.

We can share with our spouses how we both grieve for what is lost in the midst of a health struggle. It affirms that we wanted more time with them, more romance, more mobility, or more times to talk. Illness gets in the way of that. We can share this without blaming them for the illness that has befallen them.

Perhaps you cannot change the illness, but you can go through it together, holding hands instead of silently holding your feelings and placing extra stress on both of your immune systems. There's real value in that.

Third Category of Grieving: "Old Wounds"

Every human sustains one emotional injury or another during their childhood, because we are raised by imperfect parents. They were typically just doing their best with the equipment that they had at the time, but sometimes they fell short in meeting our attachment needs. "Old Wound" is my nickname for the repeated injury that you received as a result of your childhood, and this wound is often reactivated in your marriage in the present day.

The fact that you were wounded in that area as a child tends to make you hypersensitive to any instance where your spouse is bumping up against that scar. You might see your interactions in a way that is tainted by your past experience with that old wound. Paradoxically, the wound keeps resurfacing because you are so wary about getting hurt again in that area.

There is no shame in having old wounds, but I want you to know and understand a bit more about your wounds so you can communicate them to your spouse. Your spouse will have a better understanding of your needs when you can talk to him or her about the grief that still comes up at times from your old wounds, along with things that he or she may do that reactivate the wounds.

Old wounds stem from a breakdown in the process of attachment to your parent. Rather than having a secure attachment to one or both of your parents, you may have felt abandoned, invisible, overwhelmed, alone, or shamed for even having needs. You may have felt unprotected, blamed, misunderstood, inadequate, or unlovable. When your spouse brushes up against one of these hurt places, it is hard for you to see straight. You may be blinded by your pain in the current situation and also leftover pain from the past. This makes it difficult to objectively view the position of your spouse at the time.

There is no way to totally prevent the experience of having your old wounds getting reactivated, but you may share them with your beloved in the moment so that you both can grieve this experience together. Consider:

> Honey, when you pulled away from me during our conversation, it made me feel rejected—just like I did with my mom as a child.
>
> Babe, when you took a two-hour TV break this afternoon, I felt anxious again…like the chores were all up to me. It was overwhelming just like I felt at home with my parents.

> Sweetheart, when you talked to your friends about our private conversation, I felt betrayed and unprotected—just like it was when my parent leaked out my personal information to my brother.

We cannot erase the past old wounds, but we can openly share them with our spouses and grieve them together. In this way, the wounds don't get to carry on silently and painfully inside us. Our spouses can grieve with us and help us complete more of the process of neutralizing the old wounds' power by accepting us in the here and now.

There is power in being able to name what happened to us and externalize it, much like we discussed in the Power Play section back in the First Key. It helps us make sense of some of the strong reactions that we may be having to our spouses, since they can stem from a current incident *and* a historic experience. Our spouses can comfort us and be more sensitive to our needs as we vulnerably share our old wounds with him or her.

Grieving Exercises

I will offer exercises for sharing every facet of life in our next chapter about face-to-face time. But, as I mentioned in the beginning of this chapter, I invite you to become an expert in using powerful language tools that will draw your spouse to you in moments of pain and grieving.

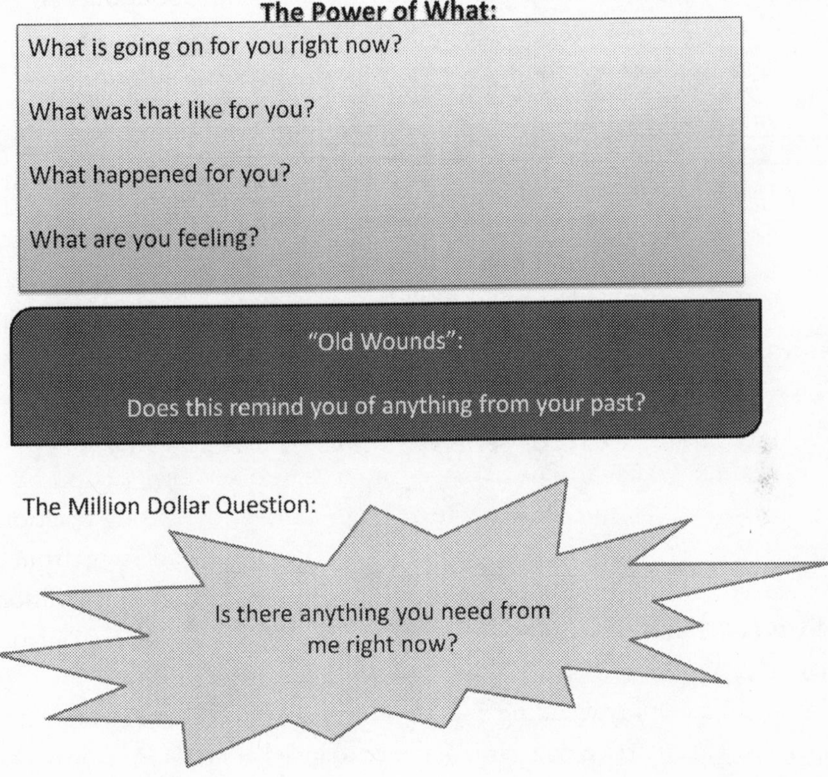

I invite you to write these phrases out on an index card, one for you and one for your spouse. You may also copy the phrases from the chart. I'd like you to find ways each day to incorporate them more into your dialogue with your spouse. Be especially tuned to these when your spouse is coming to you with distress from something that you did or left undone. You will also find them helpful when your spouse is talking about losses that stem from sources outside the marriage in the present or past

CHAPTER 9

Fifth Key—Schedule Face-to-Face Time

Starting off Face-to-Face

I still remember my wedding day. My wife, April, and I were so blessed to be able to get married in a garden. I have to give her credit for coming up with this terrific location to make our vows together. Under the shade of massive oak trees with fragrant roses blowing in the late summer breeze, we stood in the company of our friends and family. It seemed as though all Heaven was smiling down on us that day.

We had each taken time to write our own vows to one another, our words of secure commitment to one another for that day and all the times that would come. We promised in our own words "to have and to hold," to cling to one another in the times of storm, and to rely on God when our own strength was not enough to sustain one another. I will always treasure these words and hold them as foundational.

Most of us are healthy and strong on our wedding day, and yet we intentionally speak about "sickness and in health." Our language affirms our strong resolve to be ever-present. Our language on our wedding day acknowledges that we will face times of need, sickness, and struggle.

We will have times of frailty, mistakes, fears and failures, along with joys and triumphs.

We pledge to bring all these things to our spouses and to embrace our spouses when they bring their needs to us. What a secure feeling this brings us, to rest in these spoken promises. We will have and hold each other, face-to-face, through it all.

Defining Face-to-Face Time

I want you and your spouse to get into the habit of spending regular face-to-face time together throughout your week. Face-to-face time is my term for intentional time that you spend looking at your spouse, talking to your spouse with vulnerable language, and touching one another. In the previous chapters, we examined the importance of sharing a mirroring gaze with your loved ones and how this builds secure attachment. We also spoke about the importance of touch and contact comfort. You will need all these ingredients to have successful face-to-face time.

Face-to-face time does not always have to be in a quiet setting, but you want to have as few interruptions as possible during that time together. We're going to look at things that get in the way of face-to-face time before we examine ways to cultivate this time into the daily rhythms of our married lives.

Face-to-Face Time Barriers

We learned earlier in our discussion about infatuation—intoxicating love—that God gives us some chemical help to drive us to face-to-face connection during the early part of our dating relationship. Dopamine, norepinephrine, and low serotonin make us driven to look deeply into our beloved's eyes and pursue them intensely. We can't rest until we have them in our sights.

It's a form of hyper-attachment, and it drives us to form a bond quickly. It drives us to feel an initial sense of security in our love for one another. After the infatuation wears off, we still can have moments of bliss and high, but we must enter into a deeper form of love if we are to be truly secure in our marriage.

Infatuation fades so that experience and time may bring something deeper in our walk together. It is by working through pain and misunderstandings that we are deepened and strengthened into a more mature bond together. Unfortunately, many of us end up expressing our pain in ways that push or pull us away from our beloved.

Negative Cycle Barrier

You have read a lot here about the negative cycle and how it forms due to an inability to convey to our spouses that we are fighting for closeness with them. Instead of expressing love, we send signals that they are inadequate or that we don't care. That fuels the cycle, and is the number one barrier to face-to-face time with our spouses.

When I was just beginning in marital therapy, I recall asking couples to go on a date together so that they could work on their marriage relationship. I had high hopes that working on their communication would help them solve their distress. Most of them came back to me and said that they had not followed through with my request.

Of course not! How could they? When the negative cycle is rolling along, couples don't want to be with one another. It's just too painful and stressful. They don't enjoy time spent together because they are getting blasted by the cycle. They love each other, but they might not even like the other person at that time. They are still walking on eggshells around each other, insecure about where they stand.

But now you are changing that by dismantling your negative cycles as explained in earlier chapters of this book. You have been using the gift of vulnerable language to help you affirm to your spouse how much you need him or her and want to feel valued. Every conflict that arises is a fight for a better marriage connection with your spouse. And you are learning how to grieve together for the disconnections that arise, instead of blaming your spouse for them.

If you are still struggling to want to spend time together, I might encourage you to go back through the last three chapters to see where you are still stuck in your negative cycle. Examine whether the avoider has really used the gift of vulnerable language to reengage and speak of how important the protester is. Examine whether the protester is really affirming love for the avoider and the need to have connection time with him or her instead of being critical. You can look at your diagram of the negative cycle if it helps you. Ideally, you would be using your gift of vulnerable language all the way through the diagram instead of the hurtful patterns that are diagrammed there.

All of this sets the stage for you and your spouse to be ready to spend face-to-face time together and to actually enjoy that time. I see this shift in the couples I work with, as they flow from having face-to-face time in the marital therapy sessions toward a desire to have this time outside of the sessions.

Sheri and Paul: Moving Away from the Negative Cycle

I remember one couple where the wife, Sheri, felt nagged and criticized by her husband, Paul. He missed her, but he came across as angry and irritable. We were talking one day about this pattern. Paul was not much of a talker, and he especially did not like having to talk "over the children at the supper table." Paul felt unimportant and pushed aside when he had to compete with the children for Sheri's attention at supper.

Sheri: I like that Paul is nagging at me less, and he's not as critical. It makes me want to be close to him. It even makes me want to do things with him, instead of just avoiding him.

Jesse (therapist): Paul, what is different for you now with Sheri? Can you tell her about that?

Paul: It helps me to sit down and talk alone with you face-to-face, Sheri. I like that much better than trying to talk to you over the children at supper. I get irritated, then I'm rushing and getting angry while I try to say things before I forget them. I guess that's why I nag. It's much better knowing that I get to talk to after supper face-to-face, so I'm not as irritated with you later on. I never thought about how that works before.

Paul went on to share how he likes in the evening when they sit together and review the day. He tells her the happenings of his day and hears the happenings of hers. He likes to hear her happenings every bit as much as he likes to tell his, as this makes him feel connected to her. He said that they had not done that as much during the past year, but they used to do it earlier in their marriage.

Reggie and Yvette: Beyond the Negative Cycle

I remember another couple whom we'll call Reggie and Yvette. Reggie was the avoider and Yvette was the protester. We pick up with them in a session that took place just before they completed marital therapy. By this point they had done great work in removing barriers to their connection and were now establishing their ongoing bond.

Reggie: We have been making regular time together on Saturday nights, to talk about our marriage and anything that came up this week.

Yvette: Yes, my sister suggested that we do it like this, carving out time when the kids are watching their favorite show.

Reggie: It really helps me to have this guaranteed time. It helps me gear up for anything I need to say to Yvette. I don't like conflict and it gives me time to prepare for what I need to say and to be ready to hear Yvette.

Yvette: I think Reggie wouldn't confront me about the things he needs to say if we didn't have this set time where we *have* to do that.

You get the picture that Reggie and Yvette have really moved past their negative cycle and are finding a way to stay out of it. The face-to-face time on Saturday nights helped them to connect, but it also served to guarantee that Reggie would not hold things inside and let them build up.

Children Barrier

If you are married with one or more children, you may know already where I am going in this section. We adore our children and love spending time with them. Yet their little needs are pressing and continuously changing, especially when they are infants and toddlers. As they mature, we still invest significant amounts of time in them each day, caring for their physical needs, hearing about their days, playing with them, and helping with homework. There literally aren't enough hours in the day to do it all, but we do our best and entrust the rest to their heavenly Father.

Having children changes the dynamic of even a very good marriage connection. When we spend a lot of time with our children each day, it is imperative that we acknowledge how this affects each spouse's perceptions of the relationship. We must discuss how it is changing us and even grieve the loss of the way things used to be, while we embrace something so wonderful and new.

It is only in sharing about the changes, the ways they make us feel, and grieving for what has changed that we can approach face-to-face time anew as two people who are married with children. It takes creativity, commitment, and honesty in order to make this happen.

Dana and Jim: Evening Child's Play

Dana and Jim had three young children, and at times this was very overwhelming to them both. They each coped in different ways, relying on the strategies that they had learned from their own childhoods. Dana was more apt to be anxious and tried to control the circumstances around her. She was very vocal, and she often did this in the form of questioning things. Jim was more avoidant, and he would busy himself with tasks as a way to cope with all the stresses of life. He was somewhat withdrawn to start with, but the pressures and time demands of parenting contributed to him pulling further away.

Jim and Dana worked with me for several months. They did good work in dismantling their negative cycle, and we now join them in a session where they are sharing vulnerably about a misunderstanding that took place the evening before. It had been a warm and breezy midsummer evening, perfect for chasing fireflies and burning off steam before bedtime. Their youngest child was already deep in slumber.

Dana: Last night I was spending some quiet time in the living room while Jim played with the children in the yard. He came indoors three times and walked behind the sofa (where she was sitting) without saying anything to me! He should have at least asked me how I was doing.

Jesse (therapist): What was that like for you, Dana?

Dana: I felt like he didn't notice me. I felt like he didn't care and I wasn't a priority to him.

Jim: Dana, I'm sorry that I made you feel that way. I was honestly just so focused on getting things for the children…Jimmy wanted a jar to collect fireflies and Jenny wanted a drink. I was like a man on a mission. You know how I get.

Dana: But three times? Jim. Couldn't you have at least said hello or checked in with me on one of those times that you came inside?

Jim: I can see that was really bad for me to ignore you three times! (He turns and looks at her straight on.) I'm really sorry for that, Dana. I don't remember exactly, but I do know that one time I was looking over at you, and I thought you were asleep on the sofa. So I just let you be. I thought, *She must really need a rest,* so I tiptoed past.

Dana: It really helps me, Jim, when you look at me and tell me what was going on for you yesterday in the yard with the children. (Dana starts to get tears in her eyes.)

Jesse: What's going on for you right now, Dana?

Dana: I like knowing that Jim was thinking of me…and also our children. (She turns to Jim.) I like this face-to-face time that we do here [in marriage sessions]. We don't do this at home with all the busyness and hectic activities of the kids.

Dana softened at hearing these things from Jim, and especially because he immediately engaged with her concerns and sympathized with her hurts. She shifted in her view from a woman ignored to a woman who had a caring husband who was trying to look out for her. She even felt lucky to be a woman who had a devoted father in the home to play games with their children. She wanted more opportunities to connect with Jim, to have face-to-face time with him outside of the marital sessions.

What about you? Can you relate to the busyness of life and the hectic pace of raising children that Dana talked about? Does that get in the way of you having much needed face-to-face time with your spouse?

Entertainment Barrier

We have so many options now for entertainment in our modern era. There have never been so many options in the recorded history of humans. The proliferation of web-based technology gives us games, movies, electronic chatting and messaging, social network forums in an array of tantalizing choices that are almost too many to count. Most of them seem good, and many of them have a semblance of human interaction. But none of them can replace the real need that we have for face-to-face connection.

When you think about it, the human race would cease to exist if humans stopped having real forms of face-to-face connection. You can't reproduce offspring or raise them via texting or virtual chat. Your offspring would never be conceived without physical and sexual connection. Your children's brains would lack huge portions of development if they were not touched and held face-to-face. Unfortunately, our children's brains are being improperly developed due to their excessive exposure to countless hours of electronic media in the modern era.[55]

I am not trying to abolish electronic media, but I want you to be informed about the risks that they pose to your most important human connections. If you are human, the adrenaline-inducing effects of gaming and social media will draw you in and entice you. It's normal, and that is precisely why they are so popular. This can be to the detriment of your other needed activities, such as talking to your spouse in person or holding your children. If you are an avoider or a burned out protester, it is easy to use social media and gaming to console yourself, keep you company, or help you avoid dealing with the anxiety you feel in your marriage.

Again, I am not telling you to cancel your Internet service. I am just asking you to consider whether there are times that electronic media get in the way of your spending much needed face-to-face time with your spouse.

Work Barrier

It is a classic scenario when we think about the husband who works so much and is gone from the home. It may also be a wife who has a busy career that keeps her away from hearth and home, along with opportunities for face-to-face time. It is important to put food on the table for your family. It is right and fitting that we should work hard to provide for these needs. Yet, in our anxiety about providing for our families and in our need for affirmation in our careers, we may lose sight of the need to also carve out face-to-face time with our spouse and family.

I am reminded of a couple I met with recently. We'll call them Ken and Gwyn. They have done excellent work in dismantling their negative cycle. She is much softer and less critical, and he is truly engaged in a way that he has never been before.

Gwyn: I see all the ways that you are making changes, Ken. I really appreciate the effort that you are putting into us. But I still can't help feeling that I have to ask you to take time away from work to spend it with me. It's like work is definitely in the schedule, and that's the default setting.

Jesse (therapist): Where does that leave you, Gwyn?

Gwyn: It leaves me feeling lonely, and like I don't matter. It's still hard to be in that position, even though I know he cares. Sometimes, Ken, I don't even want to ask you to spend time with me because I know that *I am* going to be the one asking.

Jesse: What are you hearing Gwyn say today, Ken?

Ken: I hear that she wants to spend time with me, but that it makes her really sad to feel like she always has to ask for it.

Jesse: What's that like for you, Ken, to hear that Gwyn feels like your work is under the "protected time" category?

Ken: Well, it makes me feel badly, and even as I think about it right now, sort of foolish.

Jesse: Foolish?

Ken: Yes, I have work in the automatic setting. I've never really even thought about making a category in my schedule of protected time for our marriage. I'm going to have to look at the best times of the week to do that.

Gwyn: Ken, I'd really like it if we could do that together, instead of you trying to figure it out on your own.

Ken: Oh, yea. I see what you mean. Could we look at our calendars tonight after we get home from our daughter's ballet recital?

Gwyn: That sounds good to me.

You can see how Ken and Gwyn were able to connect around this important discussion of his work and her need to not be in the position of asking for time together. She was essentially asking for scheduled face-to-face time and the balancing of the work barrier. Now that he hears how much she wants to be with him, he is ready to look at things in a way that he never perceived them before. They get down to solving the problem of how to create meaningful connection in face-to-face time. Let's do the same in this next section.

Setting Up Your Face-to-Face Time

As you get started on this section, I want to share some encouraging news with you. Research shows that there is a strong association between high levels of marital happiness and spending just twenty minutes a day talking to your spouse. Couples who spent these twenty minutes together had drastically reduced divorce rates. Renowned family therapist, Michele Weiner-Davis recommends spending those mere twenty minutes a day together as a key "divorce buster."[56]

Please take a few minutes right now with your spouse to ask the following questions that will direct you toward finding a couple different face-to-face time slots together. Ideally, it is best to have a couple times during the weekdays when you and your spouse can be alone for twenty minutes or more without interruptions. A date once or twice a month for a few hours without interruptions is also ideal.

Face-to-Face Time Scheduling

- What are good times of the day when we are both together and are reasonably alert to listen to each other?

- Are there a couple of these times each week that we could spend together for at least twenty minutes, seated side by side or looking at each other without any distractions in the area?
- What helps us to really settle and relax so that we can tune into our own thoughts and feelings?
- What helps us to be able to listen well to the feelings of the other spouse?
- Is there a time of the week or month when we could get together for a longer date of about two hours or more?
- What helps us to get the conversation going on longer times together? Do we like to walk together, go out for coffee, read something, or have an experience together? (A movie doesn't count as face-to-face time dating unless you take time before or after to talk about it.)
- How can we arrange for childcare and scheduling to make face-to-face time something that we can reasonably expect to do on a weekly and monthly basis?
- What could get in the way of us following through with our face-to-face time together?

Ways to Enrich Your Face-to-Face Time

Now that you have worked together to set up your face-to-face time, let's talk about some key things that will enrich your experiences together. We'll look at ways to build anticipation of your time together, deepen your discussion, and prevent needless breaches in your marital connection at times of separation and reunion. All of this will help to make your face-to-face time something that you look forward to and keep returning to for years to come.

Just Thinking of You

Why is it so nice to receive a card from a loved one, especially for no reason at all? Why is it so meaningful to have a phone call or text message from your spouse that simply says, "I'm thinking of you"? It brightens our face and touches us deeply to know that we are thought of, noticed, and loved.

It's reassuring to know through the words and actions of your beloved, that you are kept in mind and held close, even when you are apart from him or her. To know that your beloved is thinking of you, even when you are apart, links you and binds your hearts despite whatever miles are between you.

I hear sad stories at least once a month where one spouse complains that the other did not phone while on a business trip or failed to let them know of a change in schedule plans that would affect the time they spent together. We are acutely aware of this loss and breach when it becomes a repeated pattern.

Peter Fonagy is a Hungarian psychiatrist who has written extensively about human attachment. He says that people feel secure when they know that *they exist in the mind* of their loved ones.[57]

That is powerful! I feel secure when I know that you hold me in your mind, in your thoughts, and in your heart. Even when we are apart, I do not cease to exist to you. You still hold on to me and are thinking of me.

God speaks this over us and over our lives. He says that He cannot forget us, and He holds on to us. Our names are written on His palms, just like a tattoo: *"See, I have engraved you on the palms of my hands..."* (Isaiah 49:16 NIV).

God says that you are ever before Him. He will not forget you, and nothing can wash you off or tear you apart from Him. In our modern culture there are a lot of tattoos that people place all over their bodies. The classic tattoo is the guy who inscribes his girlfriend's name on his shoulder or bicep.

Recently, I have seen both a mom and a dad who have their children's names tattooed on their bodies. Now, I am not telling you to go out and get your spouse or your child's name tattooed on your leg. But, the permanence of this image is the link.

Anything we do to let others know, "I'm thinking of you," serves to shore up the bond between us and let them know that we hold on to them even when we are apart. We are reassured that the relationship continues even when time and space separate us. This is very comforting and reminds us of our place in our beloved's thoughts and mind.

I consider this to be an important piece of face-to-face time in two ways. First, it is encouraging and connecting for your spouse to receive text messages, emails, inexpensive gifts, and love notes from you. Second, it is a valuable practice for us to refresh our own thoughts about our spouses with the ways that we are grateful, impressed, and enamored with all that they are to us.

There is great security in knowing that we are married to spouses who reach for us and who intentionally build up their love for us. This is part of keeping our love fresh, renewed, and current.

What are some meaningful ways you could reach out to your spouse this week? Think of some creative and also steady ways you could say, "I'm thinking of you. I saw this and thought of you. I appreciate and love this about you."

Mirror Me! Take Time to Listen

Attuned listening is another element that will enrich your face-to-face time together. I am reminded of our couple Sonda and Larry, whom we have referenced many times already in this book. You will recall this as the story where he missed the grand opening night of her small business due to being at an adult club. His job required him to travel and be away for extended periods of time, and when he went away he was tempted to cheat. She wanted him to check in over the phone to reassure her that she was still in his thoughts. It would help her be reassured in their connection and to feel less afraid. This is exactly what we just discussed, thinking of your spouse. Sonda's need was to know that she still existed in Larry's mind, even when they were apart.

Larry's needs were somewhat different from Sonda's. He had such a lonely and solitary upbringing. He didn't just want to know that he existed in *her* mind, Larry actually struggled to feel as though he *existed at all.* In his disconnected childhood, he never had anyone listen to his expressed experiences to enable him to sense that what he was going through was real and valid.

When we ask our spouses about how they are doing and then reflect it back to them, it lets them know that what they are experiencing is real and valid. They know that we care and that their experience exists, even momentarily in our minds while we listen to them.

Had you ever thought about what a great gift you offer when you take time to listen to your spouse, to mirror back to him or her and reflect experiences and feelings? You offer your spouse the gift of value. You offer your beloved the gift of existence with you by his or her side. The gift of your presence and knowing are the greatest gifts you could bring.

I want to encourage you to engage in deep and connected listening when you have your face-to-face time with your spouse. That is why it should be free from interruptions, because it is harder to get deep into listening when you have breaks in the flow of communication.

I have included the following tips for the listener when you are together with your spouse for face-to-face time.

Suggestions for the Listener

1. Put your own agenda on hold. Your turn will come soon, and your partner will be calmer to listen after you have listened and validated key feelings.
2. Maintain your attachment framework: "I want to hear your view. You're so important to me. Thank you for sharing with me, so I can meet your needs."
3. Allow your partner to speak until he or she completes a full thought.
4. Only interrupt for purposes of clarifying: "I want to make sure I'm getting what you just said before we go to the next point. Please say that last part again."
5. Repeat back to your partner what you've just heard. "What I hear you saying is…" (You can be almost like a digital recorder here in merely reflecting back what you heard him or her say.) Avoid judging or interpreting.
6. Next, ask your partner, "Did I get it? Was there anything I left out?" If there is nothing more your partner wants to say, you can move to validation.
7. Validation—After you've grasped what the speaker says, validate. Validation does not mean that you agree or see it the same as your partner. Validation means that you grasp his or her point, and put yourself in her or his shoes:
    - "It makes sense to me that you felt…" "You're right, I did that…"
    - "I can see that you would think/experience/feel that…"
    - "I really get it that for you…this happened when that took place."
    - "It's normal to feel what you're feeling. Anyone would feel that way."
    - "I can feel a little of how (insert their feeling here) that is for you."
    - "I never wanted you to feel that way."
8. The Million Dollar Question: "Is there anything you need from me?"

Ask for What You Need

When you have face time with your spouse, it is important for you to be direct with him or her about what you need. So many times I have heard one member of a couple tell me, *"I should not have to tell my spouse what I need, he (or she) should just know it!"*

There is often a lot of hurt in these words, a lot of anger. It follows from so many experiences of not being known, not having needs met. It also follows from many experiences of being locked apart by the negative cycle.

Sitting there right now, you can probably see one very logical reason why a person who states this could end up feeling unknown. If you never tell your spouse what you need, how will your spouse ever know what to do for you? Of course people in general have ideas about what is needed—kindness, affection, and attention—but the specific ways that these needs will be met are as different as the humans who populate this planet.

I have often made the following observations about people who say, "I shouldn't have to tell you what I need. You should know it!" I sense that they are really struggling with how hard it is to ask for what they need. Perhaps they never had much in the way of a parent asking them to talk about their needs in the first place. Maybe they never had the practice and valuing experience of getting to share their needs.

Perhaps they have been so lonely for so long in their marriage that they are scared to death of opening up and being rejected again. Maybe it's a little bit of both. But I have to nudge them away from the protective dream that "My spouse should just know what I need!" We all have this dream since infancy that someone would just intuitively know what we need. It would be effortless for us. We would be perfectly secure and known at all times. But there is no human on earth that can fulfill that lifelong dream and need. Only God can be in that place for us. Only God knows us that intimately, for He knit us together *"fearfully and wonderfully"* (Psalm 139:14 NIV). In our relationships with the rest of the humans on earth, we're going to have to get better at asking for what we need, especially with our spouse.

The Sock Drawer Story

I want to tell you the story of Bert and Livvy and the sock drawer. Bert and Livvy were two of my wife's friends more than a decade ago. She was privileged to share richly in their lives, the joys, triumphs, and struggles. Bert and Livvy were refreshingly honest about things that they went through. This has been a standard for April and I to aspire to in our own marriage and in our friendships.

Livvy told April this sweet story of an unexpected treasure that she found in a sock drawer. Livvy had been experiencing some times of discouragement. This was taking place in her personal life and also in her marriage. She knew that Bert loved her, but she needed to hear it more often from his lips. Bert was a busy guy who was often doing yard work, drinking coffee, and researching one or more things on the Internet.

What Livvy said to Bert is common to many of us. She told him, "Bert, I need to hear you say the words 'I love you' more often." It was a simple request, but one that could have been lost in Bert's hustle and bustle.

As the weeks passed, Livvy felt a sense of greater security and reassurance from Bert. She was hearing his affirmations of love for her on a more consistent basis. She took comfort in this and started to get more accustomed to it again. Then one day she made a discovery when she was putting away Bert's laundry.

Typically Bert put away his own laundry because he had a specific order to the way that things were positioned inside the drawer. But he had been working some late shifts that week, and Livvy wanted to bless him. She was putting some dress socks away when she discovered a little note tucked just inside the drawer. The note said: *"Don't forget to tell Livvy each day how much you love her."*

It was just as simple as that, but Livvy got the double blessing from seeing those words. First, she had asked for what she needed. Second, Bert had followed up and was being more consistent in affirming his love for her. Privately, he was making sure that he would be consistent. He did not want to let this important need slip through the cracks of life. Livvy was that important to him.

Some couples say to me, "Jesse, but wouldn't it have been better if the words 'I love you' just came naturally to him? Wasn't it kind of forced or phony if he had to remind himself?" I follow up with this question: *"Which shows more love—to do the things that come naturally for you or to go out of your way to do things for your spouse that don't come automatically?"*

Go out of your way to do things for your spouse.

I feel a greater sense of security when my spouse does something for me that requires effort, and she does it whether she feels like it or not. That kind of love is solid. I know that I can take that kind of love and build my future on it. But remember—I will never tap in to that type of love unless I take the risk to ask for what I need.

As you have your regular face time together, don't forget to ask directly for what you need. I have enclosed some tips for the speaker to get you started on your request to be heard and to put your needs forward to your spouse.

Suggestions for the Speaker

1. Ask your partner if this is a good time to talk about something important.
2. Speak about your own thoughts, your own feelings, and your desires.

3. Try to use "I" statements about your internal experience. These are easier to hear.
4. Try to be focused and "to the point" in what you are sharing. Remember that it is harder for your partner to track more than one main point at a time.
5. Maintain your attachment framework: "I got upset with you because you are the most important person in the world to me, so I felt (hurt) when I couldn't/didn't…" "I want more than anything to be close to you, so it upset me when…"
6. Correct your partner gently if he or she is not grasping what you are saying. "That isn't quite what I meant…" "That's some of it, but here's the rest."
7. Keep going until you have been understood, and your spouse gets what you mean.
8. When it feels safe, let your partner know what you need in order to feel better.

Bring Physical Touch into Your Face-to-Face Time

I want to talk to you for a moment about the importance of physical touch in your face-to-face time. At this point I am not talking about sex, per se, although positive touch during face-to-face time may serve as a very nice precursor to your sex life later that night. We will get into more depth about sex in a later chapter.

Let's talk about oxytocin, affectionately dubbed the "Cuddle Hormone," which brings a lot of benefits to your life and also to your marriage. Oxytocin is a neuropeptide hormone that strengthens attraction, the intensity of sensation in touch, bonding, attachment, and trust. It increases when you feel connected, "in love," sympathetic to others, and when you touch others. It is released during sexual activity and also during breastfeeding.[58]

When you get into a regular pattern of touching your spouse, oxytocin will increase just at the anticipation of being touched. Oxytocin helps you feel close and connected, and it helps you "want to" be close and connected. The more oxytocin you produce, the more you respond and are receptive to it. In other words, you don't build up a tolerance. You just keep getting more benefits from your ever-increasing oxytocin.[59]

Oxytocin helps to keep you from getting into conflict. It is hard to feel like fighting when your hormones are making you want to cuddle. It's a positive cycle. The more oxytocin you have, the more favorably you will view your spouse and the less you will fight.

Oxytocin provides health benefits as well.[60] Did you know that oxytocin helps to reduce cortisol, the stress hormone that is implicated in heart disease and reduced immune system functioning? So the regular practice of touching your spouse and increasing your oxytocin can help prevent heart attacks and illnesses. This is one of the benefits of being in a good marriage and also staying out of the negative cycle in your marriage.

The following is a practical list of ways to incorporate touch into your face time. This is based on an article written in 2010 by Jim Childerston and Debra Taylor,[61] who are Christian sex therapists at the Institute for Sexual Wholeness.

Suggestions for Ways to Touch Daily and Increase Oxytocin

1. Hold hands while walking. Hold hands in a lingering, sensual manner.
2. Hold one another in a longer embrace, at least two minutes. (It takes oxytocin about thirty seconds to be released, so you need a longer hug to get the benefit.)
3. Allow your body to touch your spouse when you sleep at night. Oxytocin will be released throughout the night. When you wake up in the morning, any arguments you had started will be easier to manage.
4. Take time for lingering kisses, for a full ten seconds. When we kiss passionately, we imprint positive images of our beloved in

the brain, which we tend to review throughout the day. Your spouse will look better and better to you.

Times of Separation and Reunion

In the final section of this chapter, we will look very specifically at times of separation and reunion in your daily life as a couple. At these points, it is absolutely essential that you establish regular routines and rituals for face-to-face connection. It's important to be consistent with these at the daily level, and to add extra attention in and surrounding times of extended separation from your spouse.

Do you remember the original Strange Situation experiments with infant attachment in the Ainsworth lab? The children's attachment bond and attachment style were evident during their moments of separation and reunion with their mothers. Securely attached children were upset when Mom left, but they had the settled confidence that she would return. When she returned, the children greeted her with joy, and then resumed playing. Those children were also able to branch off from Mom to play and explore the world, always knowing that they could return to her.

Secure attachment allows you to branch off from your spouse and venture into the world, knowing that while you're gone, your spouse will still carry you in his or her heart. You are confident when you return; your spouse will be there for you. You know that you can go to your spouse at any point when you are distressed, and your spouse will be present and ready to listen to you, console you, and support you.

A New England Vacation Gone Bad

I am reminded of a married couple I saw recently. He is the avoider in their marriage and she is the protester. They have done very good work in making their marriage more secure.

A striking incident happened to them. She went away on a trip to see the foliage in New England with her mom and two of her aunts. Oh the days and hours of planning that went into this trip with the girls! The husband felt slightly jealous about all the time spent away from him, but he was not vulnerable in his way of expressing it. He had just a hint of sarcasm in his voice near the time that she was leaving for her trip, "Okay, then. You just run along with your family, and I'll see you when you get back."

He genuinely wanted her to have a good time with her family, but he was also feeling slighted, which showed in his dismissive tone. She felt unwanted and left for the trip on a shaky note. They were both insecure at the moment of "separation" for this trip.

When she returned, she had not talked about her feelings, nor had he. He had to work night shift just before she returned and was still feeling tired and lethargic when she walked through the door. She assumed that he was upset with her, and they could not seem to reconnect. So, their "reunion" was incomplete.

In our session together, we processed through the insecurity that he felt, and her misunderstanding of his tone. They were both relieved that the conflict was a result of their attachment needs. He wanted to be included and to spend time with her. She desired to be wanted by him and to be missed while away. They simply had not shared that it was all about their desires to know how important each one was to the other.

This scenario clearly illustrates the need that we all have as humans to know that we will be missed when we leave our loved ones. We want to know that they will be happy to see us when we return. It is important to establish connection patterns and routines in our moments of separation and reunion with our spouse. Think about it for a minute: *What do you do when you leave your spouse for a few hours or a few days?* Ideally, you want to have a moment of face-to-face connection. You might kiss, make eye contact together, and say, "I love you. I look forward to when I get to see you again." Then you branch off for your trip or your time away.

Take time each day to tell your spouse, "I love you" when you leave for the day. Put in a lingering kiss too, so you can increase your oxytocin. Hug and kiss when you return home from your day. When you leave for a prolonged trip, make sure you say how much he or she means to you before you go. While you are apart, reach out often to say, "I'm thinking of you."

In closing this chapter, I am reminded of the words of Jesus to His disciples when He had to leave them to return to His Father. He was fully human, and fully aware of what His disciples needed as they were facing the upcoming separation and loss in their relationship with Him.

> *These things I have spoken to you so that you may be kept from stumbling. ...now I am going to Him who sent Me.... But I tell you the truth, it is to your advantage that I go away; for if I do not go away, the Helper* [Comforter] *will not come to you; but if I go, I will send Him to you. A little while, and you will no longer see Me; and again a little while, and you will see Me* (John 16:1,5,7,16).

> *...and lo, I am with you always, even to the end of the age* (Matthew 28:20).

Jesus knew exactly what His disciples would need to hear at this time of separation. He told them to take heart with His reassurance that He would comfort them, remain with them in new ways, and that He would return to them.

CHAPTER 10

SIXTH KEY—TUNE IN OFTEN AND BE QUICK TO REPAIR

Have you ever been in the presence of a really good listener? I mean someone who seems to gently see past your facades and helps you actually understand yourself better. A good listener makes eye contact and lets you have lengthy chances to talk without interrupting you. She shows you with her posture and her nonverbal signals that she's feeling what you're saying. He steadily lets you know that he cares by remaining devoted to the goal of knowing you and knowing you deeply.

When a good listener doesn't understand something, she asks another question. When a good listener gets it wrong in attempting to know you, he owns it saying, "I got that wrong. Can you help me to better understand?"

Our time and attention are the greatest gifts we can give to others. As finite human beings, that time spent is something that we can never get back or get a refund on. When someone tunes in to us, it makes us feel worthwhile and important. It makes us feel cared for, known, and somehow more whole.

Tune in Often

When you think about it, really good listeners are not with you every minute of every day. They are in your life for chunks of time, and maybe only a few times a month. But those periods of time are very attractive, very restorative, and deeply fulfilling. We internalize those experiences and hold a sense of being valued and secure, even when we are apart from those people. Though we may be far away from them, we are not separated emotionally. My Gramma has a wonderful habit of telling me, "Jesse, I hold you in my heart." This makes me feel very special.

We spoke earlier in the book about attachment theory and what it takes to build a secure bond between two humans. In order to build and maintain a secure attachment bond between a parent and child, the parent must be consistent and sensitive in his or her responses to the child.

Daniel Stern was one of the leading child developmental theorists of the late 20th century. Stern refers to the "attunement" of the caregiver, where the parent is sensitive to the verbal and nonverbal cues of the child.[62] An attuned parent responds appropriately and is able to put him or herself into the mind of the child. This doesn't mean that secure parents are 100 percent attuned. Just the opposite, the most secure parents are only about 30 percent attuned. *Wow! Isn't that astonishing? The best and most highly tuned in parents are only attuned about 30 percent of the time!*

But even though they are only accurately tuned in about a third of the time, it is enough to build a secure and steady bond between the parent and child. It is enough for the child to internalize a sense of being special. It is sufficient to help the child feel safe and secure emotionally.

Consistent Does Not Mean Perfect

If you are like me, this is tremendously reassuring. Highly attuned parents are not tuned in all the time. There are many moments when they are doing their own thing and can't get a read on their children. There are even some moments when they failed to notice what the child needed. Highly attuned parents don't get it right all the time. But they are consistently in the game.

However, when they get it wrong they also know how to repair misattunements.[63] They know how to apologize to their children and get down into their level again, to have another try at tuning in to their children's signals and needs. Highly attuned parents take the job of repair seriously. They don't want to leave their child feeling abandoned or rejected for any length of time. The relationship is so important to them. So it would not feel right to them to leave things on unsteady ground.

This faithful commitment to the process of repairing any broken places provides security for us as humans. These consistent acts of attention and care are gifts from us imperfect human beings. There is only One who is perfect, always steadfast, and always true: *"Jesus Christ is the same yesterday, today, and forever"* (Hebrews 13:8). We take great comfort in that promise, and we are strengthened by the bedrock of hope that it brings.

We are going to talk a lot more in the next chapter about the perfect presence and perfect love of Christ. We will be applying His love to our marriage relationships. In this section we will apply the findings of attunement to the marriage bond.

For those of us working daily in our marriages to build a secure face-to-face connection, it is important to know that we don't have to always get it right. It is more important to focus on being consistent with our emotional and physical presence. That is good; that is enough.

As a finite spouse, who only has a limited amount of time and attention in this lifetime, it is a tremendous gift when we listen and tune in. We are giving of the very best that we have to offer when we are *good* listeners, tuning in closely in order to know our beloved's heart and mind. It is a great gift that makes our loved one feel special, valued, treasured, and secure.

We are flawed human beings who are going to make mistakes. That is inevitable, and it is just a part of life. But when we make mistakes with our loved ones, we can turn these moments into precious opportunities to learn more about their feelings and needs. The best thing we can offer when we make a mistake is to be humble, caring, and nondefensive. We own that we hurt our spouses and that we would never want to hurt them, because we care.

These gifts of our limited time, along with our sincere apologies when we fail, are some of the closest things to the divine that we may offer. They serve to communicate safety and commitment at the deepest level, especially when we express aloud: *"I will be here. You can count on me. Even if it goes wrong; I won't run away or shut you out. I'll be with you through thick and thin."*

These type of statements provide to our spouses an experience on earth of the eternal, unchanging, never failing love of God: *"I will be with you"* (Exodus 3:12 NIV). Amid the uncertainties, frailties, and imperfections of this life, knowing we can depend on our spouses and vice versa is the greatest gift. It gives us peace and gives us courage to press forward together. We can get through anything because we know that they will be with us.

"I Will Be with You"

Rabbi Harold Kushner has written significant works about the experiences of trials and sufferings in our lives and in the lives of biblical characters including Moses.[64] Kushner speaks of Moses' fear and doubt when he encounters the living God at the burning bush. God commands Moses to go and proclaim the liberty of the Jewish slave nation in Egypt. Moses asks God, "Who am I that I should go and do this deed of deliverance?" (See Exodus 3:1-11.)

God does not reply with an affirmation of Moses' ability or gifting. Instead He reveals something deeper of *Himself.* God answers, *"I will be with you"* (Exodus 1:12). God tells Moses that no matter what you go through or what darkness you encounter, I am the light. I am with you.[65]

Kushner goes on to say that God describes to Moses that His very name, Yahweh "I Am," identifies Himself as the One who was, who is, and who is to come. That is the greatest comfort to Moses, and to all of us.

In our life's journey, it is not about our abilities or perfection. Where we lack and when we fail, God is constant and faithful. When we have doubts, His presence is the source of strength to sustain us and guide us through. And when we mistakenly look to ourselves in self-absorbed ways, He is quick to challenge us and repair our perspective, shifting our gaze once more to behold His face and rest in His constancy.

As an imperfect spouse who commits "Till death do us part," my greatest gift to my wife are my actions of *consistently tuning in* and being *quick to repair* when something goes wrong between us. It is my way of physically showing and displaying some of those attributes of God that we all find so comforting.

It is very comforting when someone steps forward to truly listen and abide with us. That constancy is what our hearts long for since infancy. It is, perhaps, God speaking to us in a language that we can understand. Could there be any doubt that God would find ways to express Himself to us in human forms? His very nature is most evident in human forms of love: *"God is love"* (1 John 4:8).

We are learning that God's love and nature embody constancy, a comfort in our past, a very real presence here and now, and a promise to be with us in the future. Love that does anything less is not complete. It is not mature.

Mature Love

I want to talk to you about another movie, although it may seem odd to continue on themes of faithfulness and constancy from Scripture by telling you about a film. Many Hollywood romance movies center on the themes of early love, infatuation, and conquest. "Intoxicating Love" was our description earlier in this book about the infatuation phase that serves to rapidly bond us to our new love object in the first nine to twelve months of a romantic relationship.

Throughout this book we have been speaking about growing into secure and mature love. One particular movie, *The Notebook,* contains a remarkable representation of secure and mature love. Seldom have I seen anything from Hollywood that so beautifully captures the essence of enduring and constant love across the span of life for two people.

It is a story of an impetuous and brazen young man who is poor and works at a lumber yard. He happens to meet a lovely, wealthy, and spirited young woman who is vacationing for the entire summer in his lakefront town. The two loved and fought passionately. In a moment when he was trying to convince her to choose him, he said, "We fight intensely and this is not going to be easy. If you want this, you're going to have to work at it every day for the rest of your life. But that's what makes it real." That's what gives it value.

He goes on to show her, even in old age, that he is a man who is faithful and devoted. All of his investment in her is reciprocated, to the point where he finds his place of comfort just being by her side. There is a point later in the film where she is very ill and his family tells him to come and stay at the family home, rather than at the medical setting.

He gives no pause in saying, "I can't go home. She is my home." What a crystalline example of the joys and benefits of constant love!

That is what happens when we know that our spouses consistently tune in to us, and that they are quick to repair when things go wrong. We get a steady and safe feeling about them in our lives. We develop a calm and joyful mood in their presence. We are beckoned to bring our thoughts and needs to them on a regular basis. May we say of our loved ones: *"You are my home. You have become my go-to person. You have become my constant one."*

We don't develop a sense of constancy and home because everything has been serene in our relationship over the years. It is not the absence of conflict that makes us grow in oneness. It is the way in which we directly tune in to each other and love one another in the midst of pain that binds us together. Our willingness to be vulnerable and quick to forgive facilitate this bonding process.

Be Quick to Repair

> *Be angry, and yet do not sin; do not let the sun go down on your anger* (Ephesians 4:26).

This Scripture passage from Ephesians 4 is familiar to many, and I have heard many folks take this phrase quite literally that you cannot have an unresolved conflict before you go to bed. You must hash it out before the morning light. This is not always wise, especially considering the fact that humans have increasingly diminished reasoning capacities as the night wears on. I suggest it may be best to "sleep on it" and resume the conversation in the morning. We may even have a clearer perspective on what was hurtful to us and to our spouse, by sheer virtue of having taken a break.

But in this section I want to frame the passage "Don't let the sun go down on your anger" in the context of being quick to repair. I believe that we are looking at Paul's (the writer of Ephesians) insistence that we not allow breaches in our relationships to fester and breed resentment.

We will get angry, and we will get hurt. However, we want to cultivate a heart that is eager to repair and yearns to restore lost connection with others. If I hurt my spouse or she hurts me, I want to be eager to restore connection. Whenever possible, I want to mimic the heart of God and run quickly to her so that we may restore our intimacy.

Of course this is difficult to do, and it is extremely hard when you are still caught in the throes of your negative cycle. However, when you dismantle the cycle, you can see past the defensive protests or avoiding actions of your spouse. It becomes easier to see the vulnerable longings of your loved one. In marriage, we all just want to be accepted and not abandoned.

Your spouse is your dearest friend, not your foe.

We must be quick to repair. We've got to bring our needs and hurts to our spouses just as soon as we are able. I recognize that there will be hurts and misunderstandings. That is just part of being married. Our ability to recognize that times of hurt and conflict are inevitable is one key part of being constant and steady. These times will be present, and they give us opportunities to show faithfulness. We need to recognize that we may even have to forgive.

We remember the story of Peter asking Jesus, "Lord, how many times should I forgive someone who hurts me? Maybe I should forgive him even seven times?" Jesus's response is a challenge to us all:

> *Jesus said to him, "I do not say to you, up to seven times, but up to seventy times seven"* (Matthew 18:22).

Jesus is letting us know that in human relationships and in marriage too, our response to hurt and offense should continually be one of forgiveness. Having the mind of Christ means that we will be quick to forgive. We will be spouses who are quick to repair relationships. There will be no tyrants or abusers when both spouses are living this motto, forgiving one another as Christ has forgiven you (Ephesians 4:32 NIV).

There won't be any tyrants, but there will be "repeat offenders," even when both spouses are engaged and trying to love one another. This is just the normal course of things. And Jesus knew that we would need a lot of forgiveness to build closeness in each of our human relationships.

Husbands need to love their wives and show them forgiveness, in a process of dying to self each day. They will create and foster a love that is so much greater than anything they could mold by clinging selfishly to their rights to repay offenses. Wives need to honor their husbands and forgive them for their mistakes, whether they are deserving of this type of honor or not.

That is what maturity is all about. This is what it takes to create a sense of constancy and security in marriage. These actions are the product of courage. Forgiveness is the substance of very strong people.

Plumbing Fix and Marriage Repair

Let me share an example from a recent session with a couple I really respect. We mentioned them earlier as John and Patsy. They have been married for many years and have been through some pretty rocky places. John initiated the marriage therapy because he wants to draw close to his wife now that they are in retirement.

John is the avoider in their marriage, and Patsy is the protester. He is a busy guy and reminds me of the classic rabbit in the "Tortoise and the Hare" story. Patsy is very intelligent, but processes things more deliberately and slowly.

There have been so many times when Patsy was unable to reach John that she has developed a sarcastic way of protecting herself from feelings of rejection. They were not quick to repair in the past because they had a negative cycle that prevented this. In the following session, they are talking about a recent conflict that arose when Patsy was trying to talk to John about what their plumber had quoted in his estimate.

Jesse (therapist): Patsy, John interrupted you as you were telling him about the plumber and you said something sarcastic. What was going on for you?

Patsy: I just felt upset that while I was trying to update him on my talk with the plumber he didn't even have time to hear me out.

Jesse: You were sharing with him and he could not even take time to hear you out. So you said something sarcastic? (She tears up.) What were you feeling?

Patsy: I just felt like he thought I was stupid, like what I had to say didn't matter more than his agenda. I was talking to the plumber for *us*.

Jesse: You felt like he put down what you had to say…like it was stupid, right when you were trying so hard to be helpful to him. That would really hurt…ouch, no wonder you said something sarcastic.

Jesse: John, what goes on for you when you hear that Patsy felt stupid in your eyes, right when she was trying so hard to be helpful to you?

John: I had no idea this was going on for her. I feel really badly that I made her feel that way. That wasn't something I would ever want.

Jesse: Can you tell Patsy how this is impacting you right now? Can you turn and tell her?

John: Patsy, I'm so sorry. I never would have wanted you to feel that way…like I thought you didn't know what you were talking about. I do respect you. That's why I asked for your help with getting the plumber.

John and Patsy are now on their way toward clearing up the misunderstanding and healing the hurt that came from his interrupting her. It takes a lot of courage and a lot of strength to share vulnerably when hurts have been triggered for either party. They are learning new ways of talking about their feelings so that it will knit their hearts instead of driving them apart.

Strength in Forgiveness

I have been speaking with you throughout this book about the principles derived from Emotionally Focused Couples Therapy.[66] This therapy involves sharing your feelings with your spouse in vulnerable ways that draw you together and cement a secure bond between you.

To an outside observer, this type of emotional sharing might sound sort of "touchy-feely or wishy-washy." One might think that emotional sharing is just about how you feel in the moment, and feelings are the guide for any situation.

That is not correct. The truth is that this vulnerable sharing is about a deepening of relationship, a oneness that actually inspires courage and accountability. When you know how much you are loved, you want to act in loving ways toward your spouse.

When you know how much you are cared for and how much he or she depends on you, it is humbling and deeply convicting. When you depend on your spouse regularly for support and to meet your needs, it is much more difficult to sin against him or her.

It is hard to be callous and indifferent when you are being vulnerable and receptive. So the mandate to forgive, *"seventy times seven,"* is not a free license for us to do whatever we feel like doing. Nor is the grace of God is an excuse to dwell or wallow in our sin.

> *Above all, keep fervent in your love for one another, because love covers a multitude of sins* (1 Peter 4:8).

In a marriage, love covers a multitude of sins. Intimacy follows from forgiveness and the willingness of each spouse to be vulnerable, serving, and receptive in the midst of hurts.

Mishaps, hurts, and misunderstandings will come our way. They could fuel our negative cycle and drive us into isolation and despair. But we have a better alternative. We can be quick to repair, and apply the mindset of being quick to forgive our spouse even *"seventy times seven."* That is what creates constancy and builds secure love.

Securely attached spouses are not immune to hurt and misunderstanding. They *are* quick to repair it. These partners are quick to own it when they have done something that was hurtful. They don't feel nearly as defensive because they are feeling affirmed in their spouse's commitment to bring them anything that needs to be dealt with.

These lovers are quick to repair. They are not scared to bring their needs because of a fear of rejection, isolation, or ridicule. Time over time, they have proven this statement to be true in their relationship: "You are the one I cling to and can bring anything to."

When repair happens quickly, it builds confident assurance in the relationship.

When repair happens quickly, it builds our sense of constancy. We can think, *We've been through hurt before, and we'll be able to get through this one too.* We have an internal working model in our heads, a map of all the times that we have brought our needs to our spouses and found acceptance. Our memory bank is full of times when we were present for our spouses too and felt good about ourselves as the go-to person on whom they can depend.

Even if something big comes up that was unexpected, we can be confident in our belief that we will make it through. We have confidence assurance in the relationship.

The Constancy of God

Psalm 27 is one of my favorite passages in the Bible. It is encouraging and strengthening throughout, and it reflects the type of secure faith that David had in God. The last few verses speak to the internal working model that David has about God's presence and strength to guide him through any challenges that come:

> *For my father and my mother have forsaken me, but the Lord will take me up. I would have despaired unless I had believed that I would see the goodness of the Lord in the land of the living. Wait for the Lord; be strong and let your heart take courage; yes, wait for the Lord* (Psalm 27:10,13-14).

God is constant and present to us no matter what our previous attachment experiences have been. He will not abandon us in this lifetime, and we have confidence that He will bring goodness to us during our days among the living. That includes experiences of goodness in our marriages.

Our constancy and presence demonstrated to our spouses are part of His plan to show them His constancy. He will strengthen us to receive hope for our own hearts and to share His constant presence with our spouses. God will be with us in this life, from beginning to the end of our days.

> *Even though I walk through the valley of the shadow of death,*
> *I fear no evil, for You are with me…* (Psalm 23:4).

Through all the seasons, we have committed to be with our spouses. In sickness and in health, we will be present together. In comfort and discomfort, we will remain. In familiarity and surprise, we will be there for them. Although our spouses may change at times due to a job loss, a health problem, or the loss of a family member, we may be shaken, but we will not be moved.

It is easy to see the parallels between the constant abiding love of God and the secure love that He beckons us into in marriage, as we tune in to our spouses and repair the hurts. You can see why this is so important for the health of a marriage, and you also see how God longs to be present to both of you in the process of building constant love.

Applications

The following are some applications of the attachment-building principles just described. As discussed in the last chapter, we have to make face-to-face time in order to build our marriages and address the growth areas. In the context of brief and lengthier face-to-face interactions, please consider the following thoughts.

Tune in Often

- Have you tuned in to your spouse today? You can do this today by sitting down together and asking, "How was your day today?"
- Try to get a feel for the joys and the struggles of your spouse's day.
- Have you been vulnerable too?
- Have you shared what you are hopeful about and the places where you are stressed?

Be Quick to Repair

- Do you have a habit of avoiding your spouse when he or she hurts your feelings?
- Are you "keeping score" of the hurtful things done instead of addressing them and offering forgiveness?
- Ahead of time, talk about phrases you each can use to indicate what issues needs to be worked on such as, "I had a hard time

with something that happened between us today and I want to get reconnected with you."

- Get in the habit of setting up a time to talk about the grievances within twenty-four hours of the occurrence.
- Ask God to strengthen you with His constant love so that you can listen and repair your bond with your spouse.

CHAPTER 11

Seventh Key—Put on Perfect Love

There is no fear in love; but perfect love casts out fear… the one who fears is not perfected in love (1 John 4:18).

When you think about it, most of the hurtful, selfish things we do in relationships are fear-driven. Our protective styles, our psychological defenses, were fashioned in order to protect us from some form of emotional pain. Frequently, the pain that we are desperately trying to avoid is that of abandonment and loss. We are insecure for one reason or another and afraid of being alone.

However, when we are caught up in the perfect love of God, we fear nothing. We are at peace. When we see the world from His perspective, it is void of fear, fretting, and all the neurotic things that we as humans do to protect ourselves from abandonment and loss. We often experience these moments of God's perfect love when we are caught up in worship, prayer, or when we behold the majesty and beauty of His creation. In those moments, we see through His eyes. We are caught up into a realm where we soar on wings of eagles, and our fears lie far below in the valleys beneath us.

Oh how we expectantly wait for the redemption of our frail minds and mortal bodies.

Oh the beauty and exhilaration of these moments in our lives! These moments are a foretaste of Heaven, a foreshadowing of what is to come when we are redeemed from this world of pain and fear. There is something within all of us that yearns and even groans with the weight that we bear in our daily lives, as we expectantly wait for the redemption of our frail minds and mortal bodies.

> *For we know that the whole creation groans and suffers the pains of childbirth together until now* (Romans 8:22).

Life without fear is good. It's the good stuff, the type of living that we were created for, going back to the Garden of Eden. Adam and Eve walked with God in newness of life, peace, and daily joy. They had contentment and the freshness of unbroken fellowship with God, prior to the Fall. They were face-to-face with their Creator and with one another. There was no fear of abandonment, rejection, or attack. Life was peaceful, and life was good.

But then sin entered the picture, and death became an imminent possibility. Subsequent to the entrance of sin and death into our world, we now cope on a daily basis with the fear of threats to our mortal bodies. We live in a world of tension and fear.

Love Deficits

We are all hardwired now to survive on this planet and to deal with potential threats. Some of us are more acutely aware of this than others. We have fearful thoughts and are apt to analyze our surroundings and troubleshoot problems before they even arise. That is the way my brain is wired. I am analytical and continuously analyzing patterns, trends, and potential pitfalls. There are many benefits to this for me in the work that I do as a professional. But, I am quite aware of the times that the analytical side of my thinking takes me away from being present emotionally in my closest relationships.

When I was dating my wife, April, I shared some things that I wanted her to know about my love for her. There were things that I wanted her to know that she could fall back on in those moments when fear (mine or hers) was crowding the view of love. I told her:

> *April, I want you to know that there will be moments when I will not perfectly love you. There will be moments when the things that I do are not what you really need. Only God will perfectly love you at all times. In those moments, please remember that I do love you and I am still finding the ways to express that love more perfectly.*

I was asking her to hold fast to my promise of commitment, even when my actions were showing my more human side. We were preparing for marriage and a lifetime of love, and yet I was already aware of my own inability to perfectly love her. I think that we are all aware of our frailty and inability to show perfect love. My sense is that marriage makes us more acutely aware of our growth areas, as we endeavor to become one with another living, breathing human.

How then are we to love? As fearful human beings who are wired for survival and with our protective barriers going up in moments of perceived threat, how are we to perfectly love our mate? It is a challenge greater than our own abilities and talents.

We need a Champion, a Guide, and a Savior to show us the way and redeem us from our fearful human ways! We need a Hero who has gone before us and paved the way through His courage and sacrifice. We need the strength, presence, and redemption of One who has lived and embodied perfect love.

We need Jesus.

Jesus was the strongest man who ever lived. His whole mission and purpose on this earth was to face death squarely and lay down His life so that we might be raised to new life.

> *Greater love has no one than this, that one lay down his life for his friends* (John 15:13).

Jesus lived above His fears and in spite of His fears, since He was fully human, just like you and I. Jesus had all the same survival tendencies that you and I have. Yet He was focused beyond those inclinations and tendencies. He was driven for the highest purpose of love, and He was given as an offering of love for the whole world to see. He was a visual representation, a model of God for us to see. He was God incarnate, Perfect Love, for us to witness and behold.

Ultimately, we came from God. The God of the universe *is* Love (1 John 4:8 NIV). We came from the timeless love and unity at the core of who God is. The Trinity embodies the whole unified relationship of the Father, Son, and Holy Spirit, eternally communing and eternally one. We humans here on earth long for a return to this loving connection with God.

We find this on earth through relationships, with God, and with one another. Jesus is the tangible expression of God's love; He is God's love incarnate for us!

> *For in Him all the fullness of Deity dwells in bodily form* (Colossians 2:9).

> *For it was the Father's good pleasure for the fullness of deity to dwell in Him* (Colossians 1:19).

It is the most wonderful and unfathomable mystery! The God of the universe would become one of us, express His perfect love to us, and lay down His life so that we could be restored to connection with Him.

Incarnational Attachment: *Receiving* Perfect Love

Jesus Christ is the tangible expression of God's love, acceptance, and presence. Jesus was and is Emmanuel, God with us (Matthew 1:23). God has promised that we will not have to go through this life alone. We have the reassurance that He will be with us; His presence will go with us and give us rest (Exodus 3:12; 33:14).

Jesus's life, sacrifice, and presence convey to us the essence of secure attachment. When we walk through the most distressing times, He promises to never abandon us.

> *...He Himself has said, "I will never desert you, nor will I ever forsake you* (Hebrews 13:5).

God has already stepped toward us to demonstrate secure and constant love. He does this through His word, love, and His Son, Jesus Christ. As you may recall from our early discussions about secure attachment, the secure bond is forged due to the reciprocal interactions between parent and child. While God has already taken the first steps toward us, we still have to respond to His prompts by reaching back to Him.

We have to step toward Him, trust His words, and embrace. We have to reach for Him in order to receive perfect love and build our security with Him. Remember that love is never known without taking a risk and sharing your life. You have to be vulnerable and give Him your heart.

Jesus told us, *"Truly I say to you, unless you are converted and become like children, you will not enter the kingdom of heaven"* (Matthew 18:3). We have to become childlike and reach up to Him with our arms wide open to receive His love and rescue in the midst of our distressed existence on this planet.

The Salvation of Childlike Dependency

Jesus wasn't talking about an insecure and anxious child. He wasn't talking about an avoidant child who no longer trusts anyone but himself. He was speaking about a secure child, a much-loved child who knows how to be dependent on her heavenly Father and to imitate Him (Ephesians 5:1 NIV).

We have to be vulnerable and express our dependency on Him in order to create security and receive His salvation. I affirm my dependency at the start of my relationship with Christ and on each day following with the words, "I need a Savior, and I need rescuing." Conversion is that moment when I trust Him with all that I am. It is that very moment when I "set my heart" upon Him.[67]

What a paradox! I am weak in order to be strong. I must become like a child in order to embrace divine maturity. I have to die in order to live. This message is such foolishness to those who do not believe, *"but to us who are being saved it is the power of God"* (1 Corinthians 1:18).

Incarnational Attachment: *Giving* Perfect Love

In marriage, God calls us to show His perfect love to one another. He calls us to love our spouses sacrificially, with reckless abandon, as Christ loved His church. He created marriage to be a symbol of the type of perfect love that He has for us as His bride. Marriage is supposed to mirror the type of love that He has for us to draw us to Him. He ordained marriage as a relationship that would help us understand His great love for us.

Secure marriage is a relationship that also helps us experience in tangible ways the love of God. In that way, marriage can be a means of incarnational love.

You are the hands and feet of Christ to your spouse.

You act as Christ's arms and His loving sacrificial embrace. Since He ordained this, He also wants to help you in marriage to embody and express His love. That is not just because He wants your marriage to succeed. It is because He wants you to actually know and experience more of His love.

Isn't that amazing? God, the Creator of the universe, is so invested in having you experience and know more of His love, that He will strengthen your spouse so that he or she can better portray His love to you.

God is so invested in having your spouse know His love that He wants to strengthen you in the toughest moments to be His arms of embrace stretched out to your spouse. He is with you in the toughest times so that you will not be alone. And He wants to move through you to show His love to your spouse. You are not just receiving His love for you—you are also receiving His love for your spouse.

I can think of no clearer illustration of the need for this in marriage than those moments when we don't actually "feel" like showing love to our spouses. I hear distressed couples say, "Well I would stop pursuing and blaming him, if he would stop pulling away." And, "I would stop pulling away, if she would stop blaming me."

This is, of course, a couple who is still stuck in their negative cycle. This is a couple where the avoider has not engaged yet nor used the gift of vulnerable language to courageously reconnect with his or her spouse. It is a couple where the protester has not used her or his gift of vulnerable language to reassure the spouse about how needed and how valuable he or she is.

And from a spiritual standpoint, this is also a couple who is *not clothed* with the perfect love of Jesus Christ. It is a couple who has not tapped in to the strength and power of God's desire to help them be His arms and His embrace to one another. I am not saying this to shame or belittle them. We are all weak in our own strength. God tells us, *"My grace is sufficient for you, for power is perfected in weakness"* (2 Corinthians 12:9). I am simply observing that there is something more for this couple than they have experienced yet. There is a level of strength and help that they have not yet known.

Bonus Power

God does not wait for us to love Him or to act in love toward Him. He reaches for us, moves Heaven and earth to redeem us, and lays down His life for us before we do anything right or deserving.

> *In this is love, not that we loved God, but that He loved us and sent His Son to be the propitiation for our sins* (1 John 4:10).
>
> *We love, because He first loved us* (1 John 4:19).

Anyone who is distressed in marriage must contend with the crippling effects of fear that spin out from the negative cycle. For all of us, whether Christian or non-Christian, it is a huge challenge to dismantle the negative cycle and to step back into the face-to-face emotional connection that God intended for our marriages.

However, as Christians, we have an added bonus availed to us in this quest. *Love is stronger than fear.* God's perfect love is ready for us to cast out all our fear. He has already come so that we could individually and collectively be set free from the strongholds of fear and so that we might be perfected in love.

Jesus stands ready and waiting to help and aid us. He is the bridge between God and humans. And Jesus's perfect love is the bridge that connects humans who are hurting, lonely, and afraid in the midst of their struggles. It's the bridge over turbulence and strife into places of rest and security in our marriage relationships.

There is no end to this love. There is no place or situation that His love cannot go to and move. He neither slumbers nor sleeps (Psalm 121:4). Jesus's perfect love empowers us to lay down our protective defenses, to die to self, so that we might enter into more abundant life and intimacy with our spouses.

Jesus was not focused merely on His own survival or on defending Himself from pain. He came not to be served but to serve and to lay down His life as a ransom for many (Matthew 20:28). He lays down His life for us as a tangible expression of the love of God. He is Incarnational Love, and He stands ready and waiting to help us show this same tangible, incarnate love of God to our spouses.

We don't have to wait until our spouses are showing us the most vulnerable facets of self. We can love them first and soften our approach to them first. We don't have to wait until our spouse fully embodies a face-to-face approach to us. Instead, we can rely on Perfect Love—God—to strengthen us and draw our spouses into the embrace of love.

I can think of no higher or more rewarding calling in marriage than this. It is a sacrifice that brings fulfillment. And, because we are one, whenever I love and strengthen my spouse, I am actually doing myself a favor. In covenant relationships, everything that we give directly returns to us in the form of an ever-increasing intimacy and an ever-growing marital bond.

There is only gain to both of us when I rely on and draw from the perfect love of Jesus in order to comfort myself in times of marital distress and embrace my spouse in those moments. Whether I am embracing her with my words, attention, patience, or my body, there is One who has my back. There is One who has this covered. He stands ready and waiting for me to call out to Him for help.

This is what incarnational love is all about, being present in the brokenness and present in the pain. Jesus entered into our brokenness and sinfulness, and He loved us just the same. We cling to His redemption and saving grace so that we can draw strength to be present for one another. We step in to be bearers of His presence so that our spouses don't have to walk through anything alone. When we are able to do this for one another, it is such a healing experience. It is a redemptive and sacred moment.

A Sacred Moment with Roger and Cloe

I'm remembering a couple I worked with whom we'll call Roger and Cloe. Cloe was a school teacher who arrived home at a decent hour each evening. Roger was highly successful at his engineering job, but he had to work long hours to achieve this. He was not successful at his marriage relationship. Whenever his wife would come to him with her urgent pleas that the two spend more time together, he felt criticized and put down. He would quickly retreat to his "cave." Many times, his "cave" took on the form of an office with a comfy high-backed chair where he would retreat and spend hours on end. Other times his "cave" was the escape he created in his own home by falling asleep soon after he walked through the front door.

Of course the more Roger retreated, the more urgent Cloe's pleas became. And the more intense her pleas, the more Roger retreated. It was a vicious cycle, and this committed Christian couple was actually thinking of divorce. What Roger could not successfully bring himself to do was stand proactively and compassionately engaged with his wife in the midst of conflict.

Roger could tackle difficult projects and assignments head-on in the workplace, but he seemed to turn into a cold and distant "cave man" whenever his wife would approach him with intensity. For the longest time, Roger blamed Cloe until he was able to hear that his response to her was increasing her anxiety and perpetuating his own experience of pain. Another shift took place when Roger clearly heard the source of Cloe's panic—she was feeling abandoned by her most important person.

Cloe grew up on Long Island, and both of her parents worked outside the home. From the age of 11 years, she was a latchkey kid, having to let herself in after school until her parents both arrived home sometime around six in the evening. Many nights one or both parents would phone Cloe to say that they were working late, and she would have to eat dinner without them. Cloe missed both of her parents terribly. She had so many experiences of abandonment that she was trained to be on the lookout for the workplace stealing the ones she loved. Her perception was highly attuned to look out for any factor that would suggest she was going to be abandoned forever by her husband as he went to work each day.

In fact, Cloe was so afraid of this happening that she came to criticize Roger's place of work at times and to resent him for going there. What she did not know was that Roger looked forward to coming home and having a restful evening with his wife. A safe, quiet, and nonconflictual home was his dream. However, whenever he got home late, Cloe criticized him stringently for abandoning her to his work.

We join them for a session later into therapy after Roger has had a chance to tell Cloe how criticized he feels ("I want to talk about me!"). She has grasped this and is softening to tell him what her criticism is really about ("You gave me a scare!").

Cloe: Roger, when I hear you are going to be late, I get this sick feeling in the pit of my stomach. I can't help it. It just churns up inside of me.

Jesse (therapist): You feel sick, right there in the center of who you are. Can you tell me more about what that is for you, Cloe?

Cloe: It's this panicky feeling all over again, like I'm losing him. I'm going to be alone…I'm being left alone… (trails off, starting to cry).

Jesse: It's like you're losing him…he's leaving you all alone.

Cloe: Just like when I was a girl…I could never have time with my parents. I just never could.

Jesse: Roger, what is going on for you right now as you listen to Cloe sharing about how scared and alone she feels in those moments?

Roger: I feel so badly for her. I didn't know it was like that for her. I didn't understand. I never meant to do that to her. That's the last thing I'd ever want to do.

Jesse: Can you let her know, Roger, that you care? Can you let her know right now?

Roger: (Reaches over with both arms around Cloe) I'm so sorry that I make you feel that way. I'm so sorry. I would never want that for you.

Cloe melted into his big hug. She was wracked with sobs for a couple minutes, while Roger just held her. I felt a sense that I was actually standing on "holy ground." I left the room for a couple minutes to give them time to be alone. It was a moment of healing for Cloe, both from her childhood hurt and all the hurts she had experienced from Roger's late returns from work. Her longings and the object of her desires were coming into alignment.

Things were going to be different now. That was the gift that Roger gave as he stepped forward to be the hands and feet of Christ. This was the embrace that Cloe received as she took a step of faith to be vulnerable instead of critical.

> *Therefore if anyone is in Christ, he is a new creature; the old things passed away; behold, new things have come* (2 Corinthians 5:17).

Practical Ways to Put on Perfect Love

Being present to our spouse is something that we have to work toward over time. Remember from our last chapter that *you* don't have to be perfect. You just have to stay consistent over time in order to give your spouse a secure place to rest. It is a process to daily grow to a place where we are able to show more perfect love, especially in times of need. I now offer you some practical suggestions about ways to develop a heart and mind that are ready to love your spouse.

Pray for Yourself

First of all, we all need a greater revelation of His love for us that covers a multitude of sins. He loves you and offers forgiveness to you for all the selfish, survival-based things that you have done in your life. If you have never fully depended on Him to be your source of strength, comfort, and saving grace, then that is the first place to start. You can do that with a prayer, which is simply talking to God in ways that acknowledge your complete dependence on Him.

If you have taken that first step before, and maybe have walked with Jesus for years, it is still a daily renewing process to confess your need for Him and dependence on Him. I need Him every day to help me trust and see His plans and intents for me. I need Him every day to help me love others.

It is good to pray for ourselves and ask for revelation to us about the greatness of His love and for His strength in times of need. It is amazing how much stronger we become when we daily depend on our heavenly Father. That is the paradox of dependence!

> *...for when I am weak, then I am strong* (2 Corinthians 12:10).

Confess your dependence on God. When we daily pray for ourselves and bring our needs to God, we are comforted and we gain a perspective that we are weak, but He is strong. He gives strength to the weary and increases the power of the weak. Even young people grow weary, but *"those who hope* [trust] *in the Lord will renew their strength. They will soar on wings like eagles"* (Isaiah 40:29-31 NIV).

As we seek to strengthen our awareness of God's secure presence in our lives, it is good to remind ourselves that He is constantly with us. Lord, wherever I go, I am hemmed in and behind. There is no place I can go where you are not with me. Lord, you know when I rise and when I sleep; you know me full well (Psalm 139). Jesus has promised us His abiding presence.

> *...I am with you always, to the very end of the age* (Matthew 28:20 NIV).

It takes intentional and daily focused attention to renew our minds so they rest in the security of God's love. Each one of us needs to grow in this paradigm shift from being in survival mode to a place of trusting peace. I encourage you to use the modes that most speak to you, whether it is uplifting worship music, listening to sermons on podcast, reading Scripture, or delving into grace-filled books that uplift you.

From this place of greater security and rest, ask God to help you be vulnerable with your spouse. Even when it is scary, ask God to help you convey your unwavering love for your spouse. Pray that you can always let your spouse know how much you need her in your life. Pray for courage to convey that you just want to matter to him or her and that you sometimes get afraid that he or she doesn't care.

Pray for Your Spouse

Get into the habit of praying regularly for your spouse. Jesus wants us all to come to Him, with all of our wearying and heavy burdens so that He can give us rest (Matthew 11:28 NIV). By this point in the book, you probably have a pretty clear sense as to whether your spouse is a protester who has felt abandoned too many times in life. Or you may see that your spouse is apt to avoid due to feeling criticized and inadequate.

Pray that your words will be comforting, encouraging, and building up for your spouse. If your spouse is an avoider, pray that he or she will know the deep acceptance of our heavenly Father to help him or her feel less criticized by you in moments of need. Jesus is ever-gentle with your avoidant spouse, *"A bruised reed he* [Jesus] *will not break"* (Matthew 12:20 NIV). Pray that your spouse will have the strength to tell you when she or he is feeling criticized instead of walking away. Claim that your mate can do all things through Christ who gives us strength (Philippians 4:13).

If your spouse is a protester who has been abandoned by you and others too many times, you want your mate to know that he or she is forever engraved on the palm of her heavenly Father's hand. She or he is never alone. Ask God to impress upon your spouse's heart that He will never leave nor forsake. Pray that *you* will be able to tell your protester that you are feeling badly about your ability to meet his or her needs, and it is not due to a lack of caring.

Pray Together

At this point we have completed the Seven Keys. My hope and prayer is that you have a clearer understanding of what a secure face-to-face marriage really looks like. I trust that you are better able to interrupt your negative cycle, and replace it with a deeper face-to-face connection with your spouse by using the gift of vulnerable language.

I invite you to set some time aside for you and your spouse to come together as one. I hope that you have been able to read some portions of this book together, but even if you have not, this could be a good time for an invitation to renew your commitment to a secure marriage.

Please consider making a confession to your spouse and God in a time of prayer in which you both participate. Whether you are the protester or the avoider, we all struggle to show our spouses the daily actions of perfect love. I encourage you to confess to your spouse your awareness of your "love deficits," your desire to be more present to him or her, and to conclude with a prayer that acknowledges your complete dependence on God to help you be more loving in the marriage you both share.

Example Words to Say to Your Spouse

> *I own it that I am not always there for you when you are hurting and alone. Sometimes I don't draw close to you in vulnerable ways when I'm hurting either. I have been guilty of pulling away from you and also lashing out when I feel bad. I'm sorry for these things. I want to do a better job.*

Prayer for Renewal Together

> *Dear Jesus, I thank You that You love us so much, and that You are always with us. You never leave us or forsake us. Please help us to love each other the way that You love us. Help us not to be afraid or ashamed as we come together to share our needs. Give us Your eyes to see how precious our marriage is and that each conversation is a chance to build more closeness, face-to-face. When our strength is not enough, we trust in You to be our strength and the center of our love. We are weak, but You are strong. Thank You that You are faithful and true. Amen.*

CHAPTER 12

NAKED AND UNASHAMED

For this reason a man shall leave his father and his mother, and be joined to his wife; and they shall become one flesh. And the man and his wife were both naked and were not ashamed (Genesis 2:24-25).

This Scripture passage in Genesis 2 speaks to me about the way God originally intended our relationship with Him and our spouse to be. He created us to be transparent and without hiding. We were to bring all that we are to Him and receive all that He had for us. It speaks to intimacy, walking in the cool of the day with Him, fellowshipping, knowing and being known. God's original plan for our relationship with Him was that we would live openly and without defenses. This open posture speaks to the type of intimacy, including sexual intimacy, that God designed for us in marriage.

The Garden of Eden was located in the Middle East. Scholars believe that it was positioned near the Equator, somewhere between the Tigris and Euphrates Rivers. It's kind of hard for me to relate to this garden, since I have never visited the Middle East. I am also pretty certain that climate changes over time have greatly altered the nature and quality of the lush tropical environment that once was Eden.

I invite you instead to think of a warm tropical island for a minute. Maybe you've had the opportunity to visit an island in the Caribbean. If you've never traveled to one, I bet you've at least viewed one on TV. The climate is warm, often rainy, and the vegetation is very lush, green, and abundant. Sandy beaches line the coastlines of the more popular islands, and the guests of the island can stroll leisurely along the warm sands, walking hand in hand with the ones they love.

I think that vacationing on a tropical island is something like Eden. There is no regular or routine work required of you. Beauty surrounds you on all sides. Imagine taking your honeymoon on such a warm tropical island. The whole purpose is to connect, build relationship together over the course of lingering afternoons and languid nights. Clothes are optional. This is something of what it means to be "naked and unashamed" in marriage.

When we start out on the honeymoon, hopefully, the process of connecting sexually comes with enjoyment, wonder, and newness in sharing together our bodies along with the fullness of who we are. For most of us, it is easier on our honeymoon to connect sexually. Like Eden, there were no distractions of work or children and the cares and worries of life. Many of us were still aided by the wonderful chemical reactions in our brains from the process of infatuation. These chemicals drove us to "hyperbond" with our beloved. They made us want to mate like rabbits!

Other folks have had sexual struggles in their relationships, even on their honeymoons. This would indeed be frustrating and discouraging, since most of us at least have the dream of Eden and the expectation of great sex for our honeymoon time. If you got off to a rough start, it is possible to still build a meaningful sexual connection through patience and intentional focus together.

After the honeymoon, we have to devote time, patience, kindness, and clear communication to cultivate a thriving sex life with our beloved. This is an investment that pays many dividends in our physical, emotional, and even spiritual health together in our marriage relationship. It is such an important part of being face to face, and yet it can be difficult to do when the cares and worries of finances, chores, and kids detract from our languid and lingering tropical nights together.

We also can lose our sexual connection when the stress, resentment, and rejection of the negative cycle have been at work in our midst. When we feel afraid of losing closeness due to "subpar performance," when we feel afraid of letting our spouse down, or when we have memories of betrayal from key moments with our beloved, then it can be very hard to be present to a fulfilling sexual connection with our spouse.

I devoted an entire chapter to sexual intimacy to help all who are involved in marriage relationships. The thoughts shared here can also be a help to those who have had a fulfilling sexual connection already in their marriage. I encourage you to renew your thinking about what it means to be face to face in this very special part of your marriage relationship.

If you and your spouse have struggled to connect sexually because of emotional distance and pain in your negative cycle, this chapter invites you into full restoration of being face to face. This chapter may not be sufficient for what you need if your marriage struggles from performance anxiety, sexual dysfunction, or other medical-related difficulties in the bedroom. For those reasons, I have included a list of references from some of the leading Christian sex therapists for you to do further work. These are listed as References within the Chapter 12 section of this book's Endnotes.

Cycling in the Bedroom

The negative cycle can be so painful between a couple that they don't even want to be in the same room with one another, much less "hop into the sack" together. The negative cycle can create all kinds of unpleasant mood states in two people, including resentment, insecurity, anxiety, and shame. It often contributes to a reduction in sexual drive and desire as well.

When the avoider feels inadequate and criticized, it can go a long way toward reducing his sex drive and sexual interest. He'd rather be anywhere than getting close enough to her where the arrows can stick. When the protester is having chronic experiences of feeling unwanted and unimportant, it can greatly detract from her sexual fulfillment and her drive. She may be angry on one end or very unsure of whether she is desirable on the other. In other words, the negative cycle enters the bedroom, along with every other room in the house, wreaking havoc and pain.

Safe in Your Arms

You have been working so hard on every facet of your marriage, being vulnerable with your spouse so that you could build a secure emotional connection. It is so important to cultivate a secure sexual connection as well. This is part of maintaining all the good work that you two have done, and it establishes your marriage as the relationship that you will turn to time and time again to meet your deepest needs for human connection. It is my desire that you and your spouse will have a meaningful and fulfilling sex life together.

I want you to have great, connected, face-to-face sex!

Now that you have dismantled your negative cycle and are relating emotionally in face-to-face ways, I want you to take it to the next level. The same freedom that you more often enjoy in sharing your emotional needs, your grieving, and your dreams can be applied to your sex life. It is more possible now to bring your emotions, your body image concerns, your sexual wants and needs directly to your spouse.

While sex can be almost purely physical for both genders at times, that is not the fullness of sex. What separates us from the mammals is the degree of sharing and closeness, the degree of investment, and the degree of commitment that we bring to our sex lives. The degree of risk that we take, putting all of who we are into the arms of our beloved, determines our level of intimacy and turns our sex into something physical, emotional, and sacred.

Sexual intimacy is the deepest form of intimacy. Intimacy can be mapped out on a scale from least intimate to most intimate.

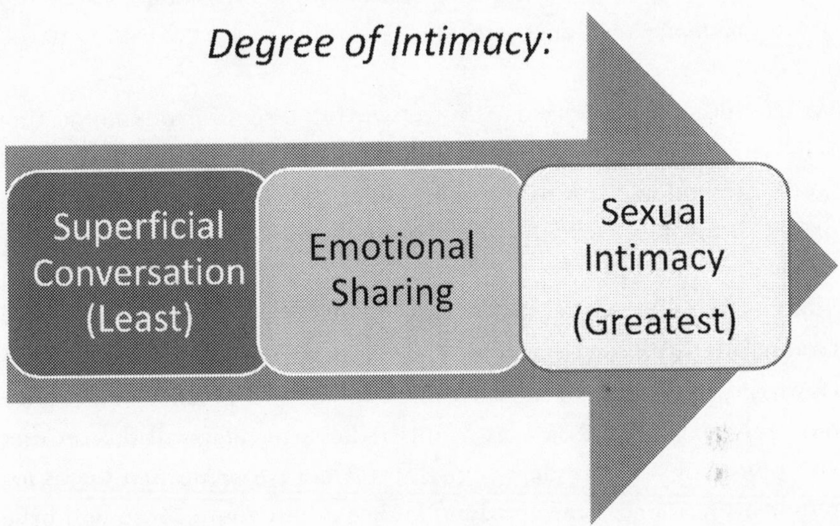

Sexual connection can be the most vulnerable form of connection between two human beings. *"They become one flesh"* (Genesis 2:24 NIV) seems to reference all the physical, emotional, and spiritual facets of oneness. Sex with our spouses has a truly spiritual dimension and connection. Many theologians believe that the bond between a husband and wife is the closest representation of the unity in the Trinity that a human can experience. Jesus prayed for us to be one, just as He is one with the Father.

> *that they may all be one; even as You, Father, are in Me and I in You, that they also may be in Us, so that the world may believe that You sent Me* (John 17:21).

It is this degree of intimacy to which we are called in marriage. This "oneness" is so sacred and wondrous that it helps to build lasting security in our marriages. It is the ultimate form of trusting and the deepest form of knowing. What a wonderful and deep gift God has given us to share with our spouses!

Made for Sex

> *God blessed them, and God said to them, "Be fruitful and multiply..."* (Genesis 1:28).

We have previously referred to this verse in our discussion on Intoxicating Love. In that chapter we spoke about infatuation, which was part of God's method and means for us to hyper-attach to our beloved. This drives us to draw close, be devoted, and make some babies with our beloved.

God naturally endowed us with the anatomy, the chemistry, the blood flow, the seed, and the eggs to make all of this possible. Even after our childbearing years are past, our bodies still retain all the abilities and physiology to connect sexually. Of course some of our sexual responsiveness and intensity slow down as the years go by, but all the basic pleasure and connections features are still in place. God did not have to make us in this enduring sexually responsive manner, but He did.

You are a sexual creature, and you are sexual by God's design. You have these gifts and features for the purpose of being fruitful and multiplying, but this hardwired sexual nature is also there for all the times that you are not intentionally trying to multiply. It is still there in the spaces before, between, and after you are trying to actually make babies.

So long as there is nothing wrong medically, your body is sexual in nature. In a relaxed and accepting setting, your body will become aroused as blood flows with warmth and awakening delight to your body's erogenous zones. In a safe and comfortable climate, the touch of your spouse can cause your body to respond with pleasurable sensations and even climax to bring you great delight.

Technically, your body can have sex with more than one partner across the span of your life. Physically, you could even have multiple sex partners in a given week. But that is not God's plan for you. Remember that our God is faithful, a God of covenant. He made a covenant with Abraham to provide fully for what he needed and to fully provide for Abraham's descendants (Genesis 15:1-17 NIV). *"I will be with you"* (Exodus 3:12) was His promise to Moses, then to Joshua, and to all believers for generations to come.

> *...Just as I have been with Moses, I will be with you; I will not fail you or forsake you* (Joshua 1:5).

God is covenantal and faithful. Among the many ways that God reveals Jesus to us, He calls Him *"Faithful and True"* (Revelation 19:11). God calls us to embark and participate in His covenantal nature with our spouses. We spoke in depth about this in our last chapter on Perfect Love. So, while you have the equipment, blood flow, and hormones to mate like rabbits, He calls you to a faithful covenant with your spouse.

It is within this faithful and intimate relationship He has designed us to be naked and unashamed. This is where a face-to-face sexual connection comes into clearer focus. When we are face to face and secure with our spouse, we know that we can bring anything forward. Any need or any concern may be brought forward to our beloved without fear of rejection or of being dismissed.

This includes our sexual needs, dreams of an intimate bond with our spouse, and our desires. When we can truly come naked and unashamed to our beloved and know that we will be embraced, it greatly reduces our anxiety and heals our shame. As we think about building and restoring healthy intimacy and sexual response, it is important to note the ways that anxiety and shame shut down the sexual response.

Fight or Flight Spoils the Mood

We examined in Chapter 3 the ways that the fight or flight response mobilizes our entire body for action in moments of threat and danger. The fight or flight response can be triggered by the threat of conflict with our spouse, or the pain of actual conflict in the negative cycle. One spouse protests and pursues angrily (fight), while the other one avoids and withdraws (flight). This is the set-up for most of our negative cycles.

However, a couple who is not in conflict may actually experience fight or flight symptoms in the bedroom. This can be due to past experiences of childhood or relationship trauma. It can include past performance pressures from the way we were raised or from misguided information about how great lovers are supposed to perform in bed. Fight or flight can get stirred up in a spouse due to fears about what will happen "If I let go and let go of control," which is what we have to be able to do to experience orgasms.

The way that fight or flight detracts or inhibits sexual response is pretty simple when you think about it. Remember that in the moment of threat, our blood flow is slammed down to our major muscle groups, including quadriceps, hamstrings, and gluteus maximus muscles. This is so that we can run away from the source of threat or we can fight it off. So all the blood flow is moving to large muscle groups, and it is exiting your genital region along with several other areas of the body.

Our genitals need blood flow to become engorged, bring our nerves closer to the surface, and allow for good sensitivity to pleasure. Little blood flow to the genitals means that we will have little to no pleasure.

Adrenaline and endorphins are released in huge surges during the fight or flight response. They serve to activate our muscles and also numb us from any pain that we may experience during the ensuing battle for survival. As you can imagine, the numbing effects of these two chemicals are counterproductive to having pleasurable sensitivity in our skin during moments of kissing and caressing. You don't want an analgesic to numb you when you are trying to get turned on!

Cognitively, we get tunnel vision during our moments of fight or flight. While this does help us to run away from predators, it does not allow us to open up and think of possibilities in the bedroom—or any room for that matter. It does not allow us to tune in to our own bodies or the body of our spouses. In milder moments of anxiety, you may be able to perform sexually, but you can come across as "an island" who is more tuned in to yourself or some behavioral technique instead of being a free flowing river that commingles with the waters of your spouse.

The fight or flight response is a huge part of the sympathetic nervous system, which is high strung and focused on basic components of survival. When the sympathetic nervous system is activated, our bodies are saying, *"Reproduction is not essential right now; I just have to focus on my own survival!"*

We are inherently self-absorbed during anxious moments. Contrast this with the parasympathetic nervous system that involves relaxed functions of the body, such as digestion, restoration of cells, tears in our eyes, and reproduction. This parasympathetic response is much more conducive to relational connection and intimacy.

We want to be in a parasympathetic state as we engage our beloved in the bedroom. If performance fears, chronic stress, or even a significant deficit in sleep are parts of our internal state as we approach making love, then our bodies say, "Reproduction is not essential right now. Shut down and just focus on survival."

We want to reduce all anxiety and performance fears in the bedroom. We want to make it a safe place for expressing ourselves and letting go. We want to care for ourselves throughout the week, so we have reduced stress and solid rest to draw from, instead of running on stress hormones that make us feel empty.

It kind of takes you back to Eden doesn't it? Prior to the onset of sin and death, life was much more leisurely and much less hectic. Food was plentiful, naps were abundant, and we did not need to perform to gain any survival-based benefits for us or our families. There was no "survival of the fittest" conflict going on because no one was going to be cut off or die. That was indeed a lush and fertile place, an excellent climate for being naked and unashamed.

Shame Steals Your Play and Wonder

Shame is the other primary emotional state that interrupts our sexual flow. The function of shame as an emotion is to make us shut down, withdraw, and relentlessly evaluate what we did that was unacceptable to our loved ones. When our loved ones disapprove of our behaviors or our advances toward them, shame is the base emotion that we feel.

Ever since the Fall in Eden, humans are driven for survival on planet Earth. We are designed to be attached to other humans and to rely on our families and tribe for survival support. So there *is* an adaptive function to shame.

If you are truly doing things that are upsetting to your family and tribe, then you need to know that so that you don't alienate yourself from them. You need them on a daily basis, and you might need them to fight on your behalf someday. There is a benefit to having some shame and to being ashamed when you do things that are bad for you and your loved ones.

But shame, just like anxiety and fear, is often misguided and misdirected. Shame often gets associated more broadly with facets of ourselves or behaviors that have nothing to do with our essential survival and nothing to do with our true worth or connection with others.

If your parents were stressed or busy when you were a child, you may have developed a sense of shame when you brought your desires to play and frolic to them. If your parents were angry or depressed, you may have developed shame about sharing more vulnerable emotions. If your playful advances or vulnerable expressions of emotion were met with distance or rejection, you could have gotten the false impression that it is shameful to be playful and vulnerable. Maybe you heard comments such as:

> "Grow up! Stop kidding around! You're much too big for that silly stuff!"
>
> "Quit complaining! You have nothing to be upset about…I had it ten times worse when I was your age!"
>
> "Stop crying before I give you something to cry about!"

Of course, these are harsh examples of verbal responses given to a child. You may never have heard such utterances from your folks as a child. Or you may have heard these very phrases, and you are getting in touch with pain right now. Remember that most of the communication we receive from our loved ones is nonverbal. So a child can get these distinct impressions of being unwanted or rejected, even if words were absent. A parent can send off these dismissive or disinterested signals through body language and because of being overwhelmed or tired.

Again, I am not here to bash parents. Most of them were doing the best they could with the life experiences they had been through. But I want you to be aware of some ways that your natural playfulness and natural vulnerability may have been squashed as a child. This can take away from your God-given sense that you are beautiful, marvelous, a wonder, and a delight.

You can lose sight of the fact that your body is wonderful and your emotions are treasures to be cared for both inside the bedroom and out.

> *I will give thanks to You, for I am fearfully and wonderfully made; wonderful are Your works, and my soul knows it very well* (Psalm 139:14).

The way God created you is precious and perfectly marvelous. You are a miracle from God's own heart and hand. Your body is an amazing creation—a wondrous, fruitful design. Your desires for play and closeness are valid and good. They were part of God's original plan for your life and were fully realized back in Eden when creation was unfettered with sin and survival fears. God created you to be naked and unashamed, and He wants you to experience that in your love life with your spouse.

Shame is not helpful in the bedroom, whether it is shame about your body image, your performance, or shame about your core self. Shame causes you to shut down, shrink back, and hide yourself. Shame shuts us down from playing, feeling, exploring, and taking interest. It keeps you from seeing your value and stepping forward. When shame is absorbing your mind, you don't open up to receive touch, and you don't press forward to connect with your lover.

Shame is self-absorbing, much like fear. It makes it hard for us to love and enjoy ourselves, and it detracts from our ability to tune in to our spouses' body and signals toward us. Shame keeps us from flowing back and forth with our spouse, and moving as one. We can learn to push back effects of shame by receiving the total acceptance of our value and worth to our heavenly Father. It is so healing to receive the open embrace of our spouses for who we are and all that we bring to the marriage.

Flirting and Affirming

When you hear the words "Your body is fearfully and wonderfully made," it can reassure you of your body's worth and value. We all need that settled in our core being and to know that God made no mistakes when He created you. This is an important place to start. But it is a whole other thing when your spouse tells you that he or she loves your body and finds you exciting.

"Come here, big boy…I'm gonna take care of you!"
"Baby, I love your curves! I can't take my eyes off you."

Flirting tells us that we are not only accepted, but we are eagerly desired and wanted by our most important person. When your spouse flirts with you, he or she lets you know that you are not only wanted and desired, but you also have nothing to fear from by way of rejection or criticism. Your spouse thinks you are the hottest thing and wants to make you feel good. Your beloved knows she or he is going to feel good with you too.

Flirting and affirming are sensuous ways to draw your spouse back into your arms and heal shameful feelings that may have cropped up over the years. Song of Solomon in the Old Testament provides us with many poetic and beautiful examples of delighting in our spouse. It highlights the spiritual depth and the unfolding adventure of cultivating a healthy sex life together.

The following are just a couple examples of the flirting and affirming that the bride and bridegroom offer to one another. These words of acceptance and desire would have gone a long way toward turning off any fear or shame and would have ignited some steamy Middle Eastern nights!

> *How beautiful you are, my darling! Oh, how beautiful! Your eyes behind your veil are doves. Your hair is like a flock of goats descending from the hills of Gilead. Your lips are like a scarlet ribbon; your mouth is lovely. Your temples behind your veil are like the halves of a pomegranate. Your breasts are like two fawns, like twin fawns of a gazelle…. Until the day breaks and the shadows flee* [I will be with you]. *You*

> *are altogether beautiful, my darling; there is no flaw in you* (Song of Solomon 4:1,3,5-7 NIV).
>
> *My beloved is radiant and ruddy, outstanding among ten thousand. His head is purest gold; his hair is wavy and black as a raven. His cheeks are like beds of spicy yielding perfume His lips are like lilies dripping with myrrh. His arms are rods of gold set with topaz. His body is like polished ivory.... His legs are pillars of marble.... His mouth is sweetness itself; he is altogether lovely. This is my beloved, this is my friend...* (Song of Solomon 5:10-11,13-16 NIV).

Undoing Performance Fear and Shame

Sex therapists say that a great love life begins with education, understanding, and acceptance of our bodies and sexual functioning. Another facet of a great sex life is our open communication about everything that we need and experience sexually. Communicating in vulnerable ways about our emotions and needs during the day provides some of the best "foreplay" leading up to time in the bedroom. When we reach the bedroom, this same vulnerable face-to-face communication must also continue for us to have deeply fulfilling and secure sex with our spouses.

When we were shamed by our spouses' criticism of us or when we felt ashamed that we were not lovable to them, it put us in a place where it was difficult to function at the highest sexual level. It would have been difficult to open up to our spouses before, due to anxiety, feeling abandoned, or feeling ashamed.

As you have begun to open up throughout the past few weeks, my hope is that you are feeling much safer and much more secure in taking risks with your spouse. It may be very natural at this point to talk about your sexual needs, questions, curiosities, and insecurities. Maybe you have already begun to talk with him or her about these things. But if you have not yet begun to take those risks, I encourage you to start doing that very soon.

Exposure Tasks

In my line of work, we train people every week how to overcome anxiety. In therapy, we also provide a place of safety so that people can come forward to their therapist or to their spouse and be accepted. Each time a client takes that step forward to talk about something that is personal or even embarrassing, we try to provide them with a new and positive experience.

Spouses have taken a risk, and we want them to feel safe, secure, honored, and accepted. Therapists call this an "Exposure Task," and it is the research-proven method to reprogram the brain away from anxiety and away from shame. It somehow seems very appropriate in this chapter on sex to invite you to "expose yourself" to your spouse. Before you do this in a literal sense, let me ask you to run through some opening up sorts of questions that you might share with your spouse about your sex life.

Exposure Questions

1. What are some areas of our sex life that I think are going very well?
2. When are my favorite times sexually with my spouse?
3. What are some areas of our sex life that have changed?
4. What do I miss about our sex life in the ways that it used to be?
5. What are some areas about myself as a lover that I am pleased with?
6. What are some areas that I would like to be more in sync with my spouse as a lover? What are some areas I wish he or she would be more in sync with me?
7. What would I like to be different in our sex life?
8. Are there any changes in timing, initiation, or foreplay I would like to see?
9. Are there any changes to stimulation, entry, and releasing that I would like to take place or would like to try for the first time?
10. What area of my body do I enjoy being stimulated today? How would I like that area to be stimulated?
11. What area of my body am I pleased with right now? Is there an area that I really need extra acceptance for these days?

This is by no means an exhaustive list to share with your spouse. Rather, I am encouraging both of you to open a dialogue about your sexual perceptions and desires. I am asking you to be vulnerable and embracing toward one another. Remember that good communication about your sex life is the best foreplay for a wonderful time in bed together.

Exposure Tasks with Your Clothes Off

After you have taken some quality time to talk through your current feelings, uncertainties, longings, and areas for growth, you may be more ready to take it into the bedroom. Even within the bedroom it may be necessary to take it slow, especially if you have had significant gaps in your love-making, significant misunderstandings and pain, or significant performance fears.

Sex therapists teach couples to engage in sexual retraining where they begin with very basic forms of touch, getting comfortable being together in the intimate setting. The touch is sequenced from no demand and nonsexual activities all the way toward more advanced touch and very arousing sexual contact. The purpose is to gradually eliminate all anxiety and all shame within the couple. At each moment of sensing and caressing, you and your lover are valued, accepted, and embraced. You get to have a new experience, and it literally retrains your sexual response, moving you away from performance fears and from shame.

The specific techniques utilized include "sensate focus," which was originally created by Masters and Johnson.[68] Training in this technique is helpful for a variety of sexual disorders and also for reengaging a couple who have had distance and anxiety in their sexual relationship. There are sensate focus scripts in the books which I have listed in the References section of this book. You can find these References within the Chapter 12 Endnotes at the back of this book. You can also type the words "sensate focus" into any search engine on the Internet to download a sensate focus script. Most are comparable and widely available now in public domain.

Even if you have never had performance anxiety or significant shame, I highly recommend using the sensate focus script as a way to get more in touch with your body and with your sexual sensitivities. It can bring a greater degree of richness into your lovemaking time together.

Sensate focus and more recent versions of these exercises serve to bring the couple into the present moment they are sharing in their bedroom. It directs them to deliberately tune in to the "here and now" and focus on what their bodies are sensing, receiving, and experiencing. The couple is trained to not drift off from this moment through forays into fear or spirals into shame and regret.

They tune out the world and tune in to their bodies and one another. All five senses are brought into the process and awakened to the journey of pleasure and pleasuring one another. The whole brain is tuned in to the experience of making love.

In our busy and distracted lives, this can be difficult to do. It is so hard to make time for love, and to set limits on the things that get in the way of our love lives. Unfortunately, the sex life of many couples in distress is greatly challenged, not only from conflict, but sometimes due to neglect stemming from other distractions in life.

The Infrequent Sex of Ken and Barbie

My wife, April, had an experience that was very striking. She was part of a small group before we got married. One of the couples in the group had recently gotten pregnant again, and April overheard the wife cracking a little joke to the other women, "We ask ourselves, whose birthday was it that we conceived during…his or mine?"

The insinuation was that they only had sex on special occasions. April was struck by this. The couple had young children, but you also need to understand that this was a very attractive couple who had a beautiful, pure, but steamy romance story together in their early days of relationship. They were as close to "Ken and Barbie" as almost anyone April ever knew. How could this have happened to them?

I am not trying to be judgmental at all. Sexual connection is a huge challenge when you have young children. In fact, I know of one really good book that was written specifically because the authors wanted to find ways to address this challenge in their own marriages—*Babyproofing Your Marriage.*[69] However, a sexual frequency of twice per year can be very damaging to a marriage.

Sometime after Barbie's comment, the husband confided to small group that he was struggling with pornography. The men of the group took it upon themselves to love and support him as he strove for victory in this area. Many variables contribute to pornography addiction, but it makes you wonder if this couple's low frequency of sex may have contributed to him being vulnerable to this temptation.

I am not blaming the wife in this situation. I am just looking at the big picture here. There is something about the dance of intimacy and sexual connection that helps us feel valued, secure, and physically cared for. There is also something protective about this for men. When I talk to couples I often say, *"Men, sex with your wives keeps you honest."*

What I mean by this is that guys have to take care of the heart and emotions of their wives if they are going to have regular and satisfying sexual intimacy. No man ever says to himself, *When I grow up, I want to have a pornography addiction or I want to get my love from prostitutes.* These forms of voyeurism and paying for love are cheap substitutes for the real thing that all men and women really want.

Sex is all about attachment for us as adults. We long for someone to touch us, accept us, embrace us, and to be there to care for our needs. Men are often times the initiators of sexual contact in their marriages. Of course there are exceptions.

Good lovers understand they have to woo their wives' emotions to connect in a meaningful way in the bedroom.

I think it is part of God's plan and design to make sure that both partners get their needs met. Many wives have a stronger felt set of emotional needs than their male counterparts. Men are often more in touch with their physical sex drives during the course of the week.

The face-to-face dance of sexual intimacy ensures that he must take care of her emotionally, and he in turn will have fulfillment of his physical and deeper emotional needs. This connected dance ensures that the wife will have her emotional and physical needs met, and that the husband will come bringing her emotional gifts while looking to her as the one who meets his sexual needs.

I mentioned in the chapter on face-to-face time that men often feel more emotionally connected after orgasm. This is heightened by the surge of oxytocin, the cuddle hormone, which is released at approximately 500 times the normal levels just after orgasm. It is a wondrous design.

When men care for their wives emotionally, they find that their own physical and emotional needs are fully provided for. Wives need to devote physical attention to their husbands, along with open and honest communication about their needs and limits, so as to draw out the emotionally best side of him.

When we have regular sexual contact with our spouses, it draws us to them and imprints in our minds that "My husband is my go-to person for my sexual needs. My wife is my go-to person for my sexual drive." You will not need to look for others, because your spouse is the one who takes care of you in this area.

The apostle Paul understood this truth and spoke about it to the Corinthian church. He urged married couples to have consistent sex with their spouses as part of caring for one another and also staying out of temptation (see 1 Corinthians 7:3-5).

Sex through the Years

A mature perspective on sex bears with it the recognition that our sex life will go through changes as we age. Sex is about an intimate physical, emotional, and spiritual connection. It's not about performance or appearance. As we age, we don't look as hot as we once did. Our performance and responsiveness vary and also decline as we age.

Over the years our skin loses some of its firmness, which leads to wrinkles and sagging parts. As we age, men's testosterone decreases by 1 percent each year after the age of 25. Women's bodies undergo hormonal changes as well, associated with their peak seasons of reproduction and as those seasons draw to a close in menopause. These hormonal changes have huge effects on our sex drive, interest, and sexual responsiveness.

My wife, April, and I have been blessed to have many examples of mature love in our lives through the years. In this moment, I am remembering the story of a fellow whom we'll call "Skip." Skip was sort of my idealized older self when I was a teenager. He was a handsome man with a charismatic grin and a full, well-traveled life. Skip was married to "Emily" who was lovely, artsy, and very elegant all at the same time.

I was housesitting for this traveling couple to make extra income a couple decades ago, and had to fill the cat's water dish at the kitchen sink. I saw a very intriguing card sitting in the kitchen window, and I confess that I peered inside.

It was a card that Skip had written to Emily on the heels of a very painful season in their lives. Emily had a mastectomy in her victorious battle against breast cancer about 2 years prior. Skip had carefully selected a romance card to give to his wife. His words go a long way toward healing and soothing any shame or fear that Emily might have had about the loss of her figure due to the mastectomy. His words in the card embraced all of who she is:

Emily,
You light my fire. You always have and you always will.
You are still the most beautiful and sexy woman in the world to me.
Love, Skip

The beauty of this love moves me and inspires me. I am mindful of one key element of Skip and Emily's love life that overarches all the other really cool pieces of their lifelong romance. That one word is *gratitude.*

Gratitude

Gratitude is the greatest gift for a healthy sex life at any age. Embracing gratitude at the end of the day is one of the most important parts of an emotionally connected sex life. Cultivate gratitude for your spouse, along with your spouse's body and physical touching of you, as ways to enhance your connection in the bedroom.

Comparing and contrasting can come across as critical. Envying others or being jealous of what they have in the bedroom just pulls you away from embracing all that you do have. Coveting only keeps you from fully engaging with the wonderful gift of a lover whom God has given to you. Criticizing your own body or performance just shames you and shuts you down.

You can quickly see how gratitude brings acceptance and appreciation for the gift of your body and that of your spouse. When I appreciate the gift of the person God has entrusted me with, it enriches every aspect of our relationship together. Our emotional, sexual, and spiritual connection are strengthened when I see my spouse as a gift for me to cherish.

> *Every good thing given and every perfect gift is from above, coming down from the Father of lights, with whom there is no variation or shifting shadow* (James 1:17).

When I see my spouse as God's gift to me personally, it is a humbling experience and I am in reverence for His goodness to me. When I consider that God gave me the gift of sex to enjoy and share with my spouse for many years, I am in awe. I can be thankful for my body, which is fearfully and wonderfully made. I can offer this gift back to my Creator and share this with my spouse.

> *Let your fountain be blessed, and rejoice in the wife of your youth. As a loving hind and a graceful doe, let her breasts*

> *satisfy you at all times; be exhilarated always with her love* (Proverbs 5:18-19).

With gratitude in my heart I can appreciate my spouse's body for all the wonder and joy that it brings to both of us. Whether you are a husband appreciating your wife's form, or a wife appreciating your husband's features, both can revel in God's goodness to give us these gifts for this present moment and across our lifetime together.

The Beauty of Here and Now

The entire face-to-face approach to restoring and maintaining connection is anchored in the here and now. It's about two lives coming together to share the sorrows, joys, shames, and triumphs together. It's about comforting one another when we are scared or sad, and rejoicing together for all that will be.

The negative cycle is caused by remnants of the past, most distantly the ways that our brains were wired in our formative early years of childhood and more recently by the painful experiences we may have had with our spouses. These experiences cause us to ruminate about our past betrayals or hurts, and they cause us to anticipate possible hurts that may come our way in the future.

Face-to-face connection means that you are *now* able to share all of who you are with your spouse, despite what happened in your past. You have been healed, and you trust in your spouse's caring for you. Face to face means that you are no longer gripped with dread and apprehension about ways that your spouse may hurt you again. Your spouse has served as your go-to person so many times, and you have confidence your spouse will be there for you as long as God gives him or her breath. You can go to your beloved, and your beloved can come to you. There's no more fear about that.

Face-to-face connection allows your spouse to be present to you emotionally, with fewer distractions from the past where you are looking in the rear view mirror. It allows you to be present in the moment, without fear of what's ahead. Of course this applies to our emotional moments and shared daily experiences, and it has particular application to our sex lives with our spouses.

The beauty of here and now sharing with our spouse will surpass even our innate good looks or lack thereof. It is the gift of life, being sensitive, present, and shared with another person.

The beauty of here and now is the gift of life shared with your spouse.

Here and now is being fully alive, right here with you in this moment. Gratitude is one practice of being present in the here and now. Shifting out of the distractions of hectic life to be present to your body and your spouse's body is another. Reducing performance fear about loss in the future and soothing shame about our past actions are other ways to bring us back into this present moment.

If you are still struggling with worries about loss and betrayal due to the actions of your spouse, then the next chapter of the book is specifically written for you. When betrayal takes place in a marriage, there are special steps that must often be conducted in order to restore the connection.

CHAPTER 13

Never Again! Dealing with Betrayal

The Lord is near to the brokenhearted and saves those who are crushed in spirit (Psalm 34:18).

The Shattering

> *"Jesse, I'd like to get in for an appointment to see you. I feel like my whole world is falling apart. I'm losing my mind! I learned last week that my husband has been having an affair with our neighbor for the past eight years. I had absolutely no idea this was going on. I don't know who to turn to or what to do. I'm a complete wreck!"*

This was the phone call I received on a Monday morning just a few weeks ago. I was struck with sorrow and sympathy for this woman whose entire world had been turned upside down with the staggering news of a betrayal from her husband and her neighbor too. When everything she counted on and held as true came crashing down, it felt like she was losing her mind.

Our inner and outer worlds are constructed around the key relationships we have forged and cultivated over the course of time. When you think about it, the security and love that we feel with our spouses came as a result of our being able to take risks with them and finding them present to our needs. When our spouse shakes or shatters our trusted foundation, it feels like a huge part of our world has come crashing down.

There are times in a marriage when the very person we trusted and relied on is the very person who betrays us. The very person who was our source of safety and security actually became a source of danger and pain. Rather than being our "constant one" or our "safe place," our spouses made a choice or choices that left us shaken and wondering which end is up.

We are shaken to the core and left with racing thoughts, sleepless nights, anger, knots in our stomachs, and a sad hollow place where once we had confidence and safety. The process of just sorting through the shock is a hefty task. Our heads reel with the staggering realization of what has happened. We can hardly take it in or begin to make sense of it. After this we start to experience the anger, the "What if" questions, and our connection to the deep sorrow of this loss.

We may or may not be able to salvage the loss and move forward with acceptance for what this means. We may find ways to trust our beloved again, or we may find it's too difficult to place our trust in this person any more. That may be independent of whether the offending spouse demonstrates trustworthy behaviors after the betrayal.

Hypervigilance

After we have been betrayed, our brain works extremely hard to make sure that we will *never* be hurt again. God designed our brains in such a way that it goes into a hypervigilant mode of perceiving and filtering information after we have been betrayed.

We can't help ourselves in this regard.

Following a betrayal experience, our brains are apt to scrutinize our spouses' behaviors and to scrutinize ourselves at times. The mind is looking for any sign that something is going awry, or that we are about to fall once again to deception. It can be exhausting when your brain works like a security system that is scanning for any possible hint that your world is getting ready to be turned upside down again.

I have worked with very nice people who actually became quite paranoid after experiencing betrayal at the hands of their spouses. These good people responded in ways that made sense, given the circumstances, but the marital work was much harder for everyone involved. It takes longer, and there are hesitations right at key moments when a betrayed spouse gets ready to "risk it" again and trust the perpetrating spouse.

All marriages have distress at times, and most of us get into significant periods when we are stuck in our negative cycles. But when betrayal has been part of your experience in marriage, the road to building and restoring a face-to-face connection is more difficult. That is why I wanted to include a chapter here to specifically address the unique effects of betrayal and the more complex needs that must be met when you hope to restore your marriage subsequent to a betrayal.

I want to overview some of the possible types of betrayal experiences that can take place in a marriage. This may help you identify whether you have actually been through a betrayal experience, and normalize some of the responses that your brain is having as a result. Many betrayal experiences will require that both spouses actually receive professional help from a counselor who is skilled in marital therapy and the presenting issues of that specific case. I am going to outline some of these, not to discourage you, but as my way of showing extra care. I want to point you in the direction of getting the help that you and your loved ones need in those particularly difficult times.

Not all betrayals involve sexual infidelity. Arguably, sexual infidelity is among the most difficult betrayals to overcome, especially when it is coupled with an emotional bond between the unfaithful ones. But there are other forms of betrayal that can just as powerfully shake the core of our trust and our reality with our spouses.

Types of Betrayal

Financial Betrayal. This involves hiding, squandering, stealing, or gambling with the family's financial resources without consent of both spouses.

Drug or Alcohol Abuse. When a spouse becomes dependent on a substance for emotional solace, it wreaks havoc on the sense of security in the marriage.

Physical Abuse. Any form of hitting, grabbing, choking, or threatening physical harm will do serious damage to the security of the relationship.

Emotional Abuse. Demeaning speech, name calling, ridiculing, degrading or threatening speech are forms of emotional abuse. These produce enduring damage to the marital bond and to the victim's sense of self.

Sexual Abuse. This involves coercing sexual activity on a spouse by force, threat, or intimidation. It may not be possible to establish marital security after this takes place.

Abuse of Children. When a spouse strikes children with objects, leaving marks, bruises or wounds, then physical abuse is taking place. Other actions may also constitute abuse.

Sexual abuse is any form of intentional sexual contact between an adult and a child. If this happens the perpetrator must be removed from the home.

Emotional Infidelity. The sharing of confidences, longings, verbal affection, and intimate happiness between a spouse and a potential partner is a form of unfaithfulness.

Sexual Infidelity. When your spouse shares physical or sexual intimacies with anyone besides you, it is a significant betrayal of trust.

The above categories are not an exhaustive list of all possible forms of betrayal. However, if any of the above actions are taking place your marriage will often require professional assistance to guide you towards healing. In many of the above instances a marital separation would be called for, depending on the context and duration of events.

What happens to your brain when you experience betrayal? There is no way to gauge exactly how you will respond after a betrayal experience. However, most people go through a consistent set of steps and stages on the road to recovery. First, most victims will walk through the process of grieving for the loss of their secure relationship and the lost stability that comes when "your world is turned upside down." During and after the grieving, most folks find that their brains struggle with the types of hypervigilant and mistrusting responses just discussed.

Grieving

Most people will react to betrayal by going through the stages of grieving that I alluded to in the opening paragraphs of this chapter. These include: denial and shock, anger, bargaining, depression, and acceptance, followed by reinvesting in healthier relationships.[70]

You go through grieving because you are experiencing a significant loss. The person you loved and trusted has now become a source of pain for you. If he physically hurt you or threatened you, then you lost him as your safe place and came to view him as a potential source of ongoing threat. Or maybe you spent years or maybe even decades building a trusted bond with her and a secure foundation, and now all of that has been turned upside down. It's a *huge* loss for you.

So your brain will go through the stages of grieving, just as if your loved one had died. It took time to build your attachment and trust with your spouse, so it will take time for your brain to try to repair and recover from this gaping wound. The process of grieving and healing will be difficult no matter how your spouse responds to the situation. As mentioned, there are forms of betrayal so huge that it may not be possible to reconcile with your spouse.

However, if your spouse is humble, remorseful, and able to fully give up the betrayal behaviors, then this will aid you in your recovery process. If your spouse is unrepentant, defensive, or blames you and continues the behaviors, then it will be much more difficult to heal from the searing pain of betrayal. With an unrepentant spouse, it will *not* be possible to achieve true reconciliation.

The road to recovery from betrayal is a difficult one. It will take courage and strength on the part of both you and your spouse. A great deal of prayer and emotional maturity from both of you is also needed. Yet, I have seldom seen full emotional maturity in a spouse who has enacted betrayal behaviors.

If your spouse had a lot of emotional maturity to start with, then he or she probably would not have been cheating on you or betraying you when times got tough.

Emotional maturity lessens the chances of betrayal.

Typically, offending spouses have to go through their own process of growth and recovery, even while they need to be kind and caring toward their wounded spouse. It's a pretty tall order, but it can be accomplished when they invest themselves in counseling or mentorship. Such counseling must challenge them to face their original sources of pain and to grow through them as opposed to escaping into destructive behaviors.

Hypervigilance and Mistrust

When your spouse betrays you, the pain may be so great that you can scarcely bear it. Everything in your autonomic nervous system is wired to protect you from pain. Think of touching a hot stove and receiving a burn. From that point forward your body will tense up whenever you get close to a stove. You now have a vivid image in your head of the pain you felt, and you might even have moments when your limbic system re-experiences physiological responses or memories of that ill-fated burning moment.

The stakes are *much* higher if your spouse whom you trusted has become the source of pain. It's a tug of war inside of you, as part of you misses your spouse, grieves, and is also terrified to get close again. Your brain responds reactively from your amygdala, which is located at the core of the limbic system. This is where your fight or flight responses take on a life of their own.

Being close or being away from your betraying spouse may provide you with plenty of fodder to become alarmed. Your spouse may be doing something mild or may be doing nothing at all, but your amygdala is working overtime to make sure that you will err on the side of protecting yourself from getting hurt again.

Your brain is all keyed up with the express intent of protecting you from a predator. The problem is that you may still love that predator and be working toward trying to restore connection with him or her. It can be confusing and unpredictable, but you need to be aware of this process that marches right alongside all of the hard work that you and your spouse are doing to heal after the betrayal.

At times your limbic system will direct you to bring the healthy accountability that your offending spouse needs in order to stay on track. Other times your limbic system will make you doubt the hard work of your betraying spouse, commanding him or her to go through incredible hoops in order to satisfy your hypervigilant brain, declaring: *"I'll never trust you again, and I'm not going to make this easy for you!"*

Your fight or flight response may also end up punishing you at times. This takes place when you subject yourself to all sorts of checking behaviors in order to monitor your spouse. Your limbic system may also drag you through intrusive images about your offending spouse, in an attempt to protect you.

For example, you may be making love to your spouse, and an intrusive image comes to your mind about your spouse cheating with another person. Believe it or not, this is just your brain trying to protect you from getting hurt again! It brings this forward to make you question whether you want to make yourself this vulnerable again.

Your mind may experience intrusive images or thoughts as well in ways that over-simplify the true reasons for the betrayal. Remember that when your brain is in fight or flight mode, it gets tunnel vision and only sees a narrow range of options. It's not interested in analyzing the full array of contributing factors to the betrayal. It just wants to keep you from getting hurt again.

Your brain might say, "This happened because I was not good enough!" or "This happened because he was a complete con artist!" It is making snap judgments in attempts to protect you. These snap judgments may be quite limited and cruel to you, by casting total blame on you or making you feel inadequate. These judgments may also be too simplistic in understanding the plight and dilemmas of your spouse during the past few months or years.

Past Betrayals

You need to know that your response to this current event also is affected by your past. Betrayal is much worse when you have a prior history of being betrayed, abused, or neglected in earlier years. It took huge amounts of work to place trust in your beloved, if you had a trauma history. You may have proceeded very cautiously and taken great pains to ascertain whether you could trust anyone ever again, including your potential spouse. For all of us a betrayal is huge setback, but when you have a past history of trauma, then the "undoing effects" of the recent betrayal are likely to be more shattering and piercing.

The Process of Recovery

Whether you stay with your spouse or not after the betrayal, you owe it to yourself to heal and to recover. Grieving is the natural process that your brain goes through in order to recover from loss and betrayal. The process of grieving in the event of a simple loss will take you about a year. In complex grieving, which includes situations that involve confusion, guilt, and betrayal, the grieving process can be longer.

It is important to actively engage the process of grieving so that you can have a full recovery. In the event of betrayal, you are going to have to work even harder to get your emotional life and stability back. It is much better to get underway with your healing and to not allow someone else's destructive choices to weigh you down any longer than is absolutely necessary.

Begin your healing immediately—don't allow yourself to be weighed down!

Grieving takes courage as you speak out, write out, and cry out your painful feelings. It's important to be honest with yourself and with one or more people who really care about you as you go through the process. Articulate your confusion and shock, aloud and also through writing.

Something about writing helps your brain allow the loss to settle in as more "real."

Discharge your anger in healthy ways, again through spoken, creative, or written methods. Allow yourself to do your bargaining: "What could I have done differently? Where did we go wrong? If only I could turn back time, how I wish that I could!" But don't stay stuck in bargaining. Allow yourself to enter into your sadness for the enormity of the loss that has befallen you. It is truly sad, and your sadness is a tribute to how precious the bond was that you created and to how precious your life and heart are.

No matter what mistakes you made, you don't deserve to be betrayed or to hurt like this! This is really hard, and this is a tragic loss.

You will never be the same person after a betrayal. You will likely be a little more aware, a little more cautious, and perhaps a little less dreamy when you have lost your innocence. But you can be happy again, and you can reconnect with other people who are trustworthy and capable of providing you with a secure bond. You can move toward that place of acceptance and reinvesting in healthier relationships. In order to get there you will have to work at forgiveness.

Forgiveness

Forgiveness means we lay down our rights to punish our spouses for hurting us. We let go of the human instinct to make them hurt for the pain that they inflicted upon us. Forgiveness does not mean that we let the other person do destructive behaviors and walk away without natural consequences. Sometimes the natural consequence of betrayal means separation, where the offending spouse will lose prolonged periods of contact with the hurt spouse. Sometimes the offending spouse may lose his or her marriage altogether.

Forgiveness is not ignoring an offense, and forgiveness is not forgetting an offense. It is different. Forgiveness is your divine gift to set you free and help you to move through your grief and pain. It is key to helping you move forward and not have the betrayal hold you down or eat you up inside.

The first person you may have to forgive is yourself. Part of the process of forgiveness involves you coming to terms with your own humanity. You are imperfect and fallible. Despite your best efforts, you may have done things that ended up backfiring. Although you wanted a healthier relationship, you may have still chosen someone with a lot of brokenness.

And, you may have done things unwittingly to trigger your spouse's avoidance or escape behaviors. You are not responsible for his or her ultimate choice, but you may have given your spouse fuel that triggered his or her retreat. It's important to forgive yourself and to receive the grace of God for you in this time of need.

> *Therefore let us draw near with confidence to the throne of grace, so that we may receive mercy and find grace to help in time of need* (Hebrews 4:16).
>
> *Just as a father has compassion on his children, so the Lord has compassion on those who fear Him. For He Himself knows our frame; He is mindful that we are but dust* (Psalm 103:13-14).

Your spouse is feeble and frail too, and also in need of forgiveness. Again, forgiveness does not mean letting him or her right back into your life in the aftermath of betrayal. It would not be very loving to your spouse to bypass the process of honest reckoning, deep repentance, and changing behaviors. But you can forgive your spouse and release yourself to not be attached to the anger and pain of bitterness and wrath.

Forgiveness is divine, and I don't expect you to forgive your betraying spouse in your own strength. God doesn't either. He stands ready and waiting for you to call on Him for His strength and help. Jesus knows what it was like to be betrayed by a friend, someone He invested in, and someone He loved. He was betrayed unto death by Judas, so He knows a lot about what you are going through. He wants to comfort you, strengthen you, and help you forgive.

> *For we do not have a high priest who cannot sympathize with our weaknesses, but One who has been tempted in all things as we are, yet without sin* (Hebrews 4:15).

Jesus was able to forgive the very people who put Him to death on the cross. He forgave the ones who got caught up in the frenzy in Jerusalem that weekend and rallied for His death. He did not hold it against them, but viewed them as frail and lacking in knowledge.

> *...Father, forgive them, for they do not know what they are doing...* (Luke 23:34).

Forgiveness is divine, but the process of embarking on the journey of forgiveness actually involves acknowledging our own humanity in deeper ways. We are feeble, fallible, and frail. Too often our judgments are inaccurate or ill-informed. Everyone has some bit of fantasy and idealizing of the marriage that they hope to foster and the life that they will lead. In his book *Overcoming Life's Disappointments,* Rabbi Harold S. Kushner speaks of the necessity of laying down our fantasy and flawed mindsets about the perfect marriage in order to actually gain a mature marriage. He writes:

> What happens when we realize that the person we are married to is far from perfect and a lot less admirable than we thought? This realization of the difference between fantasy and reality is the first crisis of a marriage, a crisis that every married person faces. And it's not only about the shortcomings of our mate. It can be about our coming to terms with our own shortcomings as well.[71]

That is some of what we are grieving when we learn of the betrayal of our spouses in moments of infidelity. They were not strong enough to resist temptation. They were not perfectly able to follow through on their commitment to be faithful to us. And we were wrong in our estimation of them. We are not as invincible, wise, or clever as we once thought that we were. It can be a difficult pill to swallow.

Yet we find deeper levels of grace in embracing their humanity and our own. We may actually use this current crisis as an opportunity to build on a foundation that is more enduring, a foundation that is more anchored in reality. We need grace in our lives every single day. Our spouses do too. None of us have what it takes to make a marriage or to be fully faithful. We are dependent each and every day upon the grace and mercy of God.

We need the grace and mercy of God every day of our lives.

Somehow knowing that makes it just a little easier to forgive. I bring myself and my spouse to the foot of the cross. We are both equal, and we are both flawed. And yet we can both be forgiven and raised to new life. That is a huge gift to me.

Forgiveness is for you. It is a gift that mostly benefits you! In addition to the spiritual need we have for forgiveness, it is given to aid our human relational needs. It is given so that you can fully engage life again and reinvest in relationships. That is going to be a scarier prospect now, since you have been betrayed. However, it is infinitely more difficult if you don't forgive and are left walking into relationship opportunities with bitterness or a chip on your shoulder.

I want to return briefly to the woman I mentioned at the start of this chapter, the one whose husband cheated on her with their neighbor. Although she was completely falling apart when I first met her, this woman actually displayed incredible strength and forgiveness. Her strength came in part through her forgiveness. She purposed very early on to forgive her husband, and I believe that God helped her with this process. It greatly aided her healing process and opened a door for reconciliation with her husband.

Reconciliation

Forgiveness is absolutely essential if you are going to be restored to your spouse. But reconciliation involves more than just the offended spouse working through grief and applying forgiveness. Reconciliation is a shared venture where both spouses are taking huge steps toward one another. The offending spouse has to take a strong lead in the process of reconciliation for the bond to be restored.

The offending spouse has to find a way to listen to and empathize with the pain of the one he has betrayed. How else could the hurt spouse ever begin to trust in the one who caused her such great pain? The hurt spouse has to know that the offender actually grasps what was done, can label it as wrong, and target it for change.

"Never again! Never again!"

These are the words that must be spoken by the offending spouse, by way of acknowledging the hurt that was inflicted and the damage that it brought. Never again is what the hurt spouse must say to let the offender know the true impact of the choices made that resulted in betrayal. It sets a healthy boundary and expectation on the part of them both that this behavior will not be tolerated again. It affirms the value of the bond, the dignity of the hurt spouse, and the commitment to never recreate this form of loss.

In the spring of 1999, I was privileged to attend a workshop led by one of the leading family therapists of all time, Cloe Madanes. Cloe Madanes came up with a protocol that she used to dramatically express repentance and to lead the way for possible reconciliation in families where sexual abuse had taken place.

Madanes actually asked offenders to get down on one knee as they humbled themselves during their apologies to the offended. They did not have permission to ask for forgiveness, and they were only allowed to make several key statements. They would state how crushing their offense was and take ownership of their complete responsibility for the pain. Offenders were asked to apologize for the pain and the betrayal, and let the victims know that it was their choice whether they would ever forgive the offender.

In other words, the offense that took place was completely outside the control of the victim. The victim then was given complete control to determine the timing and pace of forgiveness. No expectation was placed upon the victim to be pressured into doing this in order to appease the offender. Dignity and strength were afforded once again to the victims as part of the process of restoring some of what they lost.

Madanes applied this model as well to spouses who had committed infidelity and other forms of betrayal. The humility and repentance that the offender shows in this ritual of kneeling can lay a valuable foundation for reconciliation to occur.

The Affair of Jill

Let me bring you an example of a very solid apology that came from a woman whom we'll call Jill. Jill and Barry had been married for seven years when she was unfaithful with a mutual acquaintance of the couple. Her behaviors took place in the context of what we would deem an emotional and partly physical affair.

In their negative cycle, Jill had always felt like her husband, Barry, was disinterested in her as he buried himself in his work and decompressed in front of the TV. Jill could not seem to get Barry to engage with her, and she often felt taken for granted and unnoticed. Her tendency was to try to work harder on being appealing to Barry, while she internalized the feelings of rejection. This went on for years.

A male acquaintance began to notice Jill, near the seventh year anniversary of her marriage. He was charming and deep in the ways that he spoke with her. It was like water on the barren wasteland, which was her emotional landscape for the past seven years. She opened up to this man and gushed with the pent-up feelings and longings of the past few years. Barry began to question why Jill seemed to linger at work more often. She was really meeting her guy friend for coffee, but she lied to Barry by stating that she was working on an extended project from her supervisor. Eventually, Barry intercepted an email from Jill's private account. What he read enraged him as it flowed with the blushing words of two people enamored with one another.

Jill finally ended it at that point, but the effects were devastating to Barry's trust and self-esteem. We join them some months into therapy when Jill is offering an apology. She was truly broken by what she had done and the scope of the damage to Barry. Tune in to her humility and the manner in which she does not pressure Barry but gives him full control of the process of rebuilding trust.

Deep Repentance

Jill: I don't deserve you coming to me or giving me a second chance. I know that it was hard for you to be vulnerable to start with, and I have given you baggage now to deal with that no one should ever have to deal with.

Barry: (Is quiet and looks intently at her)

Jill: (Tears up) I don't deserve you ever trusting me again. But I will be here waiting for you, forever. Even if it never comes, I will not stop being here.

Barry: (Visibly softens his posture toward Jill)

Barry softened somewhat as he received the affirmation that, despite her infidelity, Jill views him still as her whole world. They had many lengthy talks where she was able to frame that her escape behaviors were stemming from her deep feelings of loneliness and feeling neglected. She had a chronic sense that she was unlovable.

In all couples who want to repair a betrayal, the offending partner has to reengage to show the wounded partner that it is safe to open back up again. It is critical that the betraying partner follows through with two things. This includes consistently drawing close again, steady over time. It also involves the offender sharing what he or she was experiencing before and during the unfaithful behaviors. This humanizes him or her and places the behaviors in a context of pain.

It has to make sense in some new way for both of them to fulfill the confessional needs of the betraying partner and the safety needs of the one left behind. All the while, the former offender must stay close and have empathy for the one who got hurt from the betrayal. Jill demonstrates this in another session.

Honest and Empathic Sharing

Jill: (Cried as she told Barry) We were never fully honest with one another before. I never told you everything going on inside of me. I didn't even tell myself. Now I can't go forward without total honesty. I know now that I can't be alone anymore. I still feel alone when I share deeply with you, and you stay guarded and pull back to watch TV. I know that I have no right to ask you to come close to me, but that is what I need. I want closeness with you, nobody but you. Please take your time, but do let me know whether you want this with me too.

Barry: That is very scary. What if I open up to you and you decide again that you don't want me?

Trust Rebuilding

The process of recovery involves offending spouses also consistently showing trustworthiness through their actions. In the case of Jill and Barry, there were many steps consistently taken over time that demonstrated a new stability and steadiness in Jill. She participated in marital therapy where she shared in vulnerable ways, had compassion for her offended spouse, and also learned new and healthy ways to engage him.

All of this steady and faithful engagement on the part of Jill served to set the stage for the incremental risks that Barry needed to take in order to see whether he could trust again. He wrestled with this process for months, and he took many small steps along the way before he was able to entrust himself to Jill again.

Risking it Again

For reconciliation to occur, the hurt spouse must take small risks over time and find the former offender to be steady and true. The hurt spouse must talk about how hurtful the betrayal was and how much he needs to know that he will be safe again in the future.

Barry: I was still in love with you when this happened. I know that I worked too much, but I was focused on providing for our family. I know I was oblivious, but I never meant to hurt you. I never cheated on you…

Jill: I get that now; I get that. I'm so sorry.

Barry: And the thing I can't get past is that you lied to me when I got uneasy about our marriage. You lied to my face, and hid this from me. How can I ever trust you again?

Jill: I don't deserve it, but I want to earn it. I want to earn your trust each day and every day.

Barry: I guess I don't have a choice really. I can't keep holding on to this anger. It just tears me up inside. A part of me just wants to leave…like that would be easier. But I don't know that I'd feel any better being apart from you.

Jill: I can only imagine how scary this has to be for you. And I have no right to ask, but I want to be here for you. I want to

> give you what we never had before. I want that for me. I want that for us.

Jill remained very engaged with Barry for weeks to come, through her kind, helpful, and vulnerable new ways of being. They still had many things to learn, and she was not perfect. But she stayed very close and he felt safe enough to look at what he had done wrong to make Jill feel so alone. He started to take risks to trust her again in small and big ways. Pretty soon he was talking about their future and making it the best marriage it could possibly be.

Jill's new openness and gentleness helped to reprogram Barry's amygdala and frightened limbic system that was screaming inside his head, "Retreat! Retreat! Don't do it. Don't trust again!" It was quite a struggle for him, as he felt torn about giving in to her. Barry chose to be very clear with both of them that his reconnecting did not mean that he condoned her unfaithful behaviors in any way. He experienced new behaviors on both their parts, and it gradually gave him the confidence to trust Jill again.

Occasions for Divorce

Not every marriage is able to recover from the breach and the tearing that takes place in the context of betrayal. Reconciliation cannot take place when the offender fails to repent and do the very difficult work just described. Some offenses are too great to bear. There are also victims of betrayal who are wired in such a way that makes it much harder for them to integrate the choices of their spouses to be unfaithful. Consequently, there are marriages where betrayal results in divorce.

Divorce is never a good thing, though there are a few instances where it is a healthy thing. God hates divorce, and the Scriptures clearly teach us this in both the Old and New Testament of the Bible.

The Law of Moses allowed more latitude for divorce, but Jesus brought in the New Covenant, which decimates all forms of selfishness and makes us rely completely on Him as Savior. He did this across the board in the New Testament, and this included divorce. Jesus raised the bar on the criteria that allow for divorce that came through Moses, but He seems to still have left one clause for cases of adultery.

That may be because God, who is kind, is acknowledging to us how severe it is when a spouse breaches that part of the marital covenant. The marital covenant is a mirror of God's covenant with us as His church. It may also be part of God's way of making provision for how frail our minds can be in recovering from adultery. He sometimes just lets us break the ties and stop putting ourselves through the agony of trying to trust again in one who betrayed us.

This is a difficult decision, whether you are trying to reconcile or whether you are leaning toward a divorce after a severe betrayal. It is one that will affect the rest of your life, and one for which you should receive counsel from a variety of sources. This would include your clergy, best friends, trusted family members, and possibly a mental health professional who endeavors to be impartial in these matters.

It takes courage and strength to tackle this difficult decision. And it will take the grace and strength of our heavenly Father to help you heal, no matter which path you take. If you are in this difficult place of still deciding or maybe you are reconciling, I want to close this chapter with a prayer for you and all those who have been betrayed in marriage:

> *Heavenly Father, I thank You for Your precious children who are wrestling with a process and a pain that they never thought they would have to face. I pray first for Your comfort upon their hearts. Speak deeply to them about how valuable they are, and what their true worth is in Your eyes and to many others. Please heal their emotional wounds and help them to fully grieve. Please grant that they may forgive themselves and their spouses who hurt them. Provide Your "peace that passes*

understanding" in the days ahead for the places of mistrust and confusion that trouble their minds. Grant them clear direction about the next steps that they should take. Above all, please let them know that You are with them. You never leave them, and You will never forsake them. May the contrast and deeper realization of Your faithfulness be one gift that comes even in the midst of this pain. We choose to trust in You. In Jesus's name, amen.

EPILOGUE

A CHORD OF THREE STRANDS

Though one may be overpowered, two can defend themselves. A cord of three strands is not quickly broken (Ecclesiastes 4:12 NIV).

At the close of this book I want to leave you with some words of encouragement. *"A chord of three strands is not quickly broken,"* is a passage that is commonly quoted during sermons about marriage. I am bringing this image to you as well, to remind you of the strength that comes when you place Jesus at the center of your marriage bond.

In this book we have explored new ways to be vulnerable with your spouse in order to build or rebuild a secure marriage connection. In what seems to be a paradox, we are actually stronger when we become vulnerable with our spouses and bring our needs forward in more direct ways. We know more fully, and we are more fully known.

As a couple with a restored face-to-face connection, a secure attachment bond, you will find that you feel stronger than ever to face whatever challenges may befall you. The two of you will often feel like you can "take on the world." It is a good feeling, and one that you were designed to experience when you entered your marriage commitment with your spouse.

As a couple who has found secure attachment, there is a place of even greater rest, and there is a place of greater strength. There is a place of resting in the strength of the Vine Himself. Being fully dependent on Christ is the most solid foundation that a marriage could ever hope to build upon. When you are rooted in Jesus as the center of your relationship, there is the possibility to expand and go even further than the comfort that we can offer to one another.

> *I am the vine, you are the branches; he who abides in Me and I in him, he bears much fruit, for apart from Me you can do nothing. My Father is glorified by this, that you bear much fruit…* (John 15:5,8).

Picture yourselves as two vibrant and living shoots wrapped in and around one another, wrapped in and around the main Vine. You have life, strength, and security. You have strength that comes from being vulnerable, being interdependent, and from being one. This three-fold vine brings you great fulfillment and a fruitful existence. This is the essence of security with one another and security with Him.

Jesus invites us to be bonded to Him, to be grafted into Him, to draw our nourishment from Him. From that place of connection, we will regularly have times of rest and refreshment. He brings us peace, and His perfect love casts out all fear.

When we go through the storms, we know that He is with us, so we never have to face challenges in our own strength. We are not alone.

When hard times come in our marriage, His love is there for us and it also flows for us to give to our spouses. This is His design and His intent for drawing strength from the Vine. When our strength is not enough, His grace is sufficient for us. He will carry us, and He will carry us together.

In that bond, we will bear fruit for our marriage and for ourselves. Abiding together in the Vine we will also branch out and explore our world. We will be the bearers of love in the world, bringing the gospel to others who are hurting.

I want you to fully enjoy the new depths of security in your marriage that come from a face-to-face connection. I want you to enjoy new forms of vulnerable sharing, and the healing that this affords you and your spouse. I also want you to have great connected face-to-face intimacy in your emotional and sexual lives together. This is the full gift of marriage that God has given to you.

From this fruitful place you may have the experience of bringing children into the world. Or you may offer this fruitful and secure foundation to the children you already have. What a gift this secure foundation is for them to receive and to rest in!

For those with physical children and those who do not have such natural families, all of us are called to foster spiritual children and thereby bear fruit. I want to lift your sights to see that God wants your marriage to be strong, secure, and abiding in Him, because this is one of His greatest illustrations and vehicles to bring His love to the world! I want you to catch a small glimpse of this as we close this book together.

First, God loved you so much that He sent Jesus to draw you to Himself. Second, He loved you so much that He grafted you into a marriage relationship that so powerfully embodies and reflects His love for us as His bride. And the love you two share in your marriage is a gift for you, and it is a gift of love that is meant to spill over into the lives of those around you.

May you be strengthened in the love that He has given you for one another. May you grow ever deeper in your dependence upon His love—as the center Vine in which you abide and flourish. May the reality of His constant presence comfort you and bring you hope for each day in your marriage together. And may your marriage be a light amid the pain and darkness, an example that others can follow. May your secure marriage bond be so strong that it points others to the Source of love and life. Amen.

Endnotes

Chapter 1

1 John Bowlby, Attachment: Attachment and Loss Volume One (New York: Basic Books, 1969, revised 1982).

2 Ibid.

3 Daniel J. Siegel, *The Developing Mind: Second Edition: How Relationships and the Brain Interact to Shape Who We Are* (New York: Guilford Press, 2012).

4 Mary D. Salter Ainsworth, "Infant-mother attachment"; *American Psychologist, Vol. 34* (October 1979), 932-937. Susan M. Johnson, *The Practice of Emotionally Focused Couples Therapy: Creating Connection* (New York: Brunner and Routledge, 2004).

5 John Bowlby, "Forty-four Juvenile Thieves: Their Characters and Home-life" (I & II), *International Journal of Psychoanalysis, 25, 19-53* (1944), 107-128.

6 John Bowlby, "Maternal Care and Mental Health"; *Bulletin of the World Health Organization, 3,* (Geneva: World Health Organization, 1951), 13.

7 William Goldfarb, "The Effects of Early Institutional Care on Adolescent Personality"; *Child Development, 14* (1943), 212-223.

8 Harry F. Harlow and Robert R. Zimmerman, "Affectional Responses in the Infant Monkey"; *Science, Vol. 130* (August 1959), 421-432. Also found at: http://www.sciencemag.org/content/130/3373/421.extract; accessed March 9, 2015.

9 Bowlby, *Attachment.*

10 Goldfarb, "The Effects of Early Institutional Care on Adolescent Personality."

11 Bowlby, "Maternal Care and Mental Health."

12 H. Rudolph Schaffer and Peggy E. Emerson, "The Development of Social Attachments in Infancy"; *Monographs of the Society for Research in Child Development* (1964), 1-77.

13 James Robertson and John Bowlby, "Responses of Young Children to Separation from Their Mothers"; *Courier Centre International de l'Enfance, 2* (1952), 131-142.

14 Ibid.; Schaffer and Emerson, "The Development of Social Attachments in Infancy."

15 Mary D. Salter Ainsworth, (1967) *Infancy in Uganda: Infant Care and the Growth of Love*; (Oxford, England: Johns Hopkins Press).

16 Mary D. Salter Ainsworth, Mary C. Blehar, Everett Waters, and Sally Wall, *Patterns of Attachment: Assessed in the Strange Situation and at Home* (Hillsdale, NJ: Lawrence Erlbaum (1978).

17 Robertson and Bowlby, "Responses of Young Children to Separation from Their Mothers."

18 Mary Main and Judith Solomon, "Procedures for Identifying Infants as Disorganized/Disoriented during the Ainsworth Strange Situation"; in Mark T. Greenberg, Dante Cicchetti, and E. Mark Cummings (Eds.), *Attachment in the Preschool Years: Theory, Research and Intervention* (Chicago: University of Chicago Press, 1990), 121-160.

Chapter 2

19 John Bowlby, Secure and Insecure Attachment (New York: Basic Books, 1989).

20 Bowlby, *Attachment*, 346.

21 Adapted from Ainsworth, *Patterns of Attachment,* and Robertson and Bowlby, "Responses of Young Children to Separation from Their Mothers," 131-142.

22 David R. Pederson, Greg Moran, Carolyn Sitko, Kathy Campbell, Kristen Ghesquire, and Heather Acton, "Maternal Sensitivity and the Security of Infant-Mother Attachment"; paper presented at the biennial meeting of the Society for Research in Child Development, Kansas City (April 1989).

23 Main and Solomon, "Procedures for Identifying Infants as Disorganized/Disoriented during the Ainsworth Strange Situation"; in Greenberg, et al., *Attachment in the Preschool Years*, 121-160.

24 Bowlby, *Attachment,* 354.

25 Inge Bretherton, "The Origins of Attachment Theory: John Bowlby and Mary Ainsworth"; *Developmental Psychology, 28* (1992), 759-775.

26 Leah Matas, Richard A. Arand, and L. Alan Sroufe, "Continuity in Adaptation: Quality of Attachment and Later Competence"; *Child Development, 49* (1978),

547-556. Mary Main and Jude Cassidy, "Categories of Response to Reunion with the Parent at Age 6: Predictable from Infant Attachment Classifications and Stable over a 1-Month Period"; *Developmental Psychology, 24,* (1988), 415-426. Cindy Hazan and Phillip Shaver, "Romantic Love Conceptualized as an Attachment Process"; *Journal of Personality and Social Psychology, 52,* (1987), 511-524. Mary Main and Ruth Goldwyn, "Predicting Rejection of Her Infant from Mother's Representation of Her Own Experiences: A Preliminary Report"; *Monograph of the International Journal of Child Abuse and Neglect, 8* (1984), 203-217.

Chapter 3

27 Helen Fisher, Arthur Aron, and Lucy L. Brown, "Romantic Love: A Mammalian Brain System for Mate Choice"; Philosophical Transactions of the Royal Society, B., 361 (2006), 2173-2186.

28 Helen Fisher, *Why We Love: The Nature and Chemistry of Romantic Love* (New York: Henry Holt and Company, 2004).

29 F. Bryant Furlow, "The Smell of Love"; *Psychology Today* (Mar/Apr, 1996), 23-29.

30 Claus Wedekind, et al., "MHC-Dependent Preferences in Humans." *Proceedings of the Royal Society of London, 260* (1995), 245-49.

31 Helen Fisher, Arthur Aron, Lucy L. Brown, "Romantic Love: An fMRI Study of a Neural Mechanism for Mate Choice, *Journal of Comparative Neurology, 493* (2005), 58-62.

32 Helen Fisher, "Lust, Attraction, and Attachment in Mammalian Reproduction"; *Human Nature, 9* (1998), 23-52.

33 Donald G. Dutton and Arthur P. Aron, "Some Evidence for Heightened Sexual Attraction under Conditions of High Anxiety"; *Journal of Personality and Social Psychology, 30(4)* (1974), 510-517. Also found at: https://gaius.fpce.uc.pt/niips/novoplano/ps1/documentos/dutton&aron1974.pdf; accessed March 10, 2015.

34 Helen Fisher, et al., "Romantic Love: A Mammalian Brain System for Mate Choice."

35 Donatella Marazziti, et al., "Alteration of the Platelet Serotonin Transporter in Romantic Love," *Psychological Medicine, 29* (1999), 741-745.

Chapter 4

[36] Salvador Minuchin and H. Charles Fishman, Family Therapy Techniques (Harvard: Harvard University Press, 1981).

[37] Leslie S. Greenberg and Susan M. Johnson, *Emotionally Focused Therapy for Couples* (New York: Guilford Press, 1988).

[38] Susan M. Johnson, *The Practice of Emotionally Focused Couple Therapy: Creating Connection* (New York: Routledge, 2004).

[39] John M. Gottman, "The Roles of Conflict Engagement, Escalation, and Avoidance in Marital Interaction: A Longitudinal View of Five Types of Couples"; *Journal of Consulting and Clinical Psychology, 61(1)* (1993), 6-15.

[40] John Eldredge, *Wild at Heart: Discovering the Secret of a Man's Soul* (Nashville, TN: Thomas Nelson Publishers, 2001).

[41] John Eldredge and Stasi Eldredge, *Captivating: Unveiling the Mystery of a Woman's Soul* (Nashville, TN: Thomas Nelson Publishers, 2005).

[42] Erik H. Erikson, *Childhood and Society,* 2nd ed. (New York: W.W. Norton, 1968), 255.

[43] Susan M. Johnson, *The Practice of Emotionally Focused Couple Therapy,* 34.

Chapter 5

[44] Johnson, The Practice of Emotionally Focused Couple Therapy, 140.

[45] John S. March and Karen Mulle, *OCD in Children and Adolescents: A Cognitive-Behavioral Treatment Manual* (New York: Guilford Press, 1998).

[46] Steven Stosny, *Manual of the Core Value Workshop* (North Charleston, SC: Booksurge, 2003), 66.

[47] Ibid.

[48] Cindy Hazan and Phillip Shaver, "Romantic Love Conceptualized as an Attachment Process"; *Journal of Personality and Social Psychology, 52* (1987), 511-524.

[49] Susan Johnson, *Emotionally Focused Couples Therapy;* Externship: June 24-28, 2008, Ottawa, Canada.

Chapter 6

[50] Harold S. Kushner, Overcoming Life's Disappointments (New York: Alfred A. Knopf, Division of Random House, Inc., 2006), 15.

[51] Estelle Frankel, *Sacred Therapy: Jewish Spiritual Teachings on Emotional Healing and Inner Wholeness* (Boston: Shambhala, 2003), 122.

[52] Johnson, *The Practice of Emotionally Focused Couples Therapy,* 149.

Chapter 7

53 Salvador Minuchin and H. Charles Fishman, Family Therapy Techniques (Harvard: Harvard University Press, 1981).

Chapter 8

54 John Steinbeck, Of Mice and Men (New York: Covici, Friede Inc., 1937).

Chapter 9

55 Nicholas Carr, The Shallows: What the Internet Is Doing to Our Brains (New York: W.W. Norton and Company, 2010).

56 Michele Weiner-Davis, *Divorce Busting: A Step-by-Step Approach to Making Your Marriage Loving Again* (New York: Fireside Book, 1993) and *The Divorce Remedy: The Proven 7-Step Program for Saving Your Marriage* (New York: Simon and Schuster, 2002).

57 Peter Fonagy, Gyorgy Gergely, Elliot L. Jurist, and Mary Target, *Affect Regulation, Mentalization and the Development of the Self* (New York: Other Press, 2002).

58 Marie S. Carmichael, Richard Humbert, Jean Dixen, Glenn Palmisano, Walter Greenleaf, Julian M. Davidson, "Plawsma oxytocin increases in the human sexual response"; *The Journal of Clinical Endocrinology and Metabolism, 64 (1)* (1987), 27-31. Marie S. Carmichael, Valerie L. Warburton, Jean Dixen, and Julian M. Davidson, "Relationships among cardiovascular, muscular, and oxytocin responses during human sexual activity"; *Archives of Sexual Behavior, 23 (1)* (1994), 59-79.

59 James K. Childerston and Debra Taylor, "The Brain and Sex: The Science of Love and Relationships"; *Christian Counseling Today, 17(2)* (2010).

60 Markus Heinrichs, Thomas Baumgartner, Clemens Kirschbaum, and Ulrike Ehlert, "Social Support and Oxytocin Interact to Suppress Cortisol and Subjective Responses to Psychosocial Stress"; *Biological Psychiatry, 54(12)* (December 2003), 1389-1398.

61 Childerston and Taylor, "The Brain and Sex: The Science of Love and Relationships," 41-42

Chapter 10

62 Daniel Stern, The Interpersonal World of the Infant: A View from Psychoanalysis and Development Psychology (New York: Basic Books, 1985).

63 Ibid.

64 Harold S. Kushner, *Overcoming Life's Disappointments.*

[65] Ibid., 15.

[66] Johnson, *The Practice of Emotionally Focused Couples Therapy.*

Chapter 11

[67] J. W. Fowler, Stages of Faith: The Psychology of Human Development and the Quest for Meaning (New York: Harper Collins, 1981), 11.

Chapter 12

[68] William H. Masters and Virginia E. Johnson, Human Sexual Response (New York: Bantam Books, 1966).

[69] Stacie Cockrell, Cathy O'Neill, and Julia Stone, *Babyproofing Your Marriage: How to Laugh More and Argue Less as Your Family Grows* (New York: Harper Collins, 2008).

References

Penner, C. and Penner, J. *Restoring the Pleasure: Complete Step-by-Step Programs to Helping Couples Overcome the Most Common Sexual Barriers.* Nashville, TN: Thomas Nelson Publishing, 1993.

Rosenau, D. E. *A Celebration of Sex: A Guide to Enjoying God's Gift of Sexual Intimacy.* Nashville, TN: Thomas Nelson Publishing, 2002.

Chapter 13

[70] Elizabeth Kubler-Ross and David Kessler, On Grief and Grieving: Finding the Meaning of Grief through the Five Stages of Loss (New York: Scribner, 2005).

[71] Harold S. Kushner, *Overcoming Life's Disappointments,* 83

Printed in the United States
By Bookmasters